DISCOVERING CHRIST
IN
GENESIS

Discovering Christ

in

Genesis

Donald S. Fortner

EVANGELICAL PRESS

EVANGELICAL PRESS
Faverdale North Industrial Estate, Darlington, DL3 0PH,
England

Evangelical Press USA
P. O. Box 84, Auburn, MA 01501, USA

e-mail: sales@evangelicalpress.org

web: http://www.evangelicalpress.org

First published 2002

British Library Cataloguing in Publication Data available

ISBN 0 85234 504 6

Scripture quotations in this publication are from the Authorized (King James) Version

Printed and bound in Great Britain by Creative Print &
Design Wales, Ebbw Vale.

To
the members of
Grace Baptist Church
of Danville
Danville, Kentucky,
USA

Contents

Preface

It is my firm conviction that the Word of God is intended, in all its parts, to set forth one glorious message. That message is *'Jesus Christ and him crucified'*. In other words, it is the purpose of all that is written in the Sacred Scriptures to make known the person and work of the Son of God as the sinner's substitute. The whole Volume of Inspiration speaks of him (Luke 24:27,44-45; John 1:45; Acts 10:43). Jesus Christ himself is 'all the counsel of God'. (Acts 20:27; 1 Cor. 2:2). He is the Living Word of whom the written Word speaks.

This volume is not intended to be a thorough exposition of the book of Genesis. No effort is made to settle theological disputes. My only purpose is to set forth, as simply and clearly as I am able, the grace and glory of God in Christ in the opening pages of Holy Scripture.

All four gospel narratives tell of a woman who brought an alabaster box, full of precious ointment, broke it open, and anointed the Saviour for his burial. When she did, the fragrance filled the room (Matt. 26:6-7; Mark 14:3; Luke 7:36-38; John 12:3). John Gill has suggested that the Scriptures are like her box, containing the gospel of the grace of God, which is like ointment poured forth; the gospel of the sweet savour of the knowledge of Christ, which is to be diffused, throughout all the world, by the preaching of it.

That is precisely my view of Holy Scripture. May God the Holy Spirit be pleased to use what I have written in these pages to fill your heart and soul with the knowledge and the sweet aroma of the Lord Jesus Christ, as you read them.

Don Fortner
Danville,
Kentucky, USA
June 2002

1.

Creation

Genesis 1

'In the beginning God created the heaven and the earth'
(Gen. 1:1).

In 2 Corinthians 5:17, the apostle Paul tells us, 'If any man
be in Christ, he is a new creature.' The work of God in the
new creation of grace is beautifully symbolized in the creation of the world. As the creation of the world was the
work of God alone, so the making of men and women as
new creatures in Christ is the work of God alone. Let me
show you three things in Genesis 1 about God's creation.
In these things, we see the work of God clearly in the new
creation. The first thing revealed in the Book of God is:

The creation of the world

The Word of God opens with a simple statement of fact: 'In
the beginning God created the heaven and the earth' (v. 1).
That is all we are told concerning the work of creation. No
argument is given to prove the existence of God. Instead,
his existence is simply affirmed as a fact to be believed.
Nothing is given to gratify the curious minds of men. How
long did it take for God to create the world? We are not

told. How old is this world? We are not told. We are simply told, 'In the beginning God created...' The truth of God is stated simply as a fact to be received and understood by unquestioning faith.

'In the beginning God...' This is the foundation of all truth. All true doctrine, all true theology, and all true religion begin with this: 'In the beginning God...' All human religion and philosophy begin with man and work up to God. The Scriptures begin with God and work down to man.

If we are to understand salvation, we must begin with God. In the Garden of Eden, Adam sinned against God and brought about death; but God was not taken by surprise. In the beginning, before the world was created, in anticipation of the Fall, God provided his Son as 'the Lamb slain from the foundation of the world' (Rev. 13:8), 'who verily was foreordained before the foundation of the world' (1 Peter 1:20).

In the new creation, the sinner who is saved by grace repents, believes on the Lord Jesus Christ and walks with him in newness of life. But it began with God. In the beginning God chose us in Christ (Eph. 1:4), predestined us to be his children (Eph. 1:5), and today 'we love him, because he first loved us' (1 John 4:19). Everything begins with God. If we understand this fact of divine revelation, we shall not stray far from the truth.

The book of Genesis is the book of beginnings. In fact, the word 'genesis' means 'beginning'. Someone has said, 'The book of Genesis is the seed plot of the Bible.' It contains the seed of all the great doctrines and truths revealed more fully in the rest of the Inspired Volume. In the book of Genesis we find the following:

1. God is revealed

God is revealed as the Creator-God, the covenant-keeping God, the Almighty God, 'the Most High God, possessor of heaven and earth'. From the opening verse hints are given concerning the blessed Trinity and the plurality of persons in the Godhead. The very name used for God — 'Elohim' — implies a plurality of persons in the Godhead. The phrase 'Let us make man' certainly implies a plurality of persons in the Godhead.[1]

2. The origin and character of man is set forth

First, we see man as God's creature, then as a fallen sinner, then as one brought back to God, finding grace in his sight, walking with God and having been made the friend of God.

3. Satan's devices are exposed

The arch-enemy of our souls, the tempter, the deceiver seeks to ruin men by calling into question the Word of God, casting doubt upon the goodness of God, and raising suspicions about the veracity of God.

4. God's sovereign election is exhibited

God approved of Abel and rejected Cain. God chose Abram and bypassed his idolatrous neighbours. God chose Isaac and rejected Ishmael. God loved Jacob and hated Esau.

5. Salvation in Christ is displayed as a type

Our fallen parents, Adam and Eve, were sought and found by grace, and clothed with the skins of innocent victims. In order to clothe the fallen pair, blood had to be shed; the innocent victim had to die in the place of the guilty. As those innocent animals were slain for Adam and Eve, so the Lord Jesus Christ was slain for sinners that they might be robed for ever in his perfect righteousness.

6. Justification by faith is revealed

'Abraham believed God, and it was counted unto him for righeousness' (Rom 4:3). By believing God's testimony concerning his Son, faith receives righteousness, the very righteousness of God in Christ.

7. The believer's security is displayed

The believers everlasting, infallible security in Christ is beautifully displayed. As the Lord brought Noah and his family into the ark and shut them in, so every believer, being brought into Christ by almighty grace, is shut in him, sealed, preserved and kept secure by the power of God. 'They shall never perish!'

This list could go on. The incarnation of Christ is prophesied; his substitutionary death is portrayed; his resurrection and exaltation are symbolized; his priesthood is anticipated; and the blessings of Christ upon the Israel of God are declared. Genesis is the book of beginnings, and in this book of beginnings everything speaks of Christ. Christ is the tree of life in the midst of the Garden of Eden. He is the promised Seed of the woman, who crushed the serpent's head. He is the Lamb whose blood was represented in Abel's sacrifice. He is the one whom Enoch believed, by whom he pleased God. He is the ark by which sinners are saved from the flood of God's wrath. Christ is the seed of promise who came from Abraham's loins, in whom all the nations of the earth are blessed. He is the Lamb of sacrifice whom God provided to die in the place of his chosen ones. He is the ladder Jacob saw, by whom the blessings of God come down to men, and by whom men ascend to God. Christ is that priest after the order of Melchizedek, by whom God's elect are blessed. He is our Joseph, ruling over all things, in whom all things are, and from whom all things come. He is the surety portrayed in Judah. He is the lawgiver prophesied by Jacob. In the book of beginnings, 'Christ is all, and in all.'

It is my desire that all who read this book will know Christ who is the beginning of the creation of God. All things were made by him and for him. He is before all things. He is in all things. By him all things consist, and all things point to him. The new creation, which is our subject, begins with Christ. We must know the Lord Jesus Christ. He is the one who made all things in the beginning. And he is the one who declares, 'Behold, I make all things new' (Rev. 21:5).

Let us refer back to verse 1. 'In the beginning God created the heaven and the earth.' The creation was a reflection of the Creator. In verse 2, we read that the earth 'was without form, and void'. It was certainly not created that way (see Isaiah 45:18). In its pristine beauty, the earth was perfect beyond imagination. Then something happened. It became 'without form, and void; and darkness was upon the face of the deep'. In the beginning there were no groans of suffering, no worms of corruption, no darkness of iniquity and no shades of death. God reigned supreme, without rival. But then the earth became without form and void, filled with darkness. Verse 2 describes:

The ruin and confusion of God's creation

The word 'was' in verse 2 should really be translated 'became'. God did not create the world in a state of confusion (Isa. 45:18). Between verses 1 and 2, some terrible catastrophe took place. Perhaps this was the fall of Satan (Isa. 14:12-17; Ezek. 28:14-18).[2] Whatever the catastrophe was, it left the earth 'without form, and void,' a desolate, uninhabitable, ruined mass of confusion. We have no indication of how long an interval there was between the creation of the world as it is stated in verse 1 and the ruin of the world as it is described in verse 2. However, all that took place from Genesis 1:3-31 transpired in six twenty-four-hour days, probably less than seven thousand years ago.

'In six days the LORD made heaven and earth, the sea, and all that in them is' (Exod. 20:11). There is a difference between 'creating' and 'making'. In Genesis 1:1, God created the world out of nothing. In Genesis 1:2, 'the earth became without form, and void; and darkness was upon the face of the deep.' In Genesis 1:3-31, God made the earth in six days, forming it and fashioning it out of that which he had created.

A. W. Pink has said, 'Out of the chaos was brought the "cosmos", which signifies order, arrangement, beauty. Out of the waters emerged the earth. A scene of desolation, darkness, and death was transformed into one of light, life, and fertility, so that at the end all was pronounced, "very good."'

As this is a picture of the world's history, so it is a picture of man's history. At the beginning of time, on the sixth day, God created man. What a creature he was, created in the image and likeness of God, gloriously reflecting the very character of God. God himself said man was 'very good'. He had no sinful heredity behind him, no sinful principle within him, no sinful stain upon him and no sinful environment around him. Man and woman walked together with God in the bliss of perfection, contentment and mutual delight. Man was delighted with God; and God was delighted with man.

Then there was a catastrophe! It is described in Genesis 3. Sin dared to raise its horrid head against God. Man defied

God's right to be God. Sin entered into the world, and death by sin. Man died; he was separated from God. The earth was cursed. It began to bring forth thorns and thistles. God's creature became without form and void. The dark slime of the serpent corrupted the race of mankind and is now found upon the face of all the earth. This great catastrophe, the Fall, is verified in the hearts of all Adam's descendants. Man is fallen (Eccles. 7:9). He is alienated from God (Eph. 4:18); he is depraved (Jer. 17:9); he is spiritually dead (Rom. 5:12).

Genesis 1:2 describes the condition of fallen man. Just as the earth, after Satan's fall, was in a state of disorder, so man, after Adam's fall, is too. The fallen state of man is *a state of confusion*: 'The earth [became] without form.' Nothing was in harmony with God; nothing was right. So, too, fallen man is out of kilter. Nothing in him is in harmony with God; nothing in him is right or good. It is a *state of emptiness*: 'The earth was ... void' — utterly empty, incapable of life and fruitfulness. And man without Christ is spiritually void, empty and barren, incapable of life and fruitfulness towards God. It is *a state of darkness*: 'Darkness was upon the face of the deep.' To be lost is to be under the power of darkness, to be under the rule of Satan, the prince of darkness. There is not one ray of spiritual light in man by nature. Fallen man has absolute no spiritual knowledge or understanding. Until he is born again, man cannot see, know, or understand anything spiritual (1 Cor. 2:14-16; John 3:3,5). The rest of this chapter (Gen. 1:3-31) describes:

The restoration of God's creation

I shall not attempt to explain the meaning of every verse. That is not my purpose in this study. I shall simply point out the spiritual significance of these verses. The order followed by God in restoring the physical creation is the same order which is followed in the new creation, in the restoration of fallen man by God's almighty grace. The work of God in the restoration of his creation corresponds exactly to the experience of a believer. Here are seven works which God performed in the restoration of his creation, which illustrate his work of grace in the believer.

First, 'And the Spirit of God moved upon the face of the waters' (v. 2). The earth, no doubt, moved in its orbit and rotated upon its own axis, but its motions could not mend it. It had to be moved upon by the Spirit of God. Otherwise, it would remain for ever 'without form, and void'. In the same way, regeneration is not accomplished by the works of man or by the motions of his heart; it is by the working of God the Holy Spirit. The new birth is not an evolution, but a creation. 'It is not of him that willeth, nor of him that runneth, but of God that showeth mercy' (Rom. 9:16). 'It is the Spirit that quickeneth; the flesh profiteth nothing' (John 6:63). As has been said, the new birth is not accomplished by man's movement towards God, but by God's movement towards and upon the heart of man.

Second, 'And God said, Let there be light; and there was light' (v. 3). Let us note this: if the Spirit of God moves upon a man, it is by the Word of God. No fewer than ten times in this chapter do we read these words: 'and God said'. God will not work apart from his Word. Without question, God could have refashioned and restored the earth without speaking a word. But he did not do so. His purposes were worked out and his counsels were fulfilled by his word. Light came, and was produced by the word of God. These two things are inseparably joined: the ministry of the Holy Spirit and the ministry of the Word of God. The Word of God is the power of God (Rom. 1:16). It is the source of spiritual light (2 Cor. 4:6); it is the seed of life (James 1:18; 1 Peter 1:23-25); it is that which conveys faith (Rom. 10:17); it is the means of grace and salvation (1 Cor. 1:23; 1 Tim. 4:16); 'and this is the Word which by the gospel is preached unto you' (1 Peter 1:25).

Third, 'And God divided the light from the darkness' (v. 4). As God separated the light from the darkness in the creation of the world, so he separates the light from the darkness in the new creation. 'Ye are all the children of light, and the children of the day: we are not of the night, nor of darkness' (1 Thess. 5:5). By the power of the Holy Spirit working in the new man, the Word of God divides between the soul and the spirit, separates the spiritual from the natural, sinful mind (2 Cor. 6:14-18). Those who are born of God know light from darkness; and they walk in the light as he is in the light (1 John 1:5-7).

Fourth, 'And God said, Let the earth bring forth [fruit]' (v. 11). Where the work of the Spirit, the Word of God and the light of grace are found, there will be fruit for God (Gal. 5:22-23). This fruit is the result of a condition, not an effort. It is the result of what we are, not of what we do. The fruit of Christ in us is Christlikeness. Those who are born of God bear fruit after his kind. The seed within bears fruit after its kind on the earth. Apples produce apples; grapes produce grapes; and grace produces grace. The grace of God working in a man gives him a new, gracious character; and that character is seen in his conduct (Eph. 4:17 - 5:21).

Fifth, 'And God said, Let there be lights in the firmament of the heaven ... to give light upon the earth' (vv. 14-15). The lights must be above the earth if they are to shine upon it. Like the lights in the heavens, all who are are born of God have been raised above the earth. 'Ye are the light of the world' (Matt. 5:14). As the moon reflects the light of the sun, let us see that we reflect the light of Christ in this world (Matt. 5:16). This is something we must do. Good works are the only lights by which the world sees Christ in his people. Let us be careful to maintain them (Eph. 2:10; Titus. 3:8). This must be clearly understood. We are saved by grace alone, through faith alone, in Christ alone. Good works have absolutely nothing to do with salvation. But that salvation which is brought about by God always produces good works (Eph. 2:8-10).

Sixth, 'God created man in his own image' (v. 27). Here is the climax of the Creator's power. God made man in his own likeness; and he made him out of the soil of the earth, even the earth which had become 'without form, and void'. Yet there is a work even greater than the work of creation. In the new creation, the God of all grace makes sinners new in Christ (2 Cor. 5:17; Gal. 6:15; Col. 3:10). God takes men and women who are utterly 'without form, and void' spiritually, and makes them replicas of his Son. When God has finished his work in us, we shall bear the image of the Lord Jesus Christ (Rom. 8:28-29). Imagine that!

Seventh, 'And God blessed the man he had made and gave him dominion over all his creation' (vv. 29-31). Those who are born of God are blessed by God (Eph. 1:3). 'All [things] are yours, and ye are Christ's; and Christ is God's.' And one day soon, God will put all things under our feet, even as he has put all things under the feet of his dear Son (Heb. 2:6-9; Rom. 16:20). Then the purpose of God will be fulfilled. Then God will be all in all! Then the Sabbath, then God our Saviour will have finished his work.

Until we are one with Christ, we are not in harmony with God's creation. But all who come to Christ, all who believe on the Lord Jesus Christ, all who are reconciled to God in his dear Son are new creatures in Christ, in harmony with God, with his purpose, with his providence and with his creation.

2.

The first week

Genesis 1:1 - 2:3

'And God blessed the seventh day, and sanctified it: because that in it he had rested from all his work which God created and made' (Gen. 2:3).

A. W. Pink wrote, 'Christ is the key which unlocks the golden doors into the temple of divine truth.'[1] Our Lord says, 'Search the Scriptures; for ... they are they which testify of me' (John 5:39). He declares, 'In the volume of the book it is written of me' (Heb. 10:7). Christ is the subject of the Book; he is enshrined upon every page. The book of Genesis speaks of him just as much as the book of Matthew. Just as the opening verses of Genesis describe God's work of creation, so they present a type of the entire work of redemption by the Lord Jesus Christ.

In these opening verses, the great need of redemption is set forth as a type. 'In the beginning God created the heaven and the earth.' Like everything else that comes from the hand of God, the world, which he first created, was perfect, beautiful and glorious. That was the original state of man. Adam was made in the image of God. He was endowed with life by the breath of the Almighty. Concerning him, God said, he was 'very good'.

Then, as we saw in chapter 1, something happened. In verse 2 we read, 'And the earth was without form, and void,' the earth became a ruin. Between Genesis 1:1 and 1:2 a terrible thing happened which resulted in the ruin of the earth. No one can say with certainty what happened because it has not been revealed, but, perhaps, this was the time when Satan's fell, the time when sin first entered God's universe.

This much is certain: Satan, the mightiest and most excellent of God's creatures, was filled with pride. Lucifer dared to oppose the will of his Creator. 'The anointed cherub that covereth' (Ezek. 28:14) dared to defy God's right to be God. As the result of his sin, Satan was cast out of heaven, cast down to the earth. The fall of Satan had far reaching consequences. The earth, which God originally created as fair and beautiful, became 'without form, and void,' a desolate place of ruin, 'and darkness was upon the face of the deep'.

This is a striking picture of what happened in the Garden. Man, who was created in the image of God, fell into sin; and his fall had far reaching consequences. The effects of his sin reached all his posterity. Humanity was ruined. All future generations were cursed, dead, incapable of bringing forth life. 'By one man sin entered into the world, and death by sin ... for that all have sinned' (Rom. 5:12).

'And darkness was upon the face of the deep.' Darkness is the opposite of light. God is light. Satan is darkness. And man under sin, being void of all light, is engulfed in total, spiritual darkness. Separated from God, morally blind, spiritually dead, all unregenerate men and women are in a state of darkness. This is the black background against which God has chosen to display the glory of his grace in redemption by Christ. 'Where sin abounded, grace did much more abound' (Rom. 5:20). As the Lord God restored creation from ruin in those first six days of time, by the work performed on each day, so he restores his elect from the ruin of the Fall by his redemptive works in Christ.

The first day

In the work on the first day, a type of the incarnation of Christ is set forth (vv. 2-5). If fallen man was to be reconciled to God who is holy, something had to be done. But what? How could that great gulf which separated man from God be bridged? What ladder could be set up upon the earth that would reach into heaven itself? Only one answer can be given. The initial work of reconciliation and restoration had to be the incarnation of God himself. The Word had to be made flesh. God himself had to come down to the horrible pit where humanity lives in helplessness, sin and death. If ever man was to be lifted out of the miry clay and transported into heavenly glory, the God of glory had to become a man, the Son of God had to take upon himself the form of a servant and be made in the likeness of men. This is precisely what is presented as a type by the first day.

First, there is the work of the Holy Spirit: 'And the Spirit of God moved upon [brooded over] the face of the waters' (v. 2). That is exactly what happened in the incarnation of Christ (Luke 1:35). That holy body, which was created in Mary's womb, was the offspring of God the Holy Spirit, especially prepared to be a suitable sacrifice for sin (Heb. 10:4-5).

Second, the Word brought forth light: 'And God said, [there is his Word], Let there be light: and there was light' (v. 3). As soon as Mary brought forth her child, the Word, Light came into the world (Luke 2:8-9, 29-32; John 1:9).

Third, the light was given God's approval: 'And God saw the light, that it was good' (v. 4). The same word which is translated 'good' here, is translated 'beautiful' in other texts. 'He hath made everything beautiful in his time' (Eccles. 3:11). 'God saw the light, that it was good,' beautiful! And so, the Lord God looks upon his incarnate Son with delight, satisfaction and approval (Luke 2:52; Matt. 3:17).

Fourth, the light was separated from the darkness: 'And God divided the light from the darkness' (v. 4). Though the Lord Jesus was, and is, the Son of man, he was separated from the sons of men by infinity. He knew no sin (Heb. 7:26).

Fifth, the light was named by God: 'And God called the light day' (v. 5). So it was with him who is the light of the world. It was not left up to Joseph and Mary to select a name for our Saviour and theirs; God himself gave him his name (Isa. 49:1; Matt. 1:21).

The second day

In the work accomplished on the second day, the cross of Christ is foreshadowed as a type (vv. 6-8). Without question, our Lord's life of obedience as the federal head and representative of God's elect was as necessary as his death upon the cross as our substitute. We could never have been saved by Christ's life alone. His life alone could never bring about our righteousness, could never satisfy the justice of God, could never atone for our sins. Thank God for his holy life! But we are justified, redeemed, forgiven and made righteous by his blood: 'Without shedding of blood is no remission' (Heb. 9:22). Life is in the blood. We could never have lived with Christ, without his death upon the cross (John 12:24). The cross of Christ is the only place where the righteous claims of God, who is holy, could be met.

The firmament was purposed by God before it was made. In verse 6, God said, 'Let there be a firmament.' Then, in verse 7, 'God made the firmament.' Long, long before the cross was erected upon Mount Calvary, it was purposed by God in everlasting mercy (1 Peter 1:18-20; Rev. 13:8).

The firmament was set 'in the midst of the waters'. The word 'waters' is sometimes used in Scripture to represent 'people' and 'nations'. (Isa. 8:7; Rev. 17:1,15,18). The Lord Jesus Christ performed his great work of redemption in the most public manner. Christ was crucified publicly, in the midst of two thieves, in Jerusalem, in the middle of the earth. And he is made known everywhere, in the midst of men and women, by the preaching of the gospel (Gal. 3:1).

The firmament 'divided the waters'. It divided the waters under it, upon the earth, from the waters above it, in the heavens. The cross of Christ is the great divider of mankind. As it separated the one thief from the other, the penitent from the unbelieving, so it divides all men into two categories: the seed of the serpent and the seed of the woman, the children of Satan and the sons of God. On the one hand, 'the preaching of the cross is to them that perish foolishness,' but on the other hand, 'unto us which are saved it is the power of God' (1 Cor. 1:18).

As God designed and made the firmament that divided the waters, so the cross of Christ, which divides the people of the world, was designed and made by God himself (Acts 2:23; Isa. 53:9-11). His sin-atoning death was by God's design and by his hand, as were the results of his death.

The third day

In the work on the third day, our Lord's resurrection is foreshadowed (vv. 9-13). The third thing necessary in the accomplishment of redemption was the resurrection of the crucified Christ. A dead Christ could save no one. He is able to save to the uttermost all who come to God by him. For this reason, 'He ever liveth!' (Heb. 7:25).

Until the third day, death had reigned supreme. No life had appeared upon the face of the ruined earth. But on the third day, the earth was commanded to 'bring forth'. Not on the second, not on the fourth, but on the third day life appeared on the previously dead and barren earth. It was on the third day that our Lord Jesus Christ arose from the dead to give life to the world, 'according to the Scriptures'!

The fourth day

In the work done on the fourth day, our Redeemer's ascension and exaltation are portrayed (vv. 14-19). The resurrection did not complete our Saviour's mediatorial work. It was necessary for him to enter into that place not made with hands, by the merits of his own blood, that he might obtain eternal redemption for us, and appear there for ever in the presence of God on our behalf (Heb. 9:12, 24). On the fourth day, our eyes are lifted from earth to heaven. As we read these verses, these words by the Spirit of God come to mind: 'Seek those things which are above, where Christ sitteth on the right hand of God. Set your affection on things above, not on things on the earth' (Col. 3:1-2).

As we lift our eyes to heaven, we see two great lights. The greater light is Christ, the Sun of Righteousness (Mal. 4:2). The lesser light is his church, the moon to reflect his light (Rev. 12:1). These two great lights are set by God to rule over the day and over the night, to give light upon the earth.

The fifth day

In the work done on the fifth day, God gave life to the waters, foreshadowing, as a type, the results of Christ's ascension (vv. 20-23). The direct, inevitable result of Christ's sin-atoning death as their substitute is the salvation of all God's elect. As the result of our Lord's death, resurrection and ascension, all the peoples of the earth have been blessed with God's salvation (Ps. 68:18-20; John 17:2; Gal. 3:13-14).

The sixth day

In the work on the sixth day, we are given a picture of the consummation of Christ's redemptive work (vv. 24-31). Our Lord has not yet done all. He assumed our nature in the incarnation; he died in our place on the cross; he arose from the dead as our representative; he ascended to heaven from where he bestows the blessings of grace upon his elect. Yet there is still a work to be done. There is a day coming called the restitution of all things. In that great day, the present earth, cursed by sin, will be made new, to bring forth fruit to God (Rom. 8:18-23). Then, manhood, in God's elect multitude, will be made perfectly into the image of the Son of God. That is what the Bible calls 'glorification'. The everlasting glorification of God's elect is the end of election and predestination (Rom. 8:28-30; Eph. 1:3-6). Then, the Lord, our God, will give to his elect every good thing as 'heirs of God and joint-heirs with Christ'.

The seventh day

Oh, blessed be God, there is a seventh day! (2:1-3). The seventh day was a day of rest. It represents three things:

1. The rest of faith in Christ (Matt. 11:28-30; Heb. 4:3).
2. The rest of Christ, our successful Saviour (Heb. 4:10).
3. The rest of the Triune God in everlasting glory (1 Cor. 15:24-28).

As creation is a picture of grace, so it is a picture of redemption, for all grace comes to us freely through the redemption that is in Christ Jesus.

3.

The first marriage

Genesis 2:18-25

'And the LORD God said, It is not good that the man should be alone; I will make him an help meet for him. And out of the ground the LORD God formed every beast of the field, and every fowl of the air; and brought them unto Adam to see what he would call them: and whatsoever Adam called every living creature, that was the name thereof. And Adam gave names to all cattle, and to the fowl of the air, and to every beast of the field; but for Adam there was not found an help meet for him. And the LORD God caused a deep sleep to fall upon Adam, and he slept: and he took one of his ribs, and closed up the flesh instead thereof; and the rib, which the LORD God had taken from man, made he a woman, and brought her unto the man. And Adam said, This is now bone of my bones, and flesh of my flesh: she shall be called Woman, because she was taken out of Man. Therefore shall a man leave his father and his mother, and shall cleave unto his wife: and they shall be one flesh. And they were both naked, the man and his wife, and were not ashamed' (Gen. 2:18-25).

On the sixth day of creation, God said, 'Let us make man in our image, after our likeness' (Gen. 1:26), and he did. In chapter 2:7 we read, 'And the LORD God formed man of the dust of the ground, and breathed into his nostrils the breath of life; and man became a living soul.' Then, in verses 16 and 17, we read, 'The LORD God commanded the man.' He did not command men, but 'the man'. He did not command the man and the woman. The woman was not around. He commanded 'the man', Adam. The commandment was given to one man because one man was representative of all men.

There was a reason for this. God had ordained the salvation of his elect by another man, the last Adam, who is our Lord Jesus Christ. As we all fell by the act of one representative man, Adam, so God ordained that all his elect would be saved by the work of another representative man, the Lord Jesus Christ (Rom. 5:12-19).

Why was Eve created?

'The LORD God said, It is not good that the man should be alone' (v. 18). Why was it not good for man to live alone? He had no one to love. Being created in the image of God, Adam was full of love and affection. That love and affection needed to have an object. There was no one like himself with whom he could converse, no one with whom he could discuss the beauties of the Garden, no one with whom he could share his thoughts. He had no one to touch and embrace. Companionship, togetherness, is essential to those who love. We need to touch and be touched. We need to embrace and be embraced. He had no one to help him. There was no one who needed Adam's help, and no one to help Adam with his needs, as a man living in the world. The Lord God graciously took care to provide help for fallen, needy man, even before he fell and became needy. There was no one for him, with whom the man could share his blessings. Love must give, and delights to give; but Adam had no one to whom he could give what God had given him, no one to whom he could give himself. He had no one for him to comfort and no one to comfort him, no one for him to admire and no one to admire him — he was alone! Adam had no one with whom to produce others like himself. All the animals of the garden had their mates and their little ones, but Adam was alone. He had neither wife, nor sons, nor daughters (vv. 19-20). Eve was created by God specifically to be 'an help meet' for Adam.

How was Eve created?

First, we are told what the Lord God did for Adam (vv. 21-22). 'The LORD God caused a deep sleep to fall upon Adam.' This was more than a normal rest, or sleep. God himself put Adam into a coma. No one else could do this to him. While he slept, God took one of his ribs out of his side and closed up the flesh, so that there was no scar. From that rib, God made a woman. Then he brought her to the man.

God did not create the woman as he did the man; he made the woman from the man. Woman was not the beginning of a new order and a new race; she was the continuation of the race. Adam was the sole head and representative. That is God's order. She is called 'Ishshah', woman, because she was taken from 'Ish', man. The Lord did not take the woman from the man's head to reign over him, nor did he take her from man's foot to be trampled upon by him, but from his side as one who would be his equal. God took woman from the rib of man, from under his arm, to be protected by him, from near his heart, to be loved by him. Then the Lord God brought the woman to the man. She was the gift of God to man. This is God's order. It cannot be changed (1 Cor. 11:8-9).

Verses 23 and 24 tell us what Adam did: 'Adam said, This is now bone of my bones, and flesh of my flesh.' He was saying, 'This woman is part of me. She is to be loved and cherished by me, as I would love and cherish myself. We are one person.' 'Therefore shall a man leave his father and his mother, and shall cleave unto his wife: and they shall be one flesh.' Adam understood from the beginning what very few men understand today. The man who has a wife is the one responsible for the household. He is the head of the house — prophet, priest and king. He provides for the household; he rules the household; and he protects it. The woman who has such a man can rest in his care and love (1 Peter 3:7).

'And they were both naked, the man and his wife, and were not ashamed' (v. 25). They were, as God had created them, holy and upright. They did not need clothes to protect them or to conceal any part of their bodies, which God had made. They were not ashamed, because they had nothing of which to be ashamed. There was no sin in their nature, no guilt in their consciences and no wickedness in their actions. But they did not remain in this blessed condition. As soon as they sinned, they were under the curse, and they were ashamed (Gen. 3:1-7). We are all inheritors of their shame because we have all inherited their guilt (Rom. 5:12).

What does the Holy Spirit teach us here?

First, without question, there is much to be learned about true womanhood in these verses. Blessed is the woman who receives and bows to the Word of the Lord, and teaches her daughters to do so (Titus 2:3-5). Blessed is her family. She alone is a truly virtuous woman (Prov. 31:10-31). But there is something far more glorious here. The marriage performed by God in the Garden of Eden, the marriage of Adam and Eve, is a picture of the marriage performed by God in grace, the marriage of Christ and his church.

Second, there is a second representative man — Christ, our Saviour (1 Cor. 15:21-22, 45-49). He is not just the second Adam. Christ is the last Adam, the last representative man. The first Adam sinned. The last Adam obeyed God perfectly for his people. The first Adam brought death to all his race. The last Adam brought life, eternal life to all who were represented by him. As we have borne the image of the first man, so will all God's elect bear the image of the last man, the Lord from heaven, our great Saviour, the Lord Jesus Christ.

This last Adam will not be alone in his kingdom. God has declared that he will have a people to love and by whom he will be loved. He will have a people made after his likeness (Rom. 8:29-30), with whom he can be in fellowship, with whom he can walk, who will serve him and whom he will serve, who will admire him and whom he can admire, a people with whom he can share everything, and who will reign with him for ever.

Third, the Lord God made a body of flesh for his dear Son (Gal. 4:4-5; Heb. 2:17; 10:5). Woman was made from man; but here is a man who was made of woman by the hand of God, that he might redeem and save fallen men.

Fourth, God caused a deep sleep to come upon his Son. His sleep was death, death for sin. None but God could do this. At the cross, God put his Son to death for us, that we might live by his death. Just as Adam died for Eve, knowing full well what he was doing, (Gen. 3:6; 1 Tim. 2:14), so Christ freely, voluntarily laid down his life for his bride. From the side of our crucified Redeemer, there flowed blood to justify and water to sanctify his chosen bride (John 19:34; Eph. 5:22-27).

Fifth, in the fulness of time, the Lord God will bring his chosen bride to Christ, by the effectual, irresistible grace and power of his Spirit (Ps. 65:4; 110:3). He will make her submissive to him, cause her to adore him and unite her to him. Christ left all for her and cleaves to her; and she leaves all for him and cleaves to him (Eph. 5:30-32).

Sixth, they are not ashamed (1 John 2:28-29). 'He that believeth shall not be ashamed!' In verse 25, we are told that Adam and Eve had no outward clothing and they were not ashamed. The righteousness of Christ is a garment to cover us, the garment of God's salvation, which makes believers unashamed before God. Our Saviour's death has put away our sin and our guilt. His Spirit has given us his nature. By faith in him, we have confidence before God and are not ashamed, for in Christ we are holy and blameless. Yes, we still have this outward body of flesh that must be covered because of its corruption. But soon we shall lay it aside and rise in his likeness. In that last great day, we shall stand before the bar of God in the perfection of Christ, robed in white garments, clean and white, and we shall not be ashamed.

4.

Two trees

Genesis 2:9

'And out of the ground made the Lord God to grow every tree that is pleasant to the sight, and good for food; the tree of life also in the midst of the garden, and the tree of knowledge of good and evil' (Gen. 2:9).

Among the many things created by God, there were two trees planted in the midst of the garden: 'the tree of life' and 'the tree of the knowledge of good and evil'.

Had Adam eaten of the tree of life, he would have lived for ever (Gen. 3:22-24). We have no way of knowing what the tree of life was. God has not told us. But we do know what it symbolized. It symbolized the Lord Jesus Christ who is our life, from whom we have eternal life. Christ is to all who believe a tree of life planted in the midst of the paradise of God (Prov. 3:18; Rev. 2:7; 22:2). To trust the Lord Jesus Christ, to live by faith upon the merits of his blood atonement and his perfect righteousness, is to eat of the tree of life. The fruit of this tree, the result of Christ's obedience to God as the sinner's substitute, is eternal life. All who eat of the fruit of this tree will live for ever.

However, the Lord also placed another tree in the midst of the Garden. It was 'the tree of the knowledge of good and evil'. The moment that Adam ate of the fruit of that tree, he died. He died spiritually, was condemned to die eternally, and began to die physically. These things are recorded in the Scriptures by the Holy Spirit for our learning and edification. There are several important, spiritual lessons to be learned by comparing 'the tree of the knowledge of good and evil' to the cursed tree upon which the Son of God was crucified. Please read Acts 5:30 and 1 Peter 2:24.

Some points of contrast

There are six obvious points of contrast between 'the tree of the knowledge of good and evil' and the cross of our Lord Jesus Christ. There is as much to be learned from the disparity between the type and its fulfilment as there is from a comparison of the type and the antitype.

First, 'the tree of the knowledge of good and evil' was planted by God (Gen. 2:9); but the tree upon which Christ was crucified was made and set in its place by man (Matt. 27:33-35).

It is true, Christ was delivered to death by the determinate counsel and foreknowledge of God (Acts 2:23). God Almighty fixed the time of his death, the means of his death, the place of his death, the object of his death and the results of his death. But human hands devised and erected the cruel tree on Golgotha's hill, stretched out the Lord of glory upon it and crucified him. It is written: 'And they crucified him'! The death of Christ was by the will, decree, purpose and hand of God the Father; but the guilt of it lies entirely upon us. It was by the will, the hands and the work of men that the incarnate God was nailed to the cursed tree.

Second, 'the tree of the knowledge of good and evil' was pleasant to the eyes (Gen. 3:6); but everything connected with the tree of the crucifixion was hideous, repugnant and ignominious.

Though it would be idolatrous to do so, were it possible for an artist to capture the scene of our Lord's crucifixion on canvas, no one would want the picture hanging in his home. The scene was horrible. Our suffering Saviour looked more like a violently slaughtered beast than a man (Isa. 52:14; Ps. 22:11-22). Drunks and priests, thieves and scribes, harlots and Pharisees, Roman soldiers and Jewish rabbis all joined in a hellish party, taunting, jeering and laughing as they slaughtered the incarnate God. For three hours, darkness covered the face of the earth. When he was made sin for us, the Son of God was forsaken by his Father. Quivering in pain, burning with fever, covered with blood and with the reproach of being made sin for us breaking his heart, the Son of God died upon the cursed tree, having been made a curse for us. Thus he redeemed his elect from the curse of the law.

Third, God forbade man to eat of 'the tree of the knowledge of good and evil' (Gen. 2:17); but every man is freely invited, and even commanded, to eat of the fruit of that tree upon which the Saviour died.

Do not mistake my meaning. There is no value, or merit, in that wooden cross upon which Christ died. We do not value the cross, the physical cross, at all. But there is infinite merit in the sacrifice of the one who died upon the cross. The fruits of our Saviour's death are priceless. God himself calls sinners to eat of the fruit of this tree. He tells us, 'All things are ready, Come.' 'O taste and see that the Lord is good.' The leaves of this tree are for the healing of the nations, the healing of God's elect scattered throughout all the nations of the world. In the cross, in the sacrifice of our Lord Jesus Christ, is all that is needed for the healing of our souls from all the consequences of sin. It is there that we find atonement made, justice satisfied, righteousness brought in, forgiveness obtained and eternal life secured for chosen sinners.

Fourth, Satan used every cunning device to get man to eat of 'the tree of the knowledge of good and evil' (Gen. 3:1-6); but he uses every cunning device imaginable to keep sinners from eating of the fruits of Christ's death upon the tree of crucifixion.

The liar from hell deceives sinners, who are all willing to be deceived, by flattering their sinful nature. All over the world, he persuades men and women that they do not need a substitute, that they are really good enough to win God's approval, that he would not really send them to hell. With cunning craftiness, he makes men and women think they are smart, too smart to believe God, so smart that they imagine all religion to be superstition and hypocrisy.

Fifth, the eating of the fruit of 'the tree of the knowledge of good and evil' brought death to Adam and Eve (Gen. 2:17); but life comes to all who eat the flesh and drink the blood of him who died upon the cursed tree (John 6:53-56). Christ's flesh — his obedience to God in the body of human flesh — is righteousness. His blood — the pouring out of his life's blood to death — is atonement. To eat his flesh and drink his blood is to receive him by faith, thus receiving his righteousness and his atonement.

Sixth, by eating of 'the tree of the knowledge of good and evil' as a thief, Adam was cast out of paradise (Gen. 3:24); but, by eating of the fruit of the tree of crucifixion, the penitent thief entered paradise (Luke 23:39-43).

The only time it is recorded in the Scriptures that our Saviour used the word 'paradise' during his earthly ministry is in his promise to the penitent thief. It was not accidental. Like the penitent thief, all believers are reconciled to God and will be brought into eternal paradise, by believing on the Lord Jesus Christ. As he confessed his sin and just condemnation, so do we. As he acknowledged Christ as his Lord, so do we. As he trusted the mercy and grace of

Christ the Lord, so do we. As he obtained the favour of the
Lord by faith in him, so do we. As he is with Christ in
paradise, so we soon shall be.

Some marks of similarity

We have seen the points of contrast between the tree in the
Garden and the cross of Christ. Now, secondly, let us look
at some of the marks of similarity between these two trees.

First, both trees were planted in a garden (John 19:41).
The first Adam died in a garden; and so did the last Adam.

Second, both trees were planted in the midst of the
garden (Gen. 2:9; John 19:18). Our Lord Jesus Christ died
as our substitute in the midst of the world, and in the midst
of two thieves, separating one thief from the other. The blood
of Christ alone is that which distinguishes God's elect from
the reprobate. Our Lord Jesus was also crucified in the midst
of time. His death was the crisis of the world. When the
fulness of the Jews had come, and as the fulness of the
Gentiles began, the Son of God died at Calvary to ransom
the Israel of God. It is this day, and it will for ever be, the
cross of Christ which is the tree of life planted in the midst
of the heavenly paradise (Rev. 22:2); that is the centre and
glory of all things.

Third, both trees were trees of the knowledge of good
and evil. There is only one place in all the world where
sinners, such as we are, can learn the knowledge of good
and evil. These things are learned by divine revelation at
the cross. There, as we look to Christ in faith, we see the
goodness of God and the holiness of God, the love of God
and the wrath of God, the grace of God and the justice of
God, the mercy of God and the truth of God. It is only as we
look to Christ in faith, trusting him as our crucified Saviour,

that we begin to see the evil of sin, the wickedness of man and the utter depravity of our own hearts. It is looking on him whom we have pierced that melts our hearts to repentance (Zech. 12:10). It is only in the light of Christ crucified that we discern good from evil in providence. For God's elect, all things are good. For the unbeliever, all things are evil (Prov. 12:21; Isa. 3:10-11).

Fourth, both trees were good for food (Gen. 3:6). The cross of Christ — by which I mean the doctrine of the cross, the gospel — is the very meat and marrow of the believer's life. It is good as food for our souls! How pleasant it is to the eyes of faith! In the crucified Christ, in the doctrine of the cross, we see our sins blotted out. We see how it is that God is, indeed, both perfectly just and the justifier of every believer. Truly, this is 'a tree to be desired to make one wise!' The preaching of the cross is the power and the wisdom of God. It makes the believing sinner wise in the matter of salvation.

The cross of Christ was to our dear Saviour a cursed tree (Gal. 3:13); but to us it is a tree of blessing, a curse removed. As Abraham's guest was urged to take water and refreshment, and find rest 'under the tree' (Gen. 18:4), so, in the gospel, weary sinners are invited by God to take water and refreshment, and find rest for their souls under the cross. As Abraham and his guest stood together 'under the tree' (Gen. 18:8), so the Triune God and believing sinners stand together at the cross of Christ. As the tree cast into Marah's bitter waters made the waters sweet (Exod. 15:23-25), so the cross of Christ cast into our bitter lives makes them sweet. With the inspired apostle, every believer ought to make this his firm resolve: 'God forbid that I should glory, save in the cross of our Lord Jesus Christ!'

5.

The fall of man

Genesis 3:1-24

'And the LORD said, I will destroy man whom I have created from the face of the earth, both man, and beast, and the creeping thing, and the fowls of the air; for it repenteth me that I have made them' (Gen. 6:7).

If we are to understand anything about the grace of God and the workings of grace for and in elect sinners, we must understand something about the Fall. Genesis 3 is one of the most important chapters in all the Word of God. Here the foundation is laid upon which all gospel truth is built. If we trace all the rivers of truth back to their source, we shall find their source in Genesis 3. Here the revelation of the great drama of redemption begins, that drama which is being acted out upon the stage of human history. In this one chapter of inspiration:

1. the present fallen, ruined condition of our race is explained;
2. the subtle devices of the devil are disclosed;
3. the utter inability of man is recorded;
4. the effects of sin are displayed;
5. God's attitude towards fallen man is set forth;

6. man's pride and self-righteousness are demonstrated;
7. God's gracious provisions for fallen sinners are proclaimed;
8. and the necessity of a mediator is revealed.

There is no understanding of the rest of the Bible until Genesis 3 is understood. If we go wrong here, we shall err in our interpretation of all the rest of the Word of God. If, by the Spirit of God, we can grasp the message of Genesis 3, we shall not greatly err in the rest of the Book.

This much is evident: if Genesis 3 is true (and it is!), then both the science and the sociology taught in our day are wrong. The evolutionary scientists tell us that man is slowly, but surely, evolving into a perfect being, that though he began very low, he has climbed very high. God tells us that he made man perfect; but man has ruined himself. God tells us that he made man very high; but man has fallen very, very low.

Leading sociologists, psychologists, educators and philosophers have been telling us for a hundred and fifty years that man's problem is his environment. Religious leaders tell us that man has great potential. His problems are outward. God tells us that our problem is our heart. The fact is, man is a fallen, depraved creature, under the wrath and curse of the holy Lord God, in need of redemption, regeneration and grace. That is the message of Genesis 3.

The fall of man

The first six verses of this chapter reveal the fall of our father Adam, and of the whole human race in him (Rom. 5:12). Man is not an independent, self-governing creature. He did not make himself; he owes his being to God. Man was made to serve God, to glorify his Creator by obedience to him. As a symbol of God's sovereignty and of man's responsibility, a tree was planted in the midst of the Garden which man was not permitted to use for himself (Gen. 2:16-17).

The only restriction placed upon his liberty was the fruit of 'the tree of the knowledge of good and evil'. This tree symbolized the relationship in which man stood to God. Adam was created as an intelligent, responsible creature, subject to the rule of God, the Creator. But soon he became a self-seeking, self-willed, self-centred, self-serving rebel. How did this happen? It is not my purpose to give an exposition of these verses here. But there are three things that need to be understood.

1. Satan tempted, beguiled and deceived our mother Eve

Satan knew how God created Adam and how he made Eve from one of Adam's ribs. He knew that Eve was the weaker vessel and that Adam loved Eve. Therefore, he set his sights on Eve. He was confident that if he could get Eve, Adam would fall. With great subtlety, the old serpent beguiled the woman. The steps that led to her ruin were these:

> 1. She heeded the voice of the tempter. Instead of saying, 'Get thee behind me, Satan,' Eve quietly listened as the wicked one assaulted the Word of God. The door was opened when she began to discuss and debate what God had revealed with one who denied God's words.

> 2. Eve then began to make additions to the Word of God. Tampering with God's Word is always fatal. It is just as much an evil to add our words to God's as it is

to diminish his. Eve said, 'Ye shall not eat of it, neither shall ye touch it' (Gen 3:3; Prov. 30:5-6).

3. The woman proceeded to alter God's Word. God said, 'In the day that thou eatest thereof thou shalt surely die.' Eve said, 'Lest ye die' *or*, 'We might die.'

4. She disregarded God's Word altogether. She began by questioning it, and she soon disregarded it altogether. This is the way sin entered into the world. To quote the words of A. W. Pink: 'The will of God was resisted. The Word of God was rejected. The way of God was deserted.'

In verses 4-5, Satan cast doubt upon the Word of God, the justice of God and the goodness of God. In verse 6, Eve saw, she coveted and she took. She saw — perhaps Satan took a bite of the fruit. She desired the wisdom, freedom and superiority that Satan promised. She took — she took that which belonged to God alone.

2. Eve gave the fruit to Adam (v. 6)

As we have seen, Eve was deceived; but Adam was not (1 Tim. 2:13-14). Adam wilfully, deliberately rebelled against the express command of God. Because of his love for Eve, he defied God. Rather than lose Eve, he willingly plunged himself and all his posterity into spiritual ruin and enmity against God.

3. When Adam sinned, we all became sinners and died spiritually

We were all separated from God (Rom. 5:12). Adam was a representative man, a covenant head. As he represented the whole human race, we all fell through the sin and fall of our father Adam. How thankful we ought to be for our God's wise arrangement of things.[1] Had there been no Fall, there would always have been the possibility of one. Had there been no Fall, we could never have known the wonders and beauties of redeeming love and saving grace (1 Peter 1:12), and we could never have been brought into union with God in Christ, the God-man. Since we fell by a representative, there is the hope that we might rise again by a representative (Heb. 2:16).

The record of the Fall, given in Genesis 3, is the only plausible explanation for the condition of the human race. Original sin is revealed here. It is verified everywhere. How else can anyone explain the universality of sin, the universality of sickness and sorrow, and the universality of death? These things are universal because we all have our being from one man, Adam. We all sinned in him; we all died in him; and we all received our nature from him.

The great power and subtlety of our adversary the Devil

Satan appears here for the first time in the Bible. We learn of his prior existence, his original glory and his terrible fall in Isaiah 14:12-15, Ezekiel 28:12-19 and Revelation 12:7-11. Words cannot be found which are strong enough to describe adequately the crafty deceit, subtlety and power of this creature, the devil, Satan, the serpent, the dragon of hell (Jude 9). He is too wise for us to outwit him without divine wisdom. He is too powerful for us to overcome him, apart from Christ; and he is too subtle for us to recognize him, apart from the Spirit of God and the Word of God. In this third chapter of Genesis, the Lord reveals three things to us about Satan. We should be wise and understand them.

1. The primary sphere of Satan's activity is in the spiritual, religious realm

Contrary to popular opinion, it is not Satan, but the natural depravity of the human heart that leads men and women into adultery, fornication, blasphemy, drunkenness, witchcraft, and many other sins (Mark 7:21-23; Gal. 5:19-21). Satan's chief aim is to come between us and God, to keep us from our Maker. His goal is to keep us from trusting Christ. The way he does this is by inspiring confidence in ourselves. He seeks to usurp the place of God, to make God's creatures his own subjects. His work consists of substituting his own lies for the truth of God. Beware! Satan's primary focus is not in brothels, bars and dark alleys, but in churches, pulpits, seminaries and religious activities (Eph. 4:10-12; 2 Cor. 11). Satan goes to church every Sunday; he has preachers. He tries to get men to perform deeds of righteousness, a righteousness of their own, to keep them from trusting Christ alone for righteousness. Satan will give men faith, peace and assurance. His ambition is not to keep them from being religious or even moral. It is to keep sinners who are bound for eternity from trusting Christ.

2. Satan's method is to pervert Holy Scripture and to appeal to the flesh

He throws doubt upon God's Word (v. 1). He substitutes his own word for God's (v. 4). He casts a slur upon the attributes of God (v. 5). He appeals to our flesh (v. 5). He appeals to our senses — the eye, to our emotions — the desires, to our intellect — that proud desire to be thought wise, and to our pride — that vile pride that makes men desire to be 'as gods'.

3. Our adversary, the devil, will be destroyed by the power of God (Gen. 3:15)

At Calvary, the Lord Jesus Christ destroyed the devil's dominion over the nations of the world (John 12:31; Rev. 20:1-3). He who deceived, and still deceives, the nations was bound by the crucified Christ, who now gathers his elect out of every nation, people, tribe and tongue. In the new birth — the conversion of sinners by his almighty grace — the Son of God enters into the hearts of chosen sinners by the power of his Spirit, binds the strong man, takes his house and spoils his goods (Eph. 2:1-4). In the Day of Judgement, our blessed Saviour will finally crush the serpent beneath our feet (Rom. 16:20).

The consequences of the Fall

As soon as Adam sinned against God, he began to suffer the consequences of his transgression. 'The eyes of them both were opened' (v. 7). Their eyes were not enlightened, but opened. They acquired no advanced knowledge, nothing pleasant or profitable. Their eyes were opened to distressing, evil things. Satan has deceived our race. We have lost communion and fellowship with God. By nature, we are all without God, life, light, Christ and hope (Eph. 2:11-12). 'They knew that they were naked' (v. 7). They felt things they had never known or felt before. They lost their innocence. Guilt engulfed them. Shame embarrassed them. Fear terrified them. Hatred arose between them (v. 12). 'They sewed fig leaves together, and made themselves aprons' (v. 7). The fallen pair began to try to quieten their consciences, cover their nakedness and get rid of their shame.

Then, 'Adam and his wife hid themselves from the presence of the LORD God' (v. 8). When they heard God's voice,
they ran. When they were exposed, they offered excuses
(vv. 12-13). Thus it has been with the sons and daughters of
Adam from that day to this.

Adam and Eve were cursed by God. The woman was
cursed (v. 16). The man was cursed (vv. 17-19). They were
driven from the presence of God (vv. 22-24). They died
spiritually, and we died in our father Adam (Col. 2:13; Eph.
2:1-3). They began to die physically; and the seeds of death
are passed from father to child, from generation to generation. They were sentenced to die eternally; and all the
sons and daughters of Adam are born 'children of wrath'
(Eph. 2:3).

The gracious character of our God

But Genesis 3 does not leave us at the point of our ruin in
Adam. This chapter also shows us something of the gracious character of our God. Here we are given great reasons
for praise and gratitude to the Lord our God.

The first call of grace is found in verse 9. The voice Adam
heard was not the voice of a policeman, seeking a criminal.
It was the voice of a Father's love, seeking a son who was
lost. It was a call of divine justice that cannot overlook sin;
a call of divine love that cannot be quenched; and a call of
divine grace that cannot be resisted (1 John 4:19).

Here is the first gospel sermon (v. 15). The preacher was
God himself. The audience was a pair of guilty, helpless
sinners. The subject was redemption by Christ. The sermon
speaks of conflict, enmity, and war between the seed of the
serpent and the Seed of the woman (Rev. 12). It shows God's
sovereign election and predestination, dividing the sons

and daughters of Adam into the seed of the serpent and the seed of Christ. It speaks of the incarnation of our Lord Jesus Christ (Gal. 4:4-6), his death, of his heel being bruised by the serpent, and his victory in death by which the serpent's head has been crushed. In a word, this first gospel sermon promised redemption, grace and salvation by the substitutionary sacrifice of God's dear Son at Calvary (2 Cor. 5:21).

Here is the first portrayal of redemption (v. 21). The guilty pair, under the sentence of death, stood before God. A sacrifice of blood was made — an innocent lamb. Adam and Eve were stripped of their fig-leaf aprons by the hand of God himself. The only way any sinner will ever give up his imaginary righteousness is if God himself strips away his fig-leaf aprons. Then the Lord God made a covering, without human aid, and put it on the fallen pair. Just as it is for sinners in the experience of God's saving grace, so it was for Adam and Eve — they were totally passive. God did everything; they did nothing (Eph. 2:8-9; Luke 15:22; Isa. 61:10).

Here is the first description of man's lost condition (v. 24). The fallen pair were driven from the Garden, separated from God. They were barred from the presence of God by the sword of justice. They were utterly incapable of returning to him. But God, in great mercy, love and grace, found a way to bring fallen, ruined, helpless sinners back to himself (John 14:6; Zech. 13:7-9; Heb. 10:19-22).

6.

Adam and Christ

Genesis 3:17-24

'And unto Adam he said, Because thou hast hearkened unto the voice of thy wife, and hast eaten of the tree, of which I commanded thee, saying, Thou shalt not eat of it; cursed is the ground for thy sake; in sorrow shalt thou eat of it all the days of thy life; Thorns also and thistles shall it bring forth to thee; and thou shalt eat the herb of the field; In the sweat of thy face shalt thou eat bread, till thou return unto the ground; for out of it wast thou taken: for dust thou art, and unto dust shalt thou return. And Adam called his wife's name Eve; because she was the mother of all living. Unto Adam also and to his wife did the LORD God make coats of skins, and clothed them. And the LORD God said, Behold, the man is become as one of us, to know good and evil: and now, lest he put forth his hand, and take also of the tree of life, and eat, and live for ever: Therefore the LORD God sent him forth from the garden of Eden, to till the ground from whence he was taken. So he drove out the man; and he placed at the east of the garden of Eden Cherubims, and a flaming sword which turned every way, to keep the way of the tree of life' (Gen. 3:17-24).

During the days of the Great Depression, there were soup kitchens in large cities all over America. People were hungry, poor, jobless and homeless. The only way they could eat was to be fed at one of those soup kitchens.

One day, as a man was working at a soup kitchen in Chicago, Illinois, he spotted a man in the line who stood out from the rest. At one time, this man had obviously been quite wealthy. Even though his suit was ragged and dirty, it was a well-made suit. It fitted him so well that it had to have been tailor made. His hat was soiled; but it was a handsome, well-formed hat. Though they were ragged, the man wore a matching tie and handkerchief set. The person serving the soup could not help looking at the man questioningly, as if to say, 'I wonder what your background is?' When the man held out his cup for soup, he said, 'Sir, I've seen better days.'

That is a pretty good description of humanity. Like the poor beggar in that queue, man has a stateliness even in his fallen state. Even though he is now ragged and soiled by sin, he still declares, 'I have seen better days.' We are not now what evidently we once were (Eccles. 7:29). There is no way to explain the universal condition of the human race except by the account of the Fall given in Genesis 3.

Man is capable of doing noble, self-sacrificing things for his fellow-man; but he is also capable of beastliness and monstrous cruelty. The same person who can show great moral virtue is capable of total immorality. Man is a dying creature. Yet he alone, of all God's creatures, fears to die. The reason is obvious: man alone is an immortal soul. In his inmost being, every one knows that 'the wages of sin is death'.

Why is it that the sons and daughters of princes, with the best of training and education, possess the same tendencies to evil as the children of paupers? Why do the children of God's saints, who have been raised in loving discipline, nurtured in godliness, surrounded by peace and trained in the fear of the Lord, feel the same lusts and run after them as the children of pimps, pushers and prostitutes? Why are all men and women everywhere sinful? Why is it

that family, environment, education and all the social pro-
grammes in the world are totally incapable of changing the
nature of man? Why is it that no one is capable of changing
the corruption of his own heart?

Only the Word of God can answer these questions. And
the answer God gives is this: 'All have sinned!' We all have
a common origin — our father Adam. We all have a common
heritage — the Fall. We have all received from our parents
and given to our children a common legacy — sin. We are
all possessed with a common nature — depravity.

The fall of Adam is an historic fact; and, the fall of the
human race in Adam is the only satisfactory explanation of
human history. These are facts which cannot be denied:
man is a fallen creature. Since the fall of Adam, all men are
sinners by birth, by nature and by practice. Fallen man
needs a Saviour.

By nature, man is alienated from God, under the
condemnation of his holy law, lost in darkness and sin.
What is the remedy for man's condition? The answer is a
new creation. 'If any man be in Christ, he is a new creature'
(2 Cor. 5:17). A. W. Pink says, 'It is not the cultivation of the
old nature that is needed, for that is ruined by the Fall, but
the reception of an entirely new nature which is begotten
by the Holy Spirit.' 'Ye must be born again!' (John 3:7).
Anything short of this is worthless and useless. Yet, even
in the Fall, there was a prophecy of a recovery. In Adam
there was a type and prophecy of Christ our Redeemer.

In the Garden there was one commandment given to man:
'Of the tree of the knowledge of good and evil, thou shalt
not eat of it: for in the day that thou eatest thereof thou
shalt surely die' (Gen. 2:17). Obedience to this commandment was the only thing God Almighty required of man.
Had he obeyed, he would have lived. Disobedience brought
death. In the gospel, God has given one commandment to

sinners: 'Believe on the Lord Jesus Christ, and thou shalt be saved' (Acts 16:31). This is the one thing God requires of men. All who obey it will live for ever. All who refuse to obey it must die for ever.

In the Garden there was one tree. The eating of the fruit of that tree brought death upon all men. In the gospel there is one tree, the cross of Christ. All who eat of the fruit of that tree will live for ever. In the Garden there was one man, Adam, who represented the human race before God, by whom and in whom we all died. In the gospel there is one man, Christ, the second Adam, the last Adam, who represents an elect race before God. By him and in him, all God's elect live for ever (Rom. 5:12,18-21; 1 Cor. 15:21-22). As Adam brought destruction and death upon his race, so the Lord Jesus Christ has brought redemption and life to his race, God's elect.

Adam was a type of Christ

As we read through the Scriptures, we find that Adam and Christ are uniquely linked. We would be wise to study carefully and prayerfully the comparison that is made between them (Rom. 5:12,18-21; 1 Cor. 15:21-22). Adam was made in the image of Christ, who is 'the image of the invisible God' (Col. 1:15; 2 Cor. 4:4; Heb. 1:3). Adam was a representative man, a covenant head, and so is Christ, the last Adam. All that Adam did was imputed to all his seed. All that he became was imparted to all his seed by natural generation. We are all the sons of Adam, by nature 'children of wrath' (Eph. 2:3). So, too, all that Christ did has been imputed to all his seed in justification; and all that he is as a man is imparted to all his seed by the Holy Spirit in regeneration. All believers are the sons of God by grace. In Romans 5, the

Holy Spirit tells us of these three great acts of imputation. First, Adam's sin has been imputed to all men and women. Second, the sins of God's elect were imputed to Christ. Third, Christ's righteousness has been imputed to all God's elect.

Consider what Adam did as our federal head. He repudiated the goodness and love of God (Gen. 3:5). He questioned the truth and veracity of God (Gen. 3:4). Adam knew nothing of death. Apparently, at least to some degree, he agreed with Satan and said, 'We shall not surely die. That is contrary to reason and experience.' Above all else, Adam rejected, denounced and rebelled against the authority of God!

Christ, the last Adam, the second and last federal head, completely vindicated the love, truth and majesty of God which the first man Adam had so grievously and deliberately dishonoured. Christ, as the God-man, our Mediator, honoured God in thought, word and deed all the days of his life upon the earth. He vindicated the love of God (Rom. 5:8; 1 John 3:16; 4:9-10). If ever you are tempted by the devil to question the goodness and love of God; if ever the events of providence appear to cast a cloud over God's goodness and love, look to Calvary and know that 'God is love!'

Our Lord Jesus Christ vindicated the truth of God too. When he was tempted by Satan to doubt God's goodness, truth and supremacy, he answered each time, 'It is written.' Every sabbath day he went into the synagogue to read the Word of God. As he chose his twelve apostles, he deliberately selected Judas that the Scriptures might be fulfilled. In his last moments of agony, he cried, 'I thirst,' that the Scriptures might be fulfilled. After he rose from the dead, and as he was speaking to his disciples, he opened the Scriptures to them (Luke 24). At every age, in every event, in all the details of his life, our all-glorious Saviour, federal head and substitute believed, honoured and magnified God's truth, even when it cost him dearly to do so.

The Lord of glory also fully vindicated the majesty, supremacy and sovereignty of God as our representative. He vindicated God's right to be God by his willing, voluntary submission to him at all times and by his obedience even to the point of death (Phil. 2:5-11; Gal. 4:4-5). As a man, he trusted God and lived in perfect faith. He obeyed the will of God perfectly (Heb. 10:5-7). He fulfilled the law of God completely (Rom. 10:4). He subjected his will to the Father's will. He magnified the justice of God in his death. In doing so, our blessed Saviour fulfilled all righteousness and brought in an everlasting righteousness for his people, to the praise, honour and glory of God. He was made like his brethren. He is not ashamed to call us his brethren, because we are made the righteousness of God in him.

The Son of God endured for his people all the curse pronounced upon fallen Adam

What was the punishment of Adam's sin? I shall confine my thoughts here to what is revealed in Genesis 3:17-24. The Lord shows us seven consequences of Adam's transgression. First, the ground was cursed. Second, man was cursed to eat his bread in sorrow, all the days of his life. Third, the earth brought forth thorns and thistles. Fourth, man was required to earn his bread by the sweat of his brow. Fifth, man must return to the dust of the earth. Sixth, a flaming sword barred the way to the tree of life. Seventh, Adam was separated from God in death. These were the curses that fell upon Adam because of sin; but Christ, the last Adam, suffered all the consequences of Adam's transgression.

The Son of God was made a curse for us (Gal. 3:13). The
Lord of glory was so thoroughly acquainted with grief that
he became the 'man of sorrows' (Isa. 53:3). The Lord Jesus
Christ came forth from the judgement hall wearing a 'crown
of thorns' (John 19:5), thorns which grew from the cursed
earth for cursed man. The first Adam got his bread by the
sweat of his face; but Christ, the last Adam, got his bread,
his soul's satisfaction, by the sweat of his heart. His sweat
was, as it were, 'great drops of blood falling down to the
ground' (Luke 22:44). As Adam returned to the dust, so the
dying Christ cried, 'Thou hast brought me into the dust of
death' (Ps. 22:15). That sword of justice which barred the
way to the tree of life, buried itself and was swallowed up
in the Son of God, our substitute, the last Adam (Zech. 13:7).
As Adam was driven from the presence of God in death, so
Christ, the last Adam, was separated from God in death,
crying as he died, 'My God, my God, why hast thou forsaken me?' (Matt. 27:46). Blessed, blessed, blessed Christ!
Who can describe the agonies of his holy soul for us? Let
us bow before him in wonder, love, praise and thankful
faith (1 Peter 2:24; 3:18;). He was made sin for us, made a
curse for us, died for us, and thus redeemed us. Now, because of all that he has done for sinners, in his life and in
his death, all who believe have been made the righteousness of God in Christ (Rom. 3:24-26; 2 Cor. 5:21).

The effects of the Fall reversed

By his obedience to God as our substitute, Christ, our great
Adam, has completely reversed all the effects of the Fall.
He says, 'I restored that which I took not away' (Ps. 69:4).
God alone is able to bring good out of evil and make even
the wrath of man praise him. This is what he has done for

his elect and for the glory of his name by the obedience of his Son as our substitute. The Fall of our father Adam gave God the opportunity to exhibit his wisdom and display the exceeding riches of his grace in a way that he could never have done had sin not entered the world. In the work of redemption, Christ not only reversed the effects of the Fall, but he also introduced something better (Heb. 10:9).

Here is the miracle of God's wisdom and grace in Christ. In him, God's elect have gained by the Fall; and God himself is glorified through Adam's transgression. Before the Fall, Adam lived in an earthly paradise as the creature of God. In Christ, we shall enter into a heavenly paradise and live as the sons of God, partakers not only of the divine breath, but of the divine nature (2 Peter 1:4). Before the Fall, Adam was lord of God's creation. In Christ, we are heirs of a heavenly inheritance. Indeed, as it is written: 'All [things] are yours.' Before the Fall, Adam enjoyed the happiness of innocence. In Christ, we are righteous and have entered into the joy of pardon, grace and redemption. Before the Fall, Adam was in fellowship with his Master. In Christ, we are one with God, inseparable from our Saviour (Eph. 4:30). His obedience is our obedience; his death is our death; his life is our life; his glory is our glory (John 17:5,22). 'Where sin abounded, grace did much more abound!' (Rom. 5:20).

Adam made all things mortal and evil. Christ makes all things holy, immortal and new (Rev. 21:5; 2 Cor. 5:17). The Son of God gives a new nature to chosen sinners (1 John 3:6-10), a new record of perfect righteousness (Jer. 23:6; 33:16; 50:20) and a new relationship (1 John 3:1). The kingdom of God is an entirely new creation. When we think of the Fall, let us ever adore God's wisdom and sovereignty (Ps. 76:10), providence (Rom. 8:28) and grace (Eph. 2:7). Let us ever adore God's Son, our dear Saviour, the last Adam (Col. 1:18).

7.

Adam driven from Eden

Genesis 3:22-24

'And the LORD God said, Behold, the man is become as one of us, to know good and evil: and now, lest he put forth his hand, and take also of the tree of life, and eat, and live for ever: Therefore the LORD God sent him forth from the garden of Eden, to till the ground from whence he was taken. So he drove out the man; and he placed at the east of the garden of Eden Cherubims, and a flaming sword which turned every way, to keep the way of the tree of life' (Gen. 3:22-24).

No portion of Holy Scripture is more important than the first three chapters of Genesis. As has been said, if a person truly understands and believes Genesis 1, 2 and 3, he has grasped the whole system of divine truth, for he has grasped the foundation of all truth. If we fail to understand what is revealed in these three chapters, we cannot understand anything else in the Sacred Volume. Perhaps that is the reason why Satan has always raised up false prophets to twist, pervert and deny the opening chapters of Genesis.

As we have seen, chapter 1 reveals the origin and creation of the universe, and the formation of man from the dust of the earth: 'In the beginning God...' Those four words show us that the Lord God is the Creator, Ruler and Disposer of all things. 'All things were made by him; and without him was not anything made that was made' (John 1:3).

Chapter 2 reveals the happiness, power and greatness of man before sin entered the world. In the Garden, in innocence, Adam was the object of God's favour and delight. He lived in harmony with God, the holy angels and the beasts of the field in perfect happiness. But Adam did not continue in this blessed, happy condition.

Chapter 3 reveals the temptation and fall of our father Adam, and the consequences of it. What a sad, sad picture! Man — created in the image of God, man — to whom God had given the whole world, man — the prince of God's creation rebelled against his Creator and lost everything!

When Adam and Eve had lost everything and they were trying to hide themselves from the Lord God, trying to cover the shame of their sin and their nakedness from God, the Lord God stepped in, not to destroy them, but to save them by his grace! (Gen. 3:9). As we have seen, he promised a Redeemer by whom he would destroy the enemy (3:15). He made a sacrifice for them (3:21), picturing the redemptive work of Christ promised in verse fifteen. He clothed the fallen pair with the skins of the slain sacrifice (3:21), picturing the garments of salvation with which he would clothe his elect.

Then, we are told, in Genesis 3:24, 'He drove out the man; and he placed at the east of the Garden of Eden Cherubims, and a flaming sword which turned every way, to keep the way of the tree of life.' This, too, was an act of God's grace. It was not, as many suppose, an act of his wrath. The Lord God drove Adam and Eve from the Garden, 'to keep the way of the tree of life' — that is, to preserve and protect 'the way of the tree of life'.

Who is speaking in Genesis 3:22-24?

When Moses wrote, 'The LORD God said,' whom did he have in mind? It is Jehovah-Elohim who is speaking. But he says, 'The man is become as one of us.' One person is speaking, but more than one person is represented. It is Christ speaking, the second person of the Holy Trinity, the Son of God, Jehovah-Elohim. He is speaking for the Father, for himself and for the Holy Spirit. Whenever we read of God speaking to man, or of God being revealed to man in the Old Testament, in the New Testament, or in eternity, the person speaking, the person revealed is the Son of God, our Mediator, the Lord Jesus Christ (John 5:37). The only way God deals with men, speaks to them and reveals himself to them is in his Son, the Lord Jesus Christ (John 14:6). Christ is the word and revelation of God (John 1:1-3,14,18). When Moses penned these words, 'The LORD God said, Behold, the man is become as one of us,' the Spirit of God was revealing, in this Book of Beginnings, four facts that are essential to the Christian faith.

1. The pre-existence of Christ before his incarnation (John 8:58)

'He is before all things, and by him all things consist' (Col. 1:17). Our Lord Jesus Christ is not a creature of time. He is the Creator, the 'I AM', who is, who was and who is to come.

2. The eternal deity of Christ

Our divine Mediator is called 'The Lord God,' Jehovah-Elohim, because Jesus Christ is God (Isa. 9:6; Rom. 9:5; 1 Tim. 3:16; John 10:30-33). He claimed to be God while he walked on the earth. Angels and men worshipped him as God. The Jews crucified him because he claimed that he is God (John 10:33).

3. The plurality and unity of the eternal Godhead

When the Lord God spoke and called himself 'us', he was declaring the plurality of persons in the Godhead. We are Trinitarians! We worship one God in the Trinity, or Tri-unity, of his sacred persons: Father, Son and Holy Spirit (1 John 5:7). This is a matter constantly presented to us in Holy Scripture. We see the doctrine of the Trinity in the baptismal formula given by Christ (Matt. 28:19-20), in the baptism of our Master (Matt. 3:16-17) and in the benedictions of grace (2 Cor. 13:14).

4. The mediation of Christ

The Lord Jesus Christ is our Mediator, the only Mediator between God and men; and he has been our Mediator from eternity (1 Tim. 2:5). In this third chapter of Genesis, Christ is revealed in all three of his offices as a mediator: Prophet, Priest and King. In *his kingly office*, he arraigned fallen man before his bar of judgement, convicted him of treason and passed upon him the sentence of death. In *his prophetic office*, he promised redemption and salvation to him, and told him how it would be accomplished. In *his priestly office*, he made a sacrifice for the guilty pair, and clothed our parents in the skins of an innocent victim.

The person speaking in this text is the Lord God, Jehovah-Elohim, the Lord Jesus Christ, the Word of God, the Son of God, our Mediator, our Saviour; and he is speaking to the fallen, sinful man, our father Adam.

What is the meaning of our Lord's words with respect to the condition of the man?

'The LORD God said, Behold, the man is become as one of us, to know good and evil.' What do those words mean? The text might be translated, 'Behold, the man *was* as one of us, knowing good and evil.' If the words are taken in that sense, they are an expression of great pity. God is saying, 'Behold, the man, now sinful, ruined, depraved and dead, was as one of us, knowing good and evil, but now only evil.'

Man was created in the image and likeness of God as he is revealed in Christ, who is the image of the invisible God (Gen 1:26; Col. 1:15). Adam was created in the image of God in the form and constitution of his body, and his human nature. That is to say, the first Adam was formed in the image of him who was to come as the second Adam. Adam did not crawl out of a slime pit, or drop out of a tree. He was created in the image of Christ. The Son of God came to be a partaker of our flesh and blood that we might be partakers of his flesh and of his bones (Eph. 5:30).

Adam was made in the image of God, in moral uprightness and righteousness too. Man came out of his Creator's hands a holy creature. And when God makes a man new by his grace, he restores holiness to him. This renovation of grace is called 'The new man, which after God is created in righteousness and true holiness' (Eph. 4:24).

The image of God was also reflected in man's mental capacity. Like his Creator, Adam was wise, rational and full of knowledge. We cannot begin to imagine how vast the mind of that man was in his unfallen state. He named all living things by himself! He knew his wife when she was brought to him. He knew both good and evil. Before the Fall, even though Adam, like Christ, knew no sin by experience, he knew the nature of it. He knew that it was contrary to God's being, and he knew the consequences of it. In this sense, it is certain that Adam knew both good and evil far more fully before the Fall than he did afterwards.

Again, the image of God is seen in Adam's dominion over all earthly creatures. Adam was made lord of God's creation (Gen. 1:26). The majesty of God was seen in him by the universal subjection of all creatures to him (Ps. 8:5-8).

The sense of the text is: 'Behold, the man was as one of us, but what is he now?' His body, so strong and full of life, is now feeble and dying. His soul, so pure and holy, is now depraved and vile. His mind, so full of wisdom and knowledge, is now darkened and ignorant. The man who was the darling of heaven is now alienated from God.

However, I am inclined to think that the way this verse has been translated in the *Authorized Version* is best: 'Behold, the man is become as one of us, to know good and evil.' This is a declaration of Adam's present state in Christ, and of ours too. Though fallen by nature, we are now restored by grace, as Adam was. What God says of Adam is true of every believer. Though we fell in Adam, we are restored in Christ, just like Adam was, by the call of God — 'Where art thou?', by blood atonement — the slain victim, by imputed righteousness — the skins.

Like Adam, we have been clothed in Christ's righteousness; and we are 'righteous, even as he is righteous' (1 John 3:7; Jer. 23:6; 33:16). Having been renewed by grace like Adam, we are now created in the image of Christ and have been conformed to him (Eph. 4:24). We are now reconciled to God and one with him in Christ (John 17:21). Enmity has been put away; reconciliation has been made by God. Now believing sinners are in a state of friendship with God. But more than that, in Christ, we are one with God. Like Adam, having been called from darkness to light in Christ, we know both good and evil. We know the goodness of God and we know the evil our own hearts.

What was the 'tree of life' which God would not allow Adam to take by his own hands?

Without doubt, it was a real tree in the Garden of Eden. Adam knew where it was and how useful it was as the tree of life. John Gill has said, 'It is highly probable that it might be useful for the invigorating of Adam's body ... during his state of innocence.' But it was also symbolic.

1. It was a symbol of dependence

It was a symbol of Adam's dependence upon God for his life. Every time he saw it and ate of its fruit, Adam was reminded that his life came from God, was preserved by God and belonged to God.

2. It was a symbol of preservation

It was a symbol of Adam's being preserved in life, for as long as he was obedient to the will of God. Perhaps it stood right beside the tree of the knowledge of good and evil. We do not know. But every time he passed the tree of the knowledge of good and evil and ate only of the fruit of the tree of life, the promise of life was confirmed to him for his obedience to God. The tree of life was not a tree by which Adam might have been transformed from his fallen condition into a state of eternal life (Gal. 3:21). When God prevented Adam from eating the fruit of this tree, it was not for the purpose of keeping Adam from obtaining life. It was so that he could reveal his grace in Adam and preserve, or keep, 'the way of the tree of life' (v. 24).

3. It was a picture of the Lord Jesus Christ

The tree of life was a type of the Lord Jesus Christ (Prov. 3:18; Rev. 2:7; 22:2,14). He is our life! He is the author and giver of life! As our Mediator, he asked our life of the Father. As our Redeemer, he purchased, with his own blood, a right to life for us. As our Advocate and Intercessor in heaven, he secures us in life in himself. 'Your life is hid with Christ in God (Col. 3:3; John 10:27-30).

Why was Adam prevented from eating the fruit of the tree of life after the Fall?

John Gill has said, 'The reason of this prevention was that Adam might have no hope or expectation of life from that, or anything else, but Christ the promised Messiah.' This was an act of grace. Though Adam had forfeited all claims to life, God kept open the way of life, and prevented him from seeking life anywhere else but in Christ.

If the Lord had not prevented Adam from eating the physical fruit of that physical tree, he might well have thought to himself, 'As this tree was useful before in the preservation of my life, it might still be. God has promised me a redeemer, but why should I wait for him. I can save myself by my own hands. All I have to do is to eat the fruit of the tree of life.' To keep Adam from such evil, the Lord God removed the temptation from him. He thrust him out of Eden and placed a guard around the tree of life.

The fact is, there is nothing man is more prone to do than to seek salvation and life anywhere but in Christ. We are all base idolaters by nature. We want to be saved; but we want to be saved by our own hands, our own will and effort. Fallen man will do anything to be saved, except trust Christ alone (John 5:40). He would rather take a pilgrimage, barefoot on broken glass, around the globe than trust Christ. He would rather climb the steep, dark, terrifying slopes of Sinai than simply look to the Christ of Calvary. But God has declared that Christ alone is the Saviour (1 Cor. 1:30). Sinners cannot come to God any other way. By our own works of righteousness we cannot be saved.

To quote John Gill again: 'He who seeks for righteousness and life by his own doings, runs upon the flaming sword of justice; and whilst endeavouring to ensure his own salvation, he is pulling ruin upon himself.'

Blessed be God, he still keeps 'the way of the tree of life'. He still keeps chosen sinners from self-destruction by self-righteousness. He blocks the way of his elect and graciously forces them to flee to Christ, the true Tree of Life (Hosea 2:6). Let us ever be aware of the wretched, vile nature of sin (Rom. 5:12) and of the folly and blasphemy of works religion (Gal. 2:21). Works religion is something which God has set himself against. All who seek to save themselves are fighting against God (Gal. 5:1-4). Let us ever bless, praise and magnify the Lord our God for providing Christ the Saviour for lost sinners (2 Cor. 9:15). Let us ever cease from all self-righteousness and lay hold upon Christ alone. He 'is a tree of life to them that lay hold upon [him]; and happy is everyone that retaineth him (Prov. 3:18).

8.

Cain and Abel

Genesis 4:1-16

'The LORD had respect unto Abel and to his offering: But unto Cain and to his offering he had not respect' (Gen. 4:4-5).

Though there were no children born to Adam and Eve before the Fall, there were many born to them after it (Gen. 5:4-5). Adam lived for 930 years! In all likelihood, before he died, Adam had thousands of descendants, including sons and daughters, grandchildren and great-grandchildren. Cain was his firstborn son. But how many sons and daughters Adam and Eve had between Cain and Abel, we do not know.

'And Adam knew Eve his wife; and she conceived, and bare Cain, and said, I have gotten a man from the LORD' (v. 1). When Cain was born, Eve thought that he was the promised Messiah, Redeemer and Saviour. She cried, 'I have gotten a man from the LORD!' Those words might imply that she had already had many daughters; but now she had given birth to a male child.

'And she again bare his brother Abel. And Abel was a keeper of sheep, but Cain was a tiller of the ground' (v. 2). God the Holy Spirit has singled out these two sons of Adam, Cain and Abel, to teach us, by example, the blessed gospel doctrine of redemption by blood (Lev. 17:11; Heb. 9:22) and to condemn the doctrine of salvation by works. The way of

Abel is the way of grace; the way of Cain is the way of works.

This is the line that divides the whole human race. It divides husbands and wives, mothers and daughters, fathers and sons, brothers and sisters. It probably divides your family, as it does mine. All who attempt to come to God must choose either the way of Cain or the way of Abel, the way of works or the way of grace. The two cannot be mixed at any point or to any degree (Rom. 11:6; Gal. 5:2,4).

> And in process of time it came to pass, that Cain brought of the fruit of the ground an offering unto the LORD. And Abel, he also brought of the firstlings of his flock and of the fat thereof. And the LORD had respect unto Abel and to his offering: But unto Cain and to his offering he had not respect. And Cain was very wroth, and his countenance fell
>
> (vv. 3-5).

Cain and Abel were not young boys; they were grown men. Evidently, they were heads of households, with wives and children. They had occupations. Cain was a farmer; Abel was a shepherd.

In Genesis 3 we saw the entrance of sin into the world. Here we see the progress of sin and its fruit. In Genesis 3 we saw sin against God. Here it is against man. The man who has no fear of God has no regard for his neighbour. In Genesis 3 we read about enmity between the Seed of the woman and the seed of the serpent, the sons of God and the children of the devil. Here we see that enmity displayed. Cain, the wicked man who approached God by his own works, persecuted and murdered Abel, the child of God. However, the central and primary truth revealed in this chapter is that God is to be worshipped, and that he can only be worshipped by faith in a blood sacrifice.

A prescribed place

There was a prescribed place where God was to be worshipped. We are told that both Cain and Abel brought their sacrifices to the Lord, to the place of the Lord's presence. We are not told where this prescribed place of worship was, but it was somewhere east of the Garden of Eden (Gen. 3:24).

Jamieson, Fausset and Brown's commentary translates Genesis 3:24 in this way: 'So he drove out the man; and he dwelt at the east of the Garden of Eden between the Cherubims, as a Shekinah [a fire-tongue, or fire-sword] to keep open the way to the tree of life.' In my opinion, this translation is very accurate. My reasons for saying so are as follows:

1. The word translated 'placed' in this verse is not translated 'placed' anywhere else in the Old Testament. It means 'to tabernacle,' or 'to dwell'. Eighty-three times in the Old Testament it is translated as 'dwell'.

2. The Lord God is always portrayed as the one who dwells upon the mercy-seat, between the cherubims (Exod. 25:17-18,22; 1 Sam. 4:4; 2 Sam. 6:2; 2 Kings 19:15; 1 Chron. 13:6; Pss. 80:1; 99:1; Isa. 6:1-7; 37:16; Ezek. 10:2,6-7).

3. Our great God, the God of all grace, who 'delighteth in mercy,' has kept open the way to the tree of life for sinners (Rev. 22:2). He kept the way open from eternity by our covenant surety, the Lord Jesus Christ, the Lamb of God slain from the foundation of the world (Rev. 13:8).

He kept the way open under the types and ceremonies of the law, all of which pointed to him by whom the way of access to God would be opened and maintained (Heb. 10:1-22).

When the Lord God expelled Adam from the Garden, he appears to have established an altar, a mercy-seat, protected by the cherubims. The flaming sword or, as it might be rendered, the flaming tongue, represented God's presence, the Shekinah glory. Anyone who approached God had to worship him at this place by means of a blood sacrifice. There was a prescribed place of worship.

I know that there are no holy places upon this earth. We are not idolaters. 'God is a Spirit: and they that worship him must worship him in Spirit and in truth.' True worship is spiritual. It is a matter of the heart (Phil. 3:3). We have no material altar. Christ is our altar (Heb. 13:10). We have no literal mercy-seat. Christ is our mercy-seat (1 John 4:10). Yet God has always had a prescribed place of worship: a place where men and women gather in his name; where he gives out his Word; where he meets sinners upon the grounds of mercy through blood atonement; a place where he dispenses his grace.

During the forty years Israel spent in the wilderness, the prescribed place of divine worship was the tabernacle. Later, the temple of God was established at Jerusalem. In this gospel age, the place appointed for divine worship is the local church, the public assembly of his saints (Matt. 18:20; 1 Cor. 3:16-17). This is the prescribed place of the divine presence, divine instruction and divine blessing (Ps. 122; 133; Heb. 10:23-25).

A prescribed time

It also appears that there was a prescribed time for the worship of God. In some versions of the Bible, the translation of verse 3 gives a reference in the margin which indicates that the words *'in the process of time'* can be translated *'at the end of days'*. Though there was no appointed sabbath, it

appears that at the end of every week men and women came
to the altar at the east of Eden to worship God.

In this gospel age, we do not keep a literal sabbath day.
The Holy Spirit expressly forbids any form of legal sabbath
keeping (Col. 2:8-19). Believers are not under the law, in
any sense whatsoever. Sunday is not the 'Christian Sabbath'. Our Sabbath is Christ. We rest in him. Yet Sunday is
'the Lord's day'. God the Holy Spirit says so (Rev. 1:10).
This is the day of Christ's resurrection (Matt. 28:1). This is
our appointed day of divine worship (Acts 20:7; Ps.
118:21-24). I do not suggest that the Scriptures require a
specific day or time when we must gather in the house of
God. However, it is obvious from the universal testimony
of Scripture that it is always both proper and needful for us
to have specified, appointed times set aside for the worship of God. God will not be worshipped in a haphazard way.

A prescribed means

God's ordained means of worship was, and is, blood atonement. The holy Lord God cannot be approached and will
not accept the worship of sinful, fallen man, but by means
of a blood sacrifice. It appears that the children of Adam
and Eve had been clearly instructed in the worship of God.

Adam showed his sons what he had done, how he had
sinned against the Lord. He told them plainly what God
had done for him and Eve, sacrificing the innocent victim
for them, stripping away their fig leaves, and clothing them
with the garments of salvation he had made specifically for
them. He spoke plainly to them about God's promise of redemption through the woman's seed. Adam understood and
taught his family the necessity of blood atonement.

Believing God, our father, Adam, in his fallen state, taught his children that the only way a sinner would ever be able to worship God is by faith in that one whom the Father would send to put away sin by the sacrifice of himself. Abel believed the gospel his father preached to him. Cain refused to believe.

What was wrong with Cain's sacrifice?

No doubt, this proud man brought the very best thing he could to God. Yet God despised his sacrifice. Why was that? It was because Cain brought a bloodless sacrifice! (Heb. 9:22). His sacrifice, his religion, was a denial of his need of Christ, the Redeemer. He thought he could approach God by his own merit, be his own priest, his own mediator and his own intercessor. His sacrifice was a denial of sin.

Cain denied his guilt and sin before God. He denied that he deserved condemnation and death under the wrath of God. He approached God on the grounds of his own merit and works. Cain's sacrifice, indeed his entire religious system, was a refusal of God's revelation. God had revealed the way of worship, acceptance and life (Luke 24:44-47; Eph. 1:6-7), but Cain did not believe God. This man was not an infidel. He was a proud, religious man, a self-righteous Pharisee, an unbeliever. His offering to God was the fruit of his own labour. He really thought, just as most religious people think today, that he was genuinely good enough for God.

Why did the Lord God have respect for Abel and his offering?

God accepted Abel's sacrifice because it looked to Christ. It was an offering of faith (Heb. 11:4). Abel believed God. He came to God through faith in a substitute. His offering was a confession of sin, guilt and just condemnation.

Our sins deserve the wrath of God. The only way for a holy God to justify guilty sinners is by the satisfaction of divine justice through blood atonement. That blood atonement which magnifies God's law and makes it honourable is found only in the substitutionary death of God's own dear Son, the Lord Jesus Christ.

Abel's offering was a type of Christ, the Lamb of God (Exod. 12:5-6). It was a lamb, the innocent dying for the guilty. It was a male of the first year, in the prime of life. It was a lamb without spot or blemish, as Christ is without sin. It was a lamb that was slain. Its blood was shed in a violent death. Abel's lamb was consumed by the fire of God (Lev. 9:24) because God accepted it as a type of Christ, whose blood of atonement is a sweet smelling savour to the holy Lord God, our heavenly Father. There were only two things which brought about the difference between Cain and Abel: blood and faith. These are the only two things which make the difference between God's elect and the lost world around us. The only distinction between God's elect and the reprobate is the distinction of grace (1 Cor. 4:7).

The way of Cain is the way of natural religion (Jude 10-11)

It is the religion of works. It gives no comfort, but only misery (Gen. 4:6-8). It is the way of all men and women by nature. The way of Cain is the way of ceremony and ritual. It is the way of every persecutor. The first human blood to be shed upon the earth was shed by a religious legalist; and the blood he shed was the blood of one who believed in sovereign grace, a worshipper of God. The battle still rages. The issue is still the same. The way of Cain persecutes the way of faith. Cain's way is the way of God's curse (vv. 10-12). It is the way of endless wandering (vv. 12,16). 'Cain went out from the presence of the LORD, and dwelt in the Land of Nod.' Nod means 'wandering'. There is no rest for the wicked; neither in this world, nor in the world to come.

The way of Abel is the way of life everlasting

This is the way of grace. It is the way of blood redemption, the way of faith. This is the way that is opposed and persecuted by the world, but it is the way of life, the way of acceptance with God.

Two ways are set before us. The way of Cain which is the way of a religion of works and everlasting destruction (Prov. 14:12; 16:25); and the way of Abel which is the way of free and sovereign grace in Christ, the way of everlasting salvation (John 14:6; 10:9). Which way will you go?

9.

Enoch

Genesis 5:24

'Enoch walked with God: and he was not; for God took him'
(Gen. 5:24).

My heart is motivated, driven and governed by four great concerns. Here are four things I want more than anything in this world. I am not an ambitious man. But I am ambitious for these things. In order to obtain these things, I am prepared, by the grace of God, to sacrifice everything else. I count all other things to be but rubbish by comparison.

1. I want to know Christ (Phil. 3:10)

Yes, I believe that in measure I do know him. God has revealed his grace and glory to me in the person of his dear Son. Still, I want a growing, spiritual, experimental knowledge of the Lord Jesus Christ. I want to know all that he has done for me. I want to know him, to know him fully.

2. I want to be totally committed to Christ

I want to lose my life totally to Christ and in Christ, so that I can truthfully say with the apostle Paul, 'For to me to live is Christ.' I want to be committed to Christ as he was to the Father, so that my heart says to him in all things, 'Not my will, but thine, be done.' It is my ongoing prayer that God will give me a heart committed to the Lord Jesus Christ, committed to his will, his gospel, his people and to the cause of his glory in this world.

3. I want to be like Christ

My heart longs to be like him, conformed to him; to be like him in love, tenderness, and thoughtfulness; in zeal, dedication, and devotion; in purity, holiness, and righteousness.

I know these goals are not attainable in this life. Yet they are the things for which my soul hungers and my heart thirsts. I cannot be satisfied with less. 'I count not myself to have apprehended: but this one thing I do, forgetting those things which are behind, and reaching forth unto those things which are before, I press toward the mark for the prize of the high calling of God in Christ Jesus' (Phil. 3:13-14). 'I shall be satisfied, when I awake, with [Christ's] likeness' (Ps. 17:15), but not until then.

4. I want to live in communion with Christ

Like Enoch of old, I want to walk with God (Read Genesis 5:21-24). *'Enoch walked with God'* — what a statement! To me, it is astounding. The text does not say that Enoch thought about God, or that he worshipped God, or served God, or talked with God, or talked about God, though he certainly did all those things. The Holy Spirit uses four simple words to describe the outstanding feature of this man's life: 'Enoch walked with God.' In his daily life, Enoch walked with God, realizing God's presence as his living Friend, in whom he confided and by whom he was loved. *'Enoch walked with God.'*

Some use Enoch as an example of sinless perfection, or to teach the doctrine of the deeper life. Others use him to promote self-righteous morality. But the Spirit of God explains that Enoch's life was a picture of grace, an example of faith in Christ (Heb. 11:5-6). 'Enoch walked with God' and 'he had this testimony, that he pleased God'. That is the desire of every true believer's heart. We want to walk with God in sweet fellowship and please him in all things. How can this desire be accomplished? How can you and I walk with God and please him? This is the thing we must see, if we are to understand what it is to walk with God and please him. It was not Enoch's conduct that pleased God, but his faith (Heb. 11:6). More specifically, it was Christ, the object of Enoch's faith, that pleased God.

What does the Scripture mean when it says, 'Enoch walked with God'?

How did Enoch walk with God? What does that statement imply? The author of Hebrews gives us some help by telling us that, while Enoch walked with God, 'he had this testimony, that he pleased God.' But how did this man please God? What was there about him that pleased the Lord?

Obviously, Enoch did not always please God, nor did he always walk with him. Enoch was a man like us. He was not born a saint. He did not simply decide one day that he would start walking with God. He was a fallen sinner, a son of Adam, who, like you and me, had a wicked heart, which by nature departed from God.

He was born in spiritual death. Like all others, he went astray from his mother's womb, as soon as he was born, speaking lies (Ps. 58:3). He was a man who needed pardon, cleansing, redemption, atonement, justification and regeneration, just like us. Before he could please God, his sin had to be removed and righteousness had to be imputed to him. Otherwise, God could never have accepted him, much less have been pleased with him. In order to have these things, Enoch had to believe God. He needed to have faith in Christ. For righteousness comes by faith in Christ 'unto all and upon all them that believe' (Rom. 3:22).

It was by faith that Enoch pleased God (Heb. 11:5). Enoch was not pleasing to God by virtue of his conduct, his works, his disposition, or his personal character. There was nothing at all remarkable about the man by nature that caused God to look upon him with pleasure. God was pleased with Enoch because he believed God. He believed that which God had spoken. Enoch's faith was the same as Abel's before him and Noah's after him. The faith by which Enoch walked with God and pleased him was the same faith that the dying thief possessed when he cried, 'Lord, remember me when thou comest into thy kingdom' (Luke 23:42). Indeed, it is the same faith that God's elect have today. This is very important. If we desire to walk with God, we must believe him. Walking with God is neither more nor less than believing God. The only way anyone can walk with God and please him is by faith in the Lord Jesus Christ.

Enoch had experienced a mighty change by the power and grace of God. The Lord God had changed his heart. God changed the bent, bias and direction of his will. This fallen sinner had been given life and faith in the Lord Jesus Christ (Eph. 2:1-10). This was a work of grace, without which Enoch could never have walked with God and pleased him. Long before Enoch was translated into glory, he had been translated in his heart and soul. He was delivered from the power of darkness and translated into the kingdom of God's dear Son. What the Holy Spirit commends to us is his faith in Christ, the grace of God upon him. This man believed God's revelation of himself and his will in

Holy Scripture. He believed on the Lord Jesus Christ, the Redeemer God promised in type and prophecy. He believed God's promise of immortality and eternal life in Christ (Jude 14-15). Enoch believed that God is, and that he is the Rewarder of them that diligently seek him (Heb. 11:5-6).

When we are told that 'Enoch walked with God' and that 'he pleased him', the Scriptures mean us to understand that Enoch believed God. Be sure you understand this: nothing pleases God except his Son. The only way you and I can walk with God and be pleasing to him is by faith in his dear Son, the Lord Jesus Christ (John 14:6; 1 Peter 2:4-5). This is what it is to live in the Spirit (Rom. 8:1-9), to walk in the Spirit (Gal. 5:16).

The highest measure of sanctification is exactly the same as the earliest beginnings of salvation. It is believing God. To grow in grace is to grow in faith. The strongest believer lives exactly as the weakest babe in Christ — by faith. We stand before God by faith. We grow strong only as we know ourselves to be weak and lay hold of Christ's strength by faith. Having begun in the Spirit, we are not then made perfect by the works of the flesh. We do not begin and go a certain distance by faith in Christ and then finish our course, making up the difference by the works of the law. Salvation is by grace alone. Our standing before God and our acceptance with him are by grace alone. To walk with God is to continue as we began — by faith (Col. 2:6-7).

The believer's life is a life of faith. I stress this point because it needs to be emphasized. Enoch pleased God because he believed God. He walked with God by faith. We are sometimes tempted to strive after some imaginary 'higher ground' or 'deeper life', by looking to our feelings or our works, instead of looking to Christ alone. That is wrong. Any doctrine, any religion, any sermon that leaves you looking to yourself, that turns your eyes away from

Christ is evil. We are not to look to our feelings, but to Christ. Neither should we look to our works, but only to Christ. We are not even to look to the image of Christ created in us by the Holy Spirit, but to Christ alone. Jesus Christ alone is our acceptance with God. By faith Enoch walked with God. By faith Enoch pleased God. Let us follow his example.

This man's walking with God by faith implies many things. When I read that 'Enoch walked with God' and that 'he pleased God,' my heart cries out, 'That's what I want as I make my pilgrimage through this world. I want to walk with God and please him in this world.' What does it mean to walk with God? To walk with God is to live in the realization of his presence (Phil. 4:4-5), and to enjoy communion and fellowship with him (1 Thess. 5:16-18). To 'pray without ceasing' is to live in communion with God, ever trusting Christ, seeking his will and his glory, submitting to his providence (Prov. 3:5-6).

The term 'walked' implies perseverance and continuance. Enoch persevered in faith. He walked with God for three hundred years. His religion was not in spurts. His communion with God was steady and constant. He walked with God steadily, for three hundred years.

The phrase 'walked with God' also implies progress. Enoch's faith was not stagnant, but progressive. At the end of three hundred years he stood upon the same ground, was built upon the same foundation, and was in the same company as at the beginning. But he was not in the same place, and he was not the same man. Enoch went forward in faith. At the end of his days he knew more, enjoyed more, loved more, did more, believed more, received more, and gave more than at the beginning of his walk with God. A believer walks with God in this world like a little child walks through the woods with its father. It is a loving walk, a walk of confidence and trust, an instructive walk, a happy walk and a safe walk.

What were the circumstances in which 'Enoch walked with God'?

We all have a tendency to think that Enoch lived in a different time. The world was different then and it was relatively easy for a man to walk with God in those days. Such thinking is wrong. Even though the details of Enoch's life are sketchy, we can be sure that the life of faith was not easier then than it is now. Enoch lived in the most trying, stressful and difficult times the world has ever known. He lived in those days just before the Flood. In those dark, dark days, when very few people did, 'Enoch walked with God.'

He was a public man, with great responsibilities. This patriarch was the head of a large family. As such, he was a prophet, priest and king in his household. He had public cares and responsibilities as a public leader. And Enoch had his trials. He bore the brunt of opposition from powerful men who hated the way of faith, who hated God and his truth. We know this is so because the Scriptures tell us plainly that all who live godly in this world will suffer persecution. Yet Enoch walked with God for three hundred years.

He was also a family man. Like many today, he had the responsibility of providing for, caring for, disciplining and educating a large family. He had a wife and many children. Yet 'Enoch walked with God.'

He lived in a terribly wicked, degenerate society. In those days, men commonly lived to be more than eight hundred years old. Their long lives gave them opportunity to invent many forms of evil. Sin covered the earth. The sons of God and the daughters of men made unholy alliances. There were few who believed God. Scoffers, mockers, unbelievers and infidels were abundant. The few who did profess to believe God compromised every principle and tried, as much as possible, to make a marriage of righteousness and unrighteousness. Yet 'Enoch walked with God.'

There is still more. Enoch faithfully bore witness to Christ in the midst of that wicked generation (Jude 14-15). He delivered his testimony in spite of opposition. He stood his ground firmly against the tide of blasphemy. The more men spoke against God, his Son and his truth, the more Enoch spoke for his Redeemer. 'Enoch walked with God.' He was a man of faith, and therefore a man of conviction, purpose, boldness and courage. In the midst of greater evil, greater opposition and greater trials than we can imagine, if, by the grace of God, this man could walk with God in his day, then you and I, who are saved by the same grace, washed in the same precious blood, and sanctified by the same Spirit, can walk with God today.

What was the result of Enoch's walking with God?

Enoch left the world at a comparatively young age. Compared with others in his day, he was just a young man, in the prime of life, when God took him. He was only three hundred and sixty-five years old. He seems to have finished his course early. It appears that it did not take this man, walking with God, very long to do all that God had for him to do. Be that as it may, here are three things which are the clear result of Enoch's walking with God.

First, because he walked with God, Enoch escaped death. Let us walk with God by faith, with our hearts set upon Christ, and we too shall escape death (John 11:25; Rev. 20:6).

Soon we too shall be translated to glory (2 Cor. 5:1-9; Col. 3:1-4).

Of course, everyone knows that believers die physically, just as unbelievers do. Yet the Son of God declares plainly that those who trust him will never die. The word 'death', as it relates to believers, is used only to accommodate our present weakness and lack of understanding. The fact is, the death of the body for the child of God is not death at all, but the beginning of life!

Second, because he walked with God, Enoch was greatly missed. When Enoch was gone, people began to look for him, but he 'was not found'. When men and women like Enoch, people who walk with God, are taken from us, they are missed.

Third, because he walked with God, when Enoch went to glory, he left a testimony behind him. Before he was translated 'he had this testimony, that he pleased God.' Everyone who knew Enoch knew about his God, his righteous judgement and his salvation in Christ.

Enoch's translation is a warning to all men and women. Soon we shall be swept out of this world, without warning, and ushered into eternity to meet the holy Lord God in judgement. Enoch's translation to glory is also a testimony of comfort to encourage God's pilgrims in this world. God 'is a rewarder of them that diligently seek him'.

Can you hear Enoch's voice? He is saying to every child of God in this world, 'Press on, weary pilgrims, press on. Walk with God by faith. There is a kingdom prepared for you, where there is no more sorrow, no more weeping, no more pain and no more death. There is a redeemer waiting to embrace you. There is a God waiting to crown you. There are saints and angels waiting to welcome you. There is a fountain to refresh you for ever, a tree to feed you for ever, a light to lighten your path for ever. Press on. Walk with

God. Make your steps lively, ever "Looking unto Jesus the author and finisher of our faith"'.

What are we to learn from this man Enoch, who 'walked with God'?

First, the only way any sinner can ever be accepted by God is in Christ. We must be in Christ by faith, or we shall never please God. But all who are in Christ always please God in him.

> Nearer, so very near to God,
> Nearer I cannot be,
> For in the person of His Son,
> I am as near as he.
> With his spotless garments on,
> I am as holy as God's Son.

Second, sometimes God makes great differences in his providence towards his beloved children. Both Abel and Enoch walked with God and pleased God. Both were loved, chosen by God, redeemed by the blood of Christ and saved by his grace, but Abel was murdered and Enoch was translated. Today both are seated around the throne in the presence of Christ.

Third, what God did for Enoch, he will do for all who walk with him by faith in Christ (1 Cor. 15:51-58). Some saints must die, physically, and be resurrected. Other saints will be taken alive into glory. But all will be transformed into the glorious image of Christ.

Fourth, only those who walk with God by faith in this world will live with God in that glorious eternal world called 'heaven'. So let us walk with God by faith in the Lord Jesus Christ.

10.

Noah

Genesis 6:1-22

'But Noah found grace in the eyes of the LORD'
(Gen. 6:8).

As we read the sixth chapter of Genesis, several things are obvious. First, we see sin increasing (vv. 1-5). Nine generations had now descended from Adam. We have no way of knowing how many millions of people there were upon the earth, but there were so many that they covered the face of the earth. And wherever men and women were found, sin was evident. The one thing all men had in common in those days, as they do now, was sin. Polygamy, which began with Lamech (4:19), was now commonly practised (6:1-2). The number of wives men took was limited only by the capacity they had to fulfil their lusts.

'The sons of God' — the sons of Seth — began to marry 'the daughters of men' — the daughters of Cain. Those who professed to be and had a name to be the sons of God, sacrificed their principles upon the altar of their lusts and married the beautiful, but godless, daughters of Cain (6:2). And 'there were giants in the earth in those days' (v. 4). The word 'giants' simply means 'violent, oppressive, fallen men'. They had the name of Seth, but the nature of Cain. They laid claim to God's name and his promises, because their

fathers were 'the sons of God'. But they were the sons of
Cain — fallen, cursed, violent, wicked men. Godless, religious men have always been the most violent, cruel and
wicked of men.

'God saw that ... every imagination of the thoughts of
[men's] heart was only evil continually' (v. 5). Sin had
reached its utmost depths. It was everywhere. It was the
only appetite, desire and work of the entire human race,
until it 'repented the Lord that he had made man'. Man,
who was created in the image and likeness of God, had
become repugnant to his holy Creator.

Second, we see the Holy Spirit striving with men (v. 3).
The apostle Peter helps us to understand the meaning of
this verse (1 Peter 3:20). The Spirit's striving with men is
the long-suffering God, calling sinners to repentance by the
preaching of the gospel, and granting them room for repentance. What mercy! God calls sinners who deserve his
immediate wrath to repentance. He gives sinners opportunity to repent. But he will not always call. The day is coming
when God will shut the door of mercy. When that happens,
when God leaves men and women to themselves, they cannot be saved (Prov. 1:23-33; Hosea 4:17; Luke 13:24-25).

Third, we see God repenting (v. 6). The first time repentance is mentioned in the Bible, the person repenting is God
himself. If we understand what this verse says, we shall
understand what repentance is. Repentance is a change of
mind, a change of attitude, a change of direction and a
change of action.

Obviously, this is an anthropomorphic expression. We
know this because we know that God does not change, nor
can he be changed. He is immutable (Mal. 3:6; Heb. 13:8).
He never changes his mind or alters his purpose (Job 23:13).
Yet sometimes the Lord God does alter his course of action
in providence. Israel, a nation once so greatly blessed by

God, is now a nation cursed. As a potter, who forms a vessel that does not please him and then breaks it in pieces, may be said to repent of his work, so, to show his aversion to man's wickedness, God resolved to destroy him. To express it another way, true repentance, then, is a change of direction in a man's heart, in his life, in his desires and in his behaviour.

Fourth, we see justice threatening (v. 7). 'The soul that sinneth, it shall die!' Justice demands it. A holy, righteous and just God must punish sin. As God once flooded this world in a storm of wrath, so, one day, he will consume this world and all who obey not the gospel of our Lord Jesus Christ in vengeful, flaming fire. He will punish the wicked with everlasting destruction (Ps. 11:6; 2 Thess. 1:7-10). Yet there is hope. God is just, but he is gracious too. He is 'a just God and a Saviour'!

Fifth, we see grace intervening (v. 8). Grace — what a blessed word! This is the first time grace is mentioned in the Bible. 'Noah found grace in the eyes of the LORD!' Salvation is by grace alone. The cause of Noah's salvation was God's free and sovereign grace. Our text does not say, 'God found grace in the eyes of Noah.' It says, 'Noah found grace in the eyes of the LORD!' It is never the other way round. Salvation does not begin with man; it begins with God. Grace is not the result of something man does. Grace is God's work. It is God's gift. It is God's intervention.

Because God had set his heart upon Noah from eternity and was determined to be gracious to him, he found a way to save him, even though he was resolved to destroy the world. It was grace in God, not goodness in Noah, that saved this man from the flood of God's wrath.

Grace is mentioned for the first time by divine purpose. Grace first appeared when the sin of man had reached its climax, as if to teach us from the beginning that there is nothing in man which causes God to bestow his grace. Grace is free. It is sovereign. It is unconditional. The world was lost; it was condemned; it perished; but 'Noah found grace in the eyes of the Lord.' God always has a remnant to whom he will be gracious. Noah alone was God's remnant in that day (Rom. 11:5). Noah's family was blessed because of their association with him. However, there is no indication in the Scriptures that any of them knew God at this time. It appears that only Noah believed God, that the Lord revealed himself to no one else.

Noah is truly a picture of grace. He was the grandson of Methuselah, the great grandson of Enoch, who 'walked with God: and he was not, for God took him'. His father was Lamech. His name, Noah, means 'comfort' or 'rest'. The Scriptures seem to indicate that his father was also a man of faith (5:28-29). Lamech had many, many sons and daughters. But the only one who knew God was Noah. Grace does not run in bloodlines. Only Noah believed his father's God. Noah believed the report of his father (5:28-29), who both acknowledged God's curse upon the earth and prophesied that God would work deliverance by Noah. In Genesis 6:9 and Hebrews 11:7, the Holy Spirit tells us ten things about this man Noah, who found grace in the eyes of the Lord.

1. Noah was 'just'

Here again is a word mentioned for the first time. This word does not refer to Noah's character, but to his standing before God. It is true, he behaved justly, but that is mentioned in the next line. This word, 'just', refers to Noah's justification by grace upon the grounds of Christ's obedience — that is, justification received by faith. As with all believers, it was not Noah's faith that justified him, but Christ, the object of his faith.

2. He was 'perfect in his generations'

Perfect means 'sincere and upright'. Noah was upright in his conduct, unspotted by the world and unaffected by all the generations in which he lived.

3. 'Noah walked with God'

Like Enoch before him and Abraham after him, Noah lived in the awareness of God's immediate presence. He walked with God by faith, trusting him, believing his Word, doing his will in sweet, blessed communion. Hebrews 11:7 describes Noah's faith.

4. His faith was based on the Word of God

The basis of Noah's faith was the Word of God. He was 'warned of God of things not seen as yet'. Faith must have a foundation; and the foundation of all true faith is the Word of God (Rom. 10:17). Noah believed because God had spoken it; and he believed what God spoke, even though it was contrary to reason, experience and science. God warned him of things not yet seen. Truly, his faith was remarkable. Noah believed God was about to send a universal flood, with waters covering the whole earth, though it had never rained! Even though no one had ever seen a boat, he built an ark by which he, his family and all the creatures of the earth were saved from destruction. His faith in God condemned all who would not enter the ark, all who did not believe God.

5. He feared God

The character of Noah's faith was reverence. He was 'moved with fear'. Noah feared God because he believed God. He had an awesome sense of God's wisdom, holiness, justice, truth and power. He was overwhelmed by a sense of God's goodness.

6. He was obedient

The evidence of Noah's faith was obedience. Being 'moved with fear, [he] prepared an ark'. Without delay, before the first raindrops fell, Noah began building an ark, following precisely the pattern God had given him. Faith is more than a creed. It is more than embracing historical facts and religious dogma. Faith acts upon God's revelation; it is belief in action (James 2:14).

7. His household was saved

The result of Noah's faith was the salvation of his house: He 'prepared an ark to the saving of his house'. God always honours faith. We know that there is no such thing as 'salvation by proxy'. Yet God does honour faith. Noah believed God, and God saved his family. Abraham believed God, and God gave his seed the land of promise. Rahab believed God, and God saved her household. The Canaanite woman believed God, and Christ healed her daughter. Because four men believed God, Christ healed their paralyzed friend (Matt. 9:2). The word of promise is yet to be believed: 'Believe on the Lord Jesus Christ, and thou shalt be saved, and thy house!' (Acts 16:31).

8. He confessed his faith publicly

The faith of Noah was confessed publicly. By his faith in and obedience to the Lord God, Noah 'condemned the world'. He warned the men and women of his generation of God's judgement and impending wrath. He called them to faith. By the Word of God he preached, he condemned them for their unbelief.

9. His reward is everlasting

The reward of Noah's faith is everlasting. He 'became heir of the righteousness which is by faith'. He was made an heir of the righteousness of Christ, and an heir of that which righteousness deserves: eternal glory.

10. The means of salvation — an ark

The means of Noah's salvation was an ark (vv. 13-18). Noah and his family were saved by an ark, a ship which God commanded him to build. That ark is a picture of Christ.

There are three arks mentioned in the Word of God. Each was a place of refuge, shelter and safety, a type of the Lord Jesus Christ and God's salvation in and by him. The ark which Noah built secured those who were in it from the vengeance and the violent wrath of an angry God. That is Christ our substitute. The ark of bulrushes protected God's chosen one, Moses, from the murderous designs of a wicked ruler, Pharaoh. That ark is Christ, into whom chosen sinners were placed from eternity by a loving Father. The ark of the covenant sheltered the two tables of God's holy law, and being covered with blood, was the place of atonement, mercy and acceptance with God for sinners. That ark is Christ our mercy-seat. From the beginning there has been but one place of refuge for sinners, only one way of salvation. That refuge, that salvation is Christ! If we would be saved, we must be robed in Christ's righteousness and washed in his blood. We must be in Christ by faith. Only Christ can bear our souls above the flood of God's wrath. Only Christ can save us.

11.

The ark

Genesis 7:1

'And the LORD *said unto Noah, Come thou and all thy house into the ark; for thee have I seen righteous before me in this generation'* (Gen. 7:1).

As has been stated, three arks are mentioned in the Scriptures. All three were places of refuge and the means of salvation. All three were pictures of grace and types of the Lord Jesus Christ, our Saviour. The ark of the covenant sheltered the two tables of stone upon which the law of God was written. In that ark, under the mercy-seat, were found the broken law that demanded death, the manna that gave life and the rod of power that led and protected Israel. The ark of bulrushes protected God's chosen one, Moses. The ark which Noah built was the ark of God's salvation for him and his family. This ark was also a beautiful type of Christ and a clear, instructive picture of the grace of God in him. Noah and his family were saved in the flood by a ship, an ark.

There was but one ark in the days of Noah. The whole world was drowned under the flood of God's wrath, except for those eight happy souls in the ark. So, too, the whole world will be destroyed in the everlasting wrath of Almighty God, except for those happy, blessed men and women who are in Christ. Christ alone is the Saviour of men. 'There is none other name under heaven given among men, whereby we must be saved.' If we would be saved, we must come into the ark, Christ Jesus. We must flee from the wrath of God, and fleeing, we must flee to Christ.

A planned ark

The ark was planned, purposed and provided by God (Gen. 6:13-16). Long before the Flood came, the Lord God provided for the salvation of his own. The ark was not an afterthought. God did not hurriedly put it together after the waters began to rise. It was God alone who determined the size, shape and material of the ark. He alone determined who would be saved by the ark. The ark was designed, built and stocked to house a specific number of residents, both of men and beasts. God determined where, how, and when the ark would be built.

In just this way, the Lord God planned and purposed the salvation of his people by Christ in his eternal purpose of grace. The Lord Jesus was provided in the purpose of God from eternity, long before the clouds of divine wrath began to swell against fallen men. Our salvation was not an afterthought. The Lord our God made provision for the salvation of his people in his Son long before the world began (Acts 2:23; 1 Peter 1:18-20; 2 Tim. 1:9; Eph. 1:3-6). Christ is the Lamb of God slain from the foundation of the world (Rev. 13:8).

Long before we sinned in Adam, the Lord God planned the salvation of his elect in Christ. The plan of salvation is not a path we follow to find God. It is the path God follows to find his elect. It is an eternal plan! God determined from eternity whom he would save (2 Thess. 2:13). God purposed from eternity that he would save his elect by the substitutionary sacrifice of his dear Son (Rom. 3:24-26). And God's purpose of grace is sure and immutable (Rom. 8:28-30).

In the fulness of time, God provided his own dear Son to be the salvation of sinners (John 3:16; 1 John 4:9-10; Gal. 4:4-5). As the ark was God's provision for Noah and his family, Christ is God's provision for sinners. As the ark was a provision of pure, free grace, so Christ is the provision of God's grace.

A sufficient ark

The ark which Noah built was an all-sufficient refuge for all who entered it. The ark was a huge ship. There was no lack of room in it; but there was no wasted space. There was room enough for Noah and his family, for two of every unclean bird, beast, rodent and insect in the world, and for seven of every clean animal. There was room enough in the ark to supply all the people and animals on board with food for a full year. The ark was an immense ship, about 450 feet long, 75 feet wide, 45 feet high; and it housed all kinds of creatures.

The Lord Jesus Christ,too, is a great and mighty Saviour, an all-sufficient refuge for sinners of every kind. As the ark was an immense vessel whose inhabitants floated safely through the storm of God's wrath, so Christ is an immense Saviour. His salvation is an immense salvation, delivering a vast multitude, which no man can number, from the wrath of God.

There was only one door in the ark, but that door was enough. All who entered the ark, clean and unclean, large and small, male and female, all came in through the same door. There is but one door of salvation for sinners. That door is Christ (John 10:9; 14:6). If we would be saved, we must enter in by the door, Christ Jesus. Grace is a great equalizer; it puts all on common ground. We cannot come to God, except as sinners in need of grace, trusting his Son. This one door is sufficient. All who will may enter into life eternal through the door which is Christ.

There was only one window in the ark, but that window was enough. It gave light to all and all the light that was needed. That window represents the Spirit of God through whom Christ, the Light of the world, the Sun of Righteousness, shines into the hearts of men. All who come to Christ and receive salvation by him are illuminated and taught by God the Holy Spirit (John 16:13; 6:44-45). And all who are taught of God are well taught. When God teaches, those who are taught by him learn the lesson. He teaches and convinces all his own of sin, of righteousness and of judgement — of their own sin, of righteousness accomplished by Christ's obedience, of judgement finished, atonement made and condemnation ended for ever, by the death of Christ who bore the wrath of God for us, as our substitute.

There was plenty of room in the ark for all who came into it. So, too, every needy sinner who comes to Christ finds all his needs abundantly supplied in Christ. All the grace we need is in Christ (Eph. 1:3). All the temporal blessings we need in this life are in Christ (Phil. 4:19). All the spiritual blessings we need, for all eternity, are in Christ (John 1:16; Col. 1:18; 2:9-10). Everything that God can, or will, do for sinful men and women, he has done for us in Christ. All that he can, or will, require of sinners, he has supplied in Christ. And all that he can, or will, give to sinners, he has given to us in Christ. The Lord Jesus Christ is a mighty, all-sufficient Saviour for needy sinners. He is able to do all that he has promised (Rom. 4:21), and to save to the uttermost all who come to God by him (Heb. 7:25). He is able to keep that which we have committed to him (2 Tim. 1:12), and to keep us from falling (Jude 24-25). He is also able to raise us from the dead (Phil. 3:20-21).

Called to enter

Noah and his family came into the ark by divine invitation (Gen. 7:1). I shall leave it to others to argue about whether the gospel call comes as an invitation or a command. Being the call of the sovereign God, it is certainly a call that no man is allowed to despise with impunity. That makes it a command. Yet it comes to needy sinners like the sweetest, most gracious, most magnanimous invitation imaginable.

God graciously revealed his thoughts of mercy, love and grace to Noah. Had the Lord not made himself known to Noah, Noah would have perished with the rest of the world. In the same way, the Lord graciously reveals his love, mercy and grace in Christ in the hearts of his elect by the gospel (2 Cor. 4:6).

Look at God's call to Noah and learn about the call of grace. This was a divine call. God himself spoke to Noah. It was a personal, particular, distinguishing call. 'The LORD said unto Noah, Come ... into the ark!' Noah's family benefited from the call; but only Noah was called (1 Cor. 7:14). This was a sovereign, powerful, effectual, irresistible call. Noah went in (Gen. 7:5). Most gladly, most willingly, most cheerfully, all who are called by God the Holy Spirit flee to Christ, the ark of salvation. All who hear his voice enter into the ark (Ps. 65:4; 110:3).

A picture of atonement

This ark, by which Noah and his family were saved, beautifully represents our atonement for sin in Christ. There are two things, in particular, which set forth our Lord's work of atonement.

First, Noah was commanded to pitch the ark within and without with pitch (Gen. 6:14). The word which is translated 'pitch' simply means 'to cover', or to 'take away'. At least seventy times in the Old Testament it is translated 'to make atonement'. The pitch was a covering which sheltered Noah and all who were in the ark from the terrible storm of God's wrath. As the mercy-seat sprinkled with blood covered the broken law of God on the Day of Atonement, so the pitch covered the ark. This is a picture of Christ's blood atonement. The pitch without portrays redemption accomplished (Heb. 9:12). The pitch within pictures redemption applied (Heb. 9:14).

Second, the storm of God's wrath fell upon the ark with all the fulness of its fury. As the rains descended and the depths of the earth were broken up, the angry, merciless billows of God's unmitigated wrath beat down upon the ark. Everyone in that ark went through the terrible storm of God's undiluted wrath. But it was the ark which took all the punishment.

Do you see the picture? When Christ was made to be sin for us, the terrible storm of God's wrath fell with full force upon him and beat him to death, without mercy, until God's justice and wrath were fully satisfied and totally expended. As our adorable Redeemer hung upon the cross, dying as our substitute, he cried, 'All thy waves and thy billows are gone over me' (Ps. 42:7). As those in the ark went through the Flood, so all God's elect in Christ have gone through the storm of his holy wrath. But it was Christ, our ark, who took all the punishment. Having once endured God's wrath, Noah had no cause to fear another flood. He was assured that he would never again suffer the flood of wrath. He had God's promise for it, and the bow of God's covenant to attest to it (Gen. 9:11-13). So, too, those who endured the wrath of God once in Christ, the sinner's substitute, will never endure it again, not to any degree, not at any time, not for any reason.

Safety in the ark

All who were in the ark were perfectly safe: 'The LORD shut him in' (Gen. 7:16). Though the ark passed through the horrible storm of God's wrath, all who were in the ark were perfectly safe and secure. The Lord brought them in. The Lord shut them in and he kept them in.

There were three storeys in the ark, the lower, the second, and the upper decks (Gen. 6:16). Perhaps these three storeys represent the believer's threefold salvation in Christ: past, present and future. We have been saved by election, redemption and regeneration. We are being saved by divine preservation. We shall yet be saved in our translation into heaven at the death of the body, by the resurrection from the grave, and in ultimate glorification.

Certainly, this is also a picture of the safety of all God's elect in Christ. Some who are in Christ are in the lower deck of doubt and fear. Some are in the second deck of strong faith. And others are in the upper deck of full assurance. Yet all who believe are in the ark; and all who are in the ark, Christ Jesus, are perfectly safe and secure. God has shut them in. It is not the strength of our faith that gives us security, but the strength of our Saviour, the ark (John 10:28-29; Rom. 8:31-39). All who entered the ark passed through the Flood and came out unharmed (Gen. 8:18; John 18:9; Rom. 8:29-30; Heb. 2:13). So shall it be with all who are in Christ.

The ark was a place of peace and rest for those who were in it; it had many 'rooms' (nests) (Gen. 6:14). In Christ, we have something more than a refuge; we have a resting place. We are like young birds in their nests, the objects of another's constant, loving care. As the dove found rest only in the ark, sinners cannot find rest for their souls except in Christ. Christ is our rest, our sabbath. Believing on him, we find rest (Matt. 11:28-29). Though they were tossed upon the stormy tempests, they were safe. So, too, all God's elect are safe and secure in the Christ. Like frightened birds, we nestle down in our resting place. Is it not true with you? In Christ we pass through the storms of life and trials of faith unharmed, if not unalarmed (Isa. 43:1-7). With David, we say, 'What time I am afraid, I will trust in thee.'

There is safety and security in the ark, Christ Jesus. All on board the good ship *Grace* are safe, immutably safe, and for ever safe. Satan cannot harm us. The law cannot condemn us. God has sworn that his wrath will not be poured out upon us again (Gen. 8:20-22; Isa. 54:9-10; Rev. 4:3). The Lord Jesus Christ cannot fail to save all who trust him (Isa. 42:1-4).

> Firm as his throne the gospel stands,
> My Lord, my hope, my trust.
> If I am found in Jesus' hands
> My soul cannot be lost!
> His honour is engaged
> to keep the weakest of his sheep.

All that his heavenly Father gave,
his hands securely keep.
Not death, nor hell shall ever remove
his people from his breast.
In the dear bosom of his love,
we shall for ever rest!

12.

God's covenant with Noah

Genesis 9:11

'And I will establish my covenant with you; neither shall all flesh be cut off any more by the waters of a flood; neither shall there any more be a flood to destroy the earth' (Gen. 9:11).

Noah's first act, when he came out of the ark, was not to build a house for himself, but an altar 'unto the LORD' on which he offered sacrifices as burnt offerings to God. These were received by God as a sweet-smelling savour. Having received these offerings, God declared that never again would he curse the ground for man's sake and that, as long as the earth remained, its seasons would not cease.[1]

Then we are told, 'God blessed Noah and his sons' (9:1). This is the first time we read of God blessing anyone since the fall of our father Adam. The basis of this blessing was the sacrifice God had received. That sacrifice was symbolic. It is a picture of Christ, the Lamb of God, for whose sake and through whose merits all the blessings of grace flow to sinners upon the earth. This is a new beginning. Judgement is over. Old things have passed away. All things are now new; and everything now rests upon a covenant that God made, a covenant of grace, based upon shed blood. Man had forfeited the blessing of God, and his position as lord of creation. But grace restores him and reinstates him.

God made a covenant with Noah and, in its scope, that covenant reached even to the beasts of the field, the birds of the air and the fish of the sea (9:2). This covenant was made to last for ever.

Everything about Noah's salvation by means of the ark is a type of our salvation by the Lord Jesus Christ. The whole story is full of spiritual suggestions.

1. The ark is a picture of Christ and our redemption by him.

2. The salvation of Noah and his family by water is a picture of our salvation by the washing of regeneration. Though we are in the world, we are dead to it, like Noah was. As Noah came out of the ark, out of the Flood of God's wrath, so we have come up out of the watery grave to walk with Christ in newness of life, by the power of our resurrected Redeemer.

3. As Noah came out of the ark to walk abroad in the earth, so the believer in Christ walks in freedom.

4. Noah's sacrifices to God are a picture of the believer's vocation in this world — the worship and praise of God our Saviour.

5. When the Lord commanded Noah to be fruitful and fill the earth, he demonstrated the fruitfulness of faith. Believers bear fruit, the fruit of the Spirit, to God (Gal. 5:22-23). As his witnesses in this world, believing sinners are spiritual parents to immortal souls, labouring in birth until Christ is formed in other chosen sinners by the work of God the Holy Spirit.

6. Noah's dominion over the beasts of the earth symbolized the believer's dominion over the lusts of his own nature. Grace has made us kings and priests in Christ. We are kings to rule our own spirits by the Spirit of Christ. We are priests to offer up sacrifices to God by Christ.

7. Standing before God on the grounds of God's own covenant, Noah was secure. This is a picture of every believer's security before God.

Before ever the earth was made, in eternity past, God made a covenant with his Son for the salvation of his elect. We call it the covenant of grace, or the everlasting covenant. That covenant was a solemn compact between God the Father, God the Son and God the Holy Spirit, which guarantees the salvation of God's elect. It is a covenant ordered in all things and made sure from eternity (Eph. 1:3-6; 2 Tim. 1:9). It is ratified by the blood of Christ at Calvary (Heb. 13:20) and is established and sealed to God's elect by the Holy Spirit in regeneration through faith (Eph. 1:13-14). It was this blessed covenant of grace that comforted, sustained and gave satisfaction to David on his deathbed (2 Sam. 23:5). It is this very same covenant which is the comfort and strength of believing sinners today (2 Tim. 1:9-12). The covenant that God made with Noah was a covenant of pure grace and was representative of the covenant of grace which he made for us with Christ before the world began.

Who made this covenant?

The source of this covenant was God alone. It was a covenant that God made with Noah, not one that Noah made with God (Read vv. 11,12,15). Man had no part in making it, or in keeping it; and he could not break it. So it is with the everlasting covenant of grace that God has made for us. It is a covenant of pure grace (Rom. 9:11-18). It is a covenant of unconditional, unqualified promise. God says, 'I shall' and 'you will' (Gal. 4:22-31). Believers do not stand before

God under a covenant that demands anything of them. We live under a covenant of promise. Its favours are unconditional. Its mercies are unlimited. All its blessings are made sure to all the seed by the oath and promise of God. As God kept his covenant with Noah (8:22), so the covenant of grace has been faithfully kept to this day, kept by God himself. Nothing in the covenant depends, to any degree, upon man. God says, 'I will remember my covenant,' and he does. The garments of salvation are all garments which God provides, garments of grace. None of God's people wear garments of linen and wool, of works and grace.

C. H. Spurgeon said, 'My looking to Jesus brings me joy and peace, but it is God's looking to Jesus which secures my salvation and that of all his elect; for it is impossible for God to look at Christ, our bleeding surety, and then be angry with us for sins already punished in him.'

The covenant of grace is an everlasting covenant. Time does not change God or his purpose. David rejoiced to declare on his dying bed, '[The LORD] hath made with me an everlasting covenant, ordered in all things, and sure.' Every child of God in this world can, and should, have the same joyful confidence in all his circumstances. Grace is never in jeopardy. Salvation is never in danger. God's elect cannot be lost by any means (Isa. 54:9-10). So, we say again, the covenant of grace is a covenant made by God and kept by God.

With whom was the covenant established?

The covenant touched everything in God's creation. Its benefits were given to all Noah's posterity. But the covenant was made with only one man — Noah (v. 11). The covenant of grace, too, was made with one person — the Lord Jesus Christ; but that one person was surety for many (Heb. 7:22). God made his covenant for us with Christ. Our divine surety met all the requirements of the covenant for us. In him, only in him, every believer receives all the blessings of the covenant. They are ours in Christ and for his sake (Eph. 1:3-6; 2 Tim. 1:9).

What was the foundation of the covenant?

This covenant was God's response to Noah's sacrifice (8:20-22). The covenant which God made with Noah was his answer to the 'sweet savour' that ascended to him from the altar. All the blessings of the covenant flowed to Noah, because of his sacrifice. And all the blessings of the covenant of grace flow to all of God's elect through 'the blood of the everlasting covenant' (Heb. 13:20), the blood of Christ, 'the Lamb slain from the foundation of the world' (Rev. 13:8).[2]

Why was this covenant made?

We must not pry into the secrets of Almighty God. I do not pretend to know all of God's reasoning and motivation in the covenant he made with Noah, or in the covenant he made with Christ for us. However, this much he has revealed. God made his covenant to be:

1. a wondrous display of his amazing grace (Gen. 8:21; Eph. 1:6,12,14);
2. a perpetual declaration of his glorious sovereignty (Gen. 8:22; Rom. 9:11-18);
3. a solid ground of comfort for his elect (Rom. 8:28-32).

What is included in the covenant?

In a word — everything! The covenant God made with Noah included all the elements of the world (8:22), all the creatures of the world (9:3,9,10), and all the governments of the world (9:6). The covenant of grace includes everything. 'All things are of God' (2 Cor. 5:18). 'All things are yours' (1 Cor. 3:21; Hosea 2:18; Rom. 8:28). Everything in this world is so absolutely governed by God that nothing happens, nothing is done, nothing moves, nothing lives, nothing dies, except what God has purposed for the fulfilling of his covenant in his elect.

What is the meaning of the rainbow, the token of the covenant?

Read verses 12-16. Here we see the rainbow upon the earth. But when John was caught up to heaven, he saw the rainbow encircling God's throne (Rev. 4:3), and he saw Christ, our Mediator, ruling all things for the fulfilment of God's covenant, crowned with a rainbow on his head (Rev. 10:1).

The Lord is ever mindful of his covenant. He does not need a token to remind him of it; but we do. So he gave us the rainbow. It was a symbol to Noah of God's covenant with him; and it is a symbol to us to remind us of God's covenant with us in Christ.

When may we expect to see the rainbow? The only time the rainbow is seen is when there is a cloud (v. 14). When our blessed Saviour died at Calvary, there was a dark cloud over the earth; and there, in the death of our substitute, we see God's covenant. The believer's days in this world are often filled with clouds, clouds hung by our heavenly Father: 'When I bring a cloud.' We best read the lines and promises of God's covenant when we read them written for us upon the dark and cloudy sky of adversity. A rainbow is never seen until a cloud appears. But, as A. W. Pink said, 'How blessed to know that the cloud that comes over our sky is of his bringing! And if so, how sure that some way he will reveal his glory in it!'

If we would see the rainbow, there must also be some rain. The cloud itself does not give the rainbow. We shall never see a rainbow without the crystal drops of water to reflect the light of the sun. And the rainbow cannot be seen unless the sun shines. It is only as Christ, the Sun of Righteousness, shines in our hearts by the Spirit of grace that we are able to see God's covenant and grace towards us in him.

> Shine, O Sun of Righteousness,
> Through all the clouds of time and sense;
> Display the rainbow of your grace
> And rest my soul in covenant peace.

What do we see in the rainbow, the token of the covenant? In the rainbow, we see transcendent beauty and glory. That is what we see revealed in the covenant of God's grace. In the rainbow, we see a symbol of justice and vengeance satisfied. There is the bow; but it has neither string nor arrow. God has hung up his bow. The warfare is over (Isa. 40:1-2). That is the covenant fulfilled by our surety. In the rainbow, we see streamers of joy, a banner of delight, flung across the heavens. That is what the covenant of grace is! (Jer. 31:3,31-34; 32:37-41).

13.

The rainbow

Genesis 9:13

'I do set my bow in the cloud, and it shall be for a token of a covenant between me and the earth' (Gen. 9:13).

After God destroyed the world with the waters of the Flood in his fierce anger, he promised Noah that he would never do so again. He made a covenant with Noah and set a rainbow in the sky (Gen. 9:11-16). From that day to this, the rainbow has stood as a perpetual reminder of God's covenant. It is a sign of the covenant that will stand until God our Saviour comes again and makes all things new.

The rainbow and the covenant are mentioned frequently in the Scriptures in connection with the throne of God, the glory of God and the promises of the grace of God. It is the Lord our God who declares:

This is as the waters of Noah unto me: for as I have sworn that the waters of Noah should no more go over the earth; so have I sworn that I would not be wroth with thee, nor rebuke thee. For the mountains shall depart, and the hills be removed; ... saith the LORD that hath mercy on thee

(Isa. 54:9-10).

When Ezekiel describes his vision of God's glory, he tells us that he saw a rainbow, the symbol of the covenant, encircling God's glorious throne: 'As the appearance of the bow that is in the cloud in the day of rain, so was the appearance of the brightness round about. This was the appearance of the likeness of the glory of the LORD' (Ezek. 1:28). When the apostle John was called up to heaven, to behold the throne of God, he tells us, 'There was a rainbow round about the throne, in sight like unto an emerald' (Rev. 4:3). As the throne that John saw is a symbol of God's sovereignty, so the rainbow round about the throne is a symbol of the covenant of grace.

John Gill comments, 'The rainbow is a reverberation, or a reflection of the beams of the sun upon a thin watery cloud. And the covenant of grace is owing to Jesus Christ, the Sun of righteousness.' It is Christ who made the covenant for us with the Father. He fills the covenant with all the blessings of grace. Christ is the mediator of the covenant, the surety of the covenant, and the messenger of the covenant. In Revelation 10:1, John draws a picture of Christ as one clothed with a cloud, having a rainbow upon his head. The fact is, the whole of the covenant of grace is Jesus Christ himself. He is the surety of the covenant, the ratifier of the covenant, the blessing of the covenant, and the embodiment of the covenant. God the Father said to his Son, 'I will preserve thee, and give thee for a covenant of the people' (Isa. 49:8).

An emblem of mercy and peace

The rainbow is an emblem of the covenant of grace. Its many colours might be expressive of the promises of God in the covenant. The covenant symbolized by the rainbow is the everlasting covenant of grace, of mercy and of peace (Jer. 31:31-34; 32:37-40; Heb. 8:8-13; 10:16-17; Ps. 89:19-37). This covenant of grace was made between God the Father, God the Son and God the Holy Spirit before the world was made. Our surety and representative in the covenant was the Lord Jesus Christ (Heb. 7:22; Gen. 43:8-9). In this ever-lasting covenant of grace, the salvation of God's elect was agreed upon, worked out, and accomplished in the oath, purpose and decree of God (1 Peter 1:18-20; Rev. 13:8; 2 Tim. 1:9-10; Job 33:24). In time, this covenant of grace, made in God's eternal purpose, was ratified by and fulfilled in the death of the Lord Jesus Christ in the place of his people (Heb. 9:15-17). And all the blessings and promises of the covenant are sealed to the hearts of God's elect by the Holy Spirit (Gal. 3:13-17; Eph. 1:13-14).

As the rainbow is the emblem of mercy, peace and reconciliation in God towards man, after he had destroyed the world by the Flood, so the covenant of grace is a coven-ant of mercy and peace. It comes from God's mercy; it is full of God's mercy; and it provides abundant mercy, peace and reconciliation for sinners through the blood of Christ.

The security of the world

As we have said, when God set his bow in the sky, he prom-ised that he would never again destroy the world by a flood. Can you imagine how Noah and his sons must have trembled, when they heard that first clap of thunder and saw that first bolt of lightning after the Flood? The ark was gone. Perhaps they used it for fire wood. As the rain began to fall, I do not doubt that they must have been terrified. Then the rain stopped, the sun began to shine, and the bow of God appeared in the sky! By the appearing of God's bow in the sky, their fears were dispelled.

As the rainbow is a symbol of God's covenant and his promise to Noah, so it is God's covenant of grace that holds back the hand of his justice and keeps him from destroying this earth and its inhabitants. Had it not been for the covenant of grace, God would have destroyed the human race when Adam sinned in the Garden. And were it not for that same, inalterable covenant, God would not allow the wicked to live today (2 Peter 3:9). As the angels of judgement could not destroy Sodom until Lot was safely out of the city, so the Lord God will not destroy this earth in his wrath until he has saved all the hosts of his elect (Rev. 7).

Above all else, it is the firm and everlasting covenant of grace that secures the eternal salvation of God's elect (2 Sam. 23:5). We believe in eternal security, because we believe in the immutability of God's covenant. God is faithful to his covenant. He will honour and keep his covenant. And, blessed be his name, God's faithfulness to his covenant is not in anyway dependent upon the faithfulness of his people (Ps. 89:28,34; Ezek. 16:60-62).

Encompassing the throne

The throne is the emblem of God's sovereignty, his dominion and power. The 'rainbow round about the throne' tells us that God's sovereignty is bound, hedged about, and limited by his covenant. In other words, God cannot and will not do anything contrary to, or inconsistent with, his covenant (Heb. 6:13-19). God has bound himself to his covenant. The fact that this rainbow, the covenant of grace, completely encircles the throne of God signifies three things:

1. God is always mindful of his covenant

The psalmist said, 'He will ever be mindful of his covenant' (Ps. 111:5). No matter which way he turns, the covenant is always before his eyes. He remembers it constantly for the good of his people. He keeps his covenant faithfully. No matter how he comes to his people, he comes to them by way of the covenant. In everything God does, he is fulfilling his covenant.

2. No man can come to God, except through the covenant

Strip the throne of the rainbow, and there is the august, sparkling majesty of God, a consuming fire, which no man dare approach. But that same throne, encircled with a rainbow, is inviting (Heb. 4:16). Sinners may approach the God of the covenant by a new and living way, by the blood of the everlasting covenant. We cannot draw near to God with our works. Both Cain and Uzza stand as striking examples of what becomes of those who put their own hands into the business of God's salvation. We dare not attempt to draw near to God with the strange fire of our own religious deeds and sacrifices. But sinners can approach God on the basis of the covenant, pleading the merits of Christ's righteousness and shed blood. We come to God in the covenant name, Jesus Christ. The password to God's throne is Christ. We pray in Christ's name (John 15:16), we worship in Christ's name (Matt. 18:20), and we are also saved in Christ's name (Acts 4:12).

3. The fact that this rainbow encircles the throne of God tells us that God's government of this world is determined by, and is in exact agreement with, the covenant of grace (Rom. 8:28)

God always has respect to the covenant. Everything he does is for its fulfilment. In all the great events of providence, he is simply fulfilling his covenant. As we read the Scriptures, we notice that everything was, and is, done to suit God's purposes for his chosen nation. Egypt comes across the stage, Assyria, Babylon, Greece and Rome. But all these nations are just background settings. Their pomp, grandeur and wealth are just accessories. They rise and fall; they come and go with insignificance. The central figure is Israel, the elect nation, the church of God. The rest of the nations are nothing more than props, scaffolding, and gardeners for the Lord's vineyard. God has chosen Jacob for his portion. He is only concerned with him. He does everything for Jacob. 'I believe', C. H. Spurgeon once said, 'that when kings and potentates meet in the cabinet chamber and consult together according to their ambition, a Counsellor whom they never see pulls the strings, and they are only his puppets' (Isaiah 10; 43:1-7).

The ultimate end of all the events of providence is the salvation of God's elect, the gathering of his redeemed ones, the calling of his church. God rules this world for his elect, covenant people. By secret, almighty, irresistible force, God works all things together for the good of his elect.

As this is true in all the great, momentous events of providence, so it is equally true of all the small, minute matters of daily life — the painting of the lilac, the feeding of the sparrow, the numbering of the hairs of our heads are all done by God because of his care and love for his people in Christ. The promise of the covenant is 'Surely blessing I will bless thee' (Heb. 6:14), and he always does. 'Although my house be not so with God', yet I am blessed by God. Let every child of God rejoice in this great fact of covenant grace. We are blessed by God according to the tenor of the covenant. In all our temptations (1 Cor. 10:13), in all our afflictions, in all our chastisements (Heb. 12:5; Rev. 3:19), our heavenly Father is bringing upon us his covenant blessings in and through our Lord Jesus Christ.

There is a rainbow round about the throne. Let that throne decree what it may, the decree will never run contrary to the covenant of love. Even when I am most distressed and the circumstances of my life are most painful, I shall know of a certainty, and shall testify gladly, 'Truly God is good to Israel' (Ps. 73:1).

Emerald green in colour

The rainbow has many colours. But the dominant colour is green. This is the colour of life, peace, tranquillity and joy. Truly, the most delightful, life-giving, peaceful sight in all the world is the covenant of God's grace. What can give us more cheer than to see God as our covenant God, Christ as our covenant surety, and all the blessings and promises of the covenant made sure in him? The covenant of grace, like the emerald, is evergreen. It is always new. Its promises are always fresh. Its blessings will endure for ever.

Designed to be a reminder

Though God does not need anything to bring things to his remembrance, yet he condescends to set the rainbow in the sky so that he might look at it and remember his everlasting covenant; and he allows us to put him in remembrance of his covenant, pleading the promises of the covenant with him in prayer (Isa. 43:25-26). Let every believer keep the covenant constantly in view. Our God does. Draw comfort from the covenant. Never sink so low as to entertain hard thoughts about God's providence. God's providence is only the outworking of his covenant grace. Give thanks and praise to God for his covenant (2 Sam. 23:1-5; Eph. 1:3-6).

14.

Noah and his sons

Genesis 9:18-29

'And the sons of Noah, that went forth of the ark, were Shem, and Ham, and Japheth: and Ham is the father of Canaan' (Gen. 9:18).

The entire inspired account of Noah's life after the Flood, a period of 350 years, is given to us by Moses in just twenty-nine verses in Genesis chapter 9. That fact, in itself, is remarkable, when we consider what tremendous responsibilities fell upon his shoulders. Noah led the world in the worship of God. He was the man responsible for the government of the nations which issued from his loins. In addition to his tasks as both the prophet of God and the civil magistracy of the world, Noah still had the care of his family.

Yet the Holy Spirit bypasses all the frustrations of earth he endured and the feats of faith he accomplished, and focuses our attention upon the only blemish recorded concerning his life of 950 years! There must be some special reason for this.

The Scriptures declare that 'Noah found grace in the eyes of the LORD' (Gen. 6:8). The Lord God reduced the world to one family. In the Flood, the Lord God destroyed the whole human race, except for Noah, his sons and their wives. Why was this? It was because 'Noah found grace in the eyes of the LORD'. God chose Noah, provided an ark of salvation for him and his family, put them in the ark and graciously brought Noah and all who were with him through the judgement.

In Genesis 9:1-11 Moses describes God's covenant with Noah and his sons after the Flood. In these verses God made a promise of his providential care for Noah and his family, as they went about replenishing the earth (v. 1). He put the fear of man in the beasts of the earth (v. 2). The Lord gave man all the vegetation of the earth, beasts of the land, fowls of the air and fish of the sea for his food and pleasure (vv. 3-4). God required all men, under penalty of death, to take care of one another[1] (vv. 5-6). Then, in verses 8-17, we read of God's covenant, in which he promised never to destroy the world by water again and to place the rainbow in the sky as the token of his covenant[2].

In verses 18 and 19, we are told that 'The sons of Noah, that went forth of the ark, were Shem, and Ham, and Japheth: and Ham is the father of Canaan. These are the three sons of Noah: and of them was the whole earth overspread.' We have two choices. We can either accept the ever-changing, wild guesses of those who believe in evolution, regarding the origins of man and of the nations of the world, or we can believe the revelation of God. I believe God.

According to the Book of God, all mankind descended from Noah and his wife, his three sons and their wives, and before that from Adam and Eve. It is obvious that we have many different groups or races with what seem to be greatly differing features. The most noticeable of these is skin colour. Many see this as a reason to doubt the Bible's record of history. They believe that the various groups could only have come about through an evolutionary process in which they evolved separately over tens of thousands of years.

This view has no foundation. Skin pigmentation, eye and hair colour, and the shapes of men's physical features change within immediate families in one generation. It requires nothing more than looking at any man and his children to see that fact clearly demonstrated. The races of humanity did not evolve from some cosmic ooze, or from the fish of the sea, or from some very crude early species of monkey. We may have different skin colour and may be shaped differently, but the entire human race is one race. We are all the sons and daughters of Adam, descended through Noah, Shem, Ham and Japheth. The dispersing of the nations, under the judgement of God, was the work of God's wise and adorable providence, not the luck of evolutionary accidents (Acts 17:26).

In verses 20-29, the Holy Spirit records the sad events of Noah's drunkenness and Ham's sin against his father, the curse of Canaan, Noah's prophecy regarding his sons and his death.

Noah's fall

In verses 20-21, Moses records Noah's fall for all to read. A sad, sad record this is, but it is written for our learning and admonition. So let us learn its lessons well. May God the Holy Spirit inscribe them upon our hearts. We must make neither more nor less of this than the Spirit of God does. We are told by God what kind of man Noah was. Like Job, grace had made Noah a just and upright man (Gen. 6:9). He was 'just' — both justified by the grace of God through the redemption that is in Christ and just in his dealings with God and men. He was sincere, upright and honest. The grace of God which distinguished him from the world had saved him from the corruption of his own heart and the corruptions of the world in which he lived. Noah was a child of God, a man of faith (Heb. 11:7).

Yet, as we have already said, when Moses was inspired by God to write the history of this remarkable man after the Flood, he mentions nothing about those 350 years in which he walked with God by faith in Christ, just as his great grandfather, Enoch, had done — nothing of those years, except this drunken stupor and the events surrounding it.

The intention of our heavenly Father in permitting these things and the intention of the Holy Spirit in inspiring Moses to record them here is that we might learn from them and profit by them (Rom. 15:4; 1 Cor. 10:11-13). Without question, there are many more lessons than I shall mention which could, and should, be drawn from this sad event in Noah's life; but it appears to me that there are five very obvious lessons to learn from this.

1. The Bible — the inspired Word of God

The Bible is, indeed, the inspired Word of God. One striking piece of evidence of divine inspiration is the fact that those men who wrote the Scriptures recorded, without excuse or extenuation, the most horrible failures of the greatest examples of faith and godliness. Unlike the writings of men, the Word of God deals with things honestly, even those things which are most likely to give men occasion to blaspheme and ridicule it. There is no attempt made in the Book of God to hide or excuse Noah's drunkenness, Abraham's actions before Pharaoh, David's crime, Peter's fall, or even the strife between Paul and Barnabas.

2. A Book to teach us

These things are written in the Book of God to teach us, by example, that 'Salvation belongeth unto the LORD!' Grace precedes the need for grace. God chose Noah and made a covenant with him, assuring him of his goodness before Noah needed assurance, and in anticipation of his need of it. Grace saved Noah and preserved him; and when he fell, grace restored the fallen saint, and preserved him still.

3. Men are only men

The Holy Spirit shows us here that the very best of men are only men at best. 'Man at his best estate is altogether vanity.' The fact is, though he was saved by the grace of God, Noah was still, like you and me, a sinner. The human heart is essentially evil (Jer. 17:9).

4. Only Christ's righteousness

The only righteousness any sinner has, or can have, before the holy, Lord God is the righteousness of Christ. It is the righteousness of Christ imputed to us by grace that justifies us, and the righteousness of Christ imparted to us in the new birth that sanctifies us.

5. No believer is free from temptation

No believer in this world is immune to temptation or sin. God graciously keeps his own elect from Satan, but not from sin; from death, but not from decline; from condemnation, but not from corruption; from falling away, but not from falling. Sometimes God lets one of his saints fall for the comfort of others, lest we be overwhelmed with despair when we experience the same thing. Martin Luther wrote, 'The Holy Spirit wanted the godly, who know their weakness and for this reason are disheartened, to take comfort from the offence that comes from the account of the lapses among the most perfect patriarchs. In such instances, we should find proof of our own weakness and therefore bow down in humble confession, not only to ask for forgiveness, but also to hope for it.'

Ham's sin

Next, in verses 22-23, the Spirit of God shows us Ham's sin, the terrible sin of a malicious, God-hating rebel against his father, and, more importantly, against the God of heaven, whose authority was represented by his father.

When Noah lay naked in his tent, in his drunkenness, Ham walked in on him. When he saw his father in such a condition, rather than trying to help the old man recover, rather than protecting his father's honour, he went outside and called his brothers, seizing the opportunity to defame his father, his father's God, and the worship of God that his father had taught him.

We must remember that Ham was not a boy. This was not a childish taunt. He was a grown man. He was at least 100 years old. No doubt, Noah had often upbraided him. Perhaps he had often reproved Ham for drunkenness. Ham's sin revealed his heart. The son would not have treated his father with such contempt, if he had not already murdered him in his heart.

God commands children to respect their parents, giving them the honour due to their position as parents, because it is right. Ham despised his father. Before the Flood, the whole world thought Noah was a fool, condemned him as an heretic, and looked down upon him as a mad, divisive, mean-spirited bigot, because the gospel he preached condemned them. Though he hid it, Ham was, all the while, in complete agreement with them, and now his true heart was manifest. Like Absalom after him, Ham walked in the way of Cain, ran after the error of Balaam, and perished under the gainsaying of Korah (Jude 8,10,11). Ham thought himself holy and Noah evil. Therefore, he jumped at the chance to expose Noah as a sinful wretch, despised and judged by God. He gleefully aired his father's nakedness.

This is the conflict which has been going on in the world since the beginning of time, and still continues today. The seed of the serpent is at enmity with the Seed of the woman. As Cain's murder of Abel must be traced to the enmity Satan has for Christ, so Ham's uncovering of his father's nakedness reveals the same enmity. It is this enmity of hell which inflames the rage of the entire world against Christ, his church and the gospel of the grace of God. It is this enmity which unites the whole religious world of Babylon — intoxicated with the wine of free-will, works religion — against Christ and his kingdom.

Ham was an apostate. He professed to be one with Noah and to believe the gospel Noah preached. But it was all a show of hypocrisy. In time, he turned from the way of Noah to the way of Cain. He behaved as a reprobate man, rejoicing in the iniquity of his father and making it known (1 Cor. 13:4-6; Gal. 6:1; Prov. 10:12; 12:6; 17:9). Like his father, the devil, he was a liar and a murderer.

As Shem and Japheth refused to look upon their father's nakedness and covered it, so believers protect the names, reputations and honour of others (Gen. 9:23). They took a blanket and went into the tent backwards, refusing to look upon Noah's nakedness and folly. By their actions, they said to each other, 'This is not our father. We shall not look upon his folly ourselves, or expose it to anyone else.' That is what love does when the person who is loved falls (Prov. 10:12). Believers are kind, forbearing and gracious, bearing with one another's infirmities, covering one another's faults, excusing, and making as little as possible of one another's failures. As this is true with respect to all men, so it is particularly true with respect to our brethren, and even more particularly with respect to God's servants: 'Against an elder receive not an accusation, but before two or three witnesses.' Gossiping, slandering men and women, people who rejoice in making known the faults of others (though they always preface it by saying, 'I hate to say it, but...'), simply do not know God.

Canaan's curse

In verses 24-25, we read about the dreadful curse that fell upon Canaan and all the descendants of Ham because of their father's sin. These words do not represent the wrath and vengeance of Noah, but the terrible wrath of God. The Lord God was so moved by wrath against this despicable, insolent, contemptuous rebel, that, in this text, he does not even call him by name, but calls him Canaan, after his son and the multitude of rebels which would spring from his loins.

What was this curse? What did it involve? There is no question that Ham was the father of those people known as Negroid. But it is the height of racial arrogance and it displays a terrible ignorance of Scripture to suggest that the colour of a man's skin represents the curse of God. Ham and his sons were cursed, a curse of servitude, bondage and slavery. It is true that in modern times the sons of Ham have been enslaved by other people. Some have even pointed to this text as a biblical justification for the barbaric practice of slavery. However, if we read the Bible or from history books, we shall see that cursed Ham took possession of the largest part of the earth and established the most extensive and powerful kingdoms in the world. Compared with the history of blessed Shem and Japheth, it appears to the eye of human reason that they were cursed and Ham was blessed.

The curse of God upon Canaan (Ham and his descendants) must have been something other than what men look upon and consider to be a curse. The fact is, this prophecy, like all others, is beyond the mere scope of reason. It can be understood only by the revelation of God given in Holy Scripture, and embraced by faith.

The life of the believer is a life of faith and hope. Prosperity is never an indication of blessedness. Neither is adversity an indication of wretchedness. In fact, just the opposite is true. Ham was cursed. Yet he alone became a master. Nimrod, who was his grandson by Cush, became the father of Babylon. Mizraim, another of Ham's children, became the father of Egypt (Gen. 10:6; Ps. 78:51). Shem and Japheth were blessed. Yet they appear to have been cursed. The specific curse of God upon Ham and his sons was slavery. Yet it was Ham and his descendants who held Abraham, Isaac and Jacob in slavery in Canaan and in Egypt. What, then, was God's curse upon Ham? Do we have any indication in Holy Scripture what it was? We do indeed.

You will recall that when the Lord God cursed Cain, he put a mark upon him. Cain complained that his punishment was greater than he could bear and he wanted to die. But God made him a permanent fugitive and vagabond in the earth. Yet, again, we see Cain's sons possessing great wealth and power (Gen. 4:10-18). The mark God put on Cain, like the curse placed upon Ham, was a spiritual mark and a spiritual curse. I do not know whether Cain was marked by some terrible, grotesque disease or deformity, but I really doubt it. The mark of Cain and the curse of Canaan were the same. God's mark upon Cain was the mark of the beast, the mark of the world, the mark of doomed, damned men, clinging to the religion of the world, despising God, his Son and the gospel of his grace. It is the same curse that God put upon Ham and his descendants.

The only people who are not engulfed in the religion of this world, the only ones who do not wear the mark of the beast are God's elect, whose names are in the Book of Life and who have been sealed by the Spirit of God[3] (2 Thess. 2:11-12; Rev. 13:8,17-18; 14:11; 16:2; 17:8; 19:20).
We should learn this and learn it well: God's thoughts are higher than our thoughts. His ways are higher than our ways. God's elect are blessed with a kingdom, but it is a kingdom of grace, not of the world. We possess great blessedness, but it is the blessedness of sins forgiven, of being reconciled to God, and of everlasting glory. We must set our hearts upon these things, leaving the cursed followers of Cain and Ham to possess the world and perish with it (Col. 3:1-3; Matt. 6:19-21,33).

We should learn this, too: the Lord God does visit the iniquities of the fathers upon their children, from generation to generation. God considers it no more a dishonour to his character to declare this truth than he did to declare that he will have mercy on whom he will have mercy (Exod. 33:19; 34:6-7). It should, however, be understood that while the sin of a father makes him responsible for the ruin of his family, a man's own sin is alone the cause of his punishment (Ezek. 18:20; Deut. 24:16). In the Day of Judgement we shall, each one, give account of ourselves to God.

Noah's prophecy

In verses 25-27, we read about Noah's other two sons, Shem and Japheth. What a remarkable prophecy this is. It is a prophecy which was never fully understood or explained by any other man, until the apostle Paul, writing by the same Spirit of inspiration, explained its meaning in Romans 9 - 11. Noah understood that his sons would inhabit the earth until the end of time. He prophesied that Christ (the God of Shem, the Seed of the woman) would come down to earth through Shem's seed. He prophesied too that God would bring about the fulness of Israel by gathering his elect from the Gentile world (Japheth) into the tents of Shem (the Jews). Noah also prophesied that Ham, that dominant but reprobate son, would ultimately become the servant of both Shem and Japheth.

Noah praised the God of Shem for his electing love: 'Blessed be the LORD God of Shem.' The blessings Shem enjoyed were not the result of his goodness, but of God's. Therefore it is the God of Shem who is blessed. Then the old patriarch spoke of the union of Jew and Gentile in Christ: 'God shall enlarge Japheth, and he shall dwell in the tents of Shem.' This dwelling of Japheth in the tents of Shem is not the result of war, but the blessed unity and union of believing hearts in Christ (Eph. 2:13-22).

Noah also assured his sons, who were favoured, that their oppressing, persecuting, slandering brother, with all his apparent power, would only, and always, be their servant, performing only that which would ultimately benefit them. What a promise this was! Ham built Egypt, and Egypt possessed Israel; but their redemption was portrayed in the overthrow of Pharaoh. Ham built Canaan, and Canaan became the land of Israel's inheritance by the blessing of God. Ham built Babylon, and Babylon possessed Israel; yet there redemption was portrayed in Cyrus. It was the sons of Ham (the Pharisees and the Romans) who crucified the Lord of glory; but it was by this that the Son of God redeemed his people (Acts 2:23). To this day, the sons of Ham despise, persecute and slander Shem and Japheth (God's elect); but they only serve the interests of our souls (Rom. 11:33-36).

Noah's end

In verses 28-29, the Holy Spirit records Noah's end, so that we might learn from that too. Noah lived 950 years, twenty years longer than Adam and only nineteen years fewer than Methuselah. For at least 370 of those years, he lived as a preacher of righteousness. Yet, finally, he died. Here is a man who saw great things. Happy are those who are blessed by God to see the same. Noah saw the world before the Flood, deserving the wrath and judgement of God. He saw the justice and mercy of God in bringing him through the Flood. This man saw the world after the Flood, and the splendour of God's good providence in all things. This same man, Noah, now lives in the world above and sees all things clearly, in the light of the glory of God our Saviour.

Do you see him, seated above, in the blood-washed company around the throne of God and of the Lamb? I can imagine the old patriarch singing, as he casts his crown at the Saviour's feet and worships the one who lives for ever and ever:

Thou art worthy, O Lord, to receive glory and honour and power: for thou hast created all things, and for thy pleasure they are and were created...Thou art worthy to take the book, and to open the seals thereof: for thou wast slain, and hast redeemed us to God by thy blood out of every kindred, and tongue, and people, and nation; And hast made us unto our God kings and priests: and we shall reign on the earth...Worthy is the Lamb that was slain to receive

power, and riches, and wisdom, and strength, and
honour, and glory, and blessing... Blessing, and
honour, and glory, and power, be unto him that sitteth
upon the throne, and unto the Lamb for ever and ever
(Rev. 4:11; 5:9-10,12-13).

15.

Babel — the religion of the cursed

Genesis 11:1-9

'And the whole earth was of one language, and of one speech.
And it came to pass, as they journeyed from the east, that
they found a plain in the land of Shinar; and they dwelt
there. And they said one to another, Go to, let us make brick,
and burn them throughly. And they had brick for stone, and
slime had they for mortar. And they said, Go to, let us build
us a city and a tower, whose top may reach unto heaven;
and let us make us a name, lest we be scattered abroad upon
the face of the whole earth. And the LORD came down to see
the city and the tower, which the children of men builded.
And the LORD said, Behold, the people is one, and they have
all one language; and this they begin to do: and now nothing will be restrained from them, which they have imagined
to do. Go to, let us go down, and there confound their language, that they may not understand one another's speech.
So the LORD scattered them abroad from thence upon the
face of all the earth: and they left off to build the city. Therefore is the name of it called Babel; because the LORD did there
confound the language of all the earth: and from thence did
the LORD scatter them abroad upon the face of all the earth'
(Gen. 11:1-9).

In this age of superstition and spiritual ignorance, it is fairly easy to convince even educated people that when human beings die they float around in the air looking for a new body to inhabit and come back to earth in some animal form, or as another person. It is not difficult to persuade well-read, well-educated people that there are highly intelligent little green men from Mars or Pluto flying in and out of the earth's atmosphere in UFOs, looking for friendly faces with whom to communicate.

Yet it is next to impossible to persuade men of the most self-evident, undeniable facts revealed in Scripture. Among the many things which men choose not to believe — because they do not wish to believe them — is the fact that Satan is real, his influence is real, and that his most cunning, powerful, deceptive influence has always been religious deception. This is a fact men and women ignore to the peril of their souls and to the peril of the souls under their influence.

Our adversary

Satan is today what he has been throughout the history of this world, our adversary. He is the avowed enemy of God, of Christ, the gospel and our souls. In his pride, the fiend of hell longs to occupy the place of God. He longs to sit upon the throne of total sovereignty. Because God has given that place to his Son and to chosen sinners in his Son from eternity, Apollyon has been bent upon the destruction of Christ and his people from the beginning. The red dragon of hell is determined to destroy Christ and the woman of his choice, his bride, the church (Gen. 3:15).

No other explanation can be given for the serpent's attack on Adam and Eve in the Garden, other than the serpent's hatred for God and his people. Satan's rage was displayed in Cain's murder of his brother Abel. As we have seen, Cain murdered his brother for only one reason. Abel confessed that the only way a sinner can approach God is by the blood and righteousness of the Lamb of God, the Lord Jesus Christ. Abel was the first disciple of Christ, persecuted and murdered for righteousness' sake — that is, the righteousness of Christ (Matt. 5:11-12). It was Satan's hellish influence that swelled Ham's heart with pride and hypocrisy, causing him to despise his father, Noah, and gleefully to expose his sin.

Satan's master plan by which he seeks to dominate the world, by which he strives to destroy the souls of men, by which he toils night and day to do what he knows he cannot do (i.e., to topple the throne of the Almighty and destroy the people of God's love), is deception, hellish religious deception.

Satan is the master of deception. The prince of darkness is the great imitator. The primary sphere of his activity is in the spiritual, religious realm. It is the natural depravity of the human heart which leads people into drugs, alcohol, pornography, adultery, fornication, abortion and murder. By these things men and women destroy their own lives and the lives of others. Satan's devices are far more crafty. He seeks to destroy the souls of men by religion and righteousness.

He cannot destroy the Christ of God. So he raises up false christs, antichrists. He cannot keep sinners from Christ by making them ever so wicked. So he transforms himself into an angel of light and sends preachers from hell to teach sinners how to make themselves righteous (2 Cor. 11:13-15). He cannot destroy the church and kingdom of God, the woman of Christ's choice, his virgin bride who has been made holy, beyond blame or reproach, by his grace and righteousness. So the destroyer has, from the beginning, raised up and maintained a religion to rival the worship of God, a woman to rival the church of God and to seek to destroy it.

Babylon, the great harlot

This rival religion, this rival woman, by whom the prince of darkness rules the minds of men and women throughout the world is referred to throughout the Scriptures as Babylon, the great whore, the mother of all harlot religion (Prov. 7; Rev. 16 - 18). The wine of this old, old whore's fornication, by which she keeps the heads and hearts of men in the spin of a drunken stupor is a self-righteous religion of works and free will. We are warned and commanded by God to come out of and to have nothing to do with the blasphemous, soul-damning charms of a religion which is based on works or free will. (Prov. 6:23-26; Isa. 48:20; 57:12; Jer. 50:8; 51:6,45; 2 Cor. 6:14 - 7:1; Rev. 18:4).

The religion of Babylon is the religion of the damned. The religion of this world began as an organized religious system way back in Genesis 10 and 11, during the days of Nimrod and the building of the Tower of Babel.

Nimrod, the mighty rebel

The story of Nimrod and the great Tower of Babel was prominent in medieval folklore. Regrettably, most of what people think about Nimrod, Babel and the great Tower of Babel arises, not from the account given by divine inspiration, but from medieval folklore. The myths and legends of dark ages still linger. We are told by many that the walls of Babel were nine miles high.

Men and women commonly pass over the account given in Scripture, giving it little notice and learning nothing from it, simply because they mistakenly picture a huge tower reaching upward towards heaven, so high that men hoped to walk into heaven by climbing a brick tower. How easily Satan blinds us to the warnings and teachings of Holy Scripture. The city of Babel (Babylon) was built by cursed Ham's grandson, Nimrod, in rebellion against God, as a fortress to protect unbelieving rebels from the wrath and judgement of God. The religion of Babel is the religion of the cursed, the damned, the reprobate.

The man who built this city was Nimrod, a mighty rebel against God (Gen. 10:8-10). The name 'Nimrod' means rebel, and a rebel this man was. He was the cursed son of a cursed son. Nimrod knew of the curse of God upon Ham and Canaan. He knew the reason for the curse. He knew what Ham had done to Noah. Yet, being the proud rebel that he was, Nimrod dared to set himself up as the judge of God's judgement. He was a hunter, but not just a hunter of game. This man was a bloodthirsty man. He wanted all men to be put in subjection to him; and he was determined to make it happen, no matter whom, or how many, he had to kill. God said, 'The sons of Ham will serve Japheth and Shem.' Nimrod said, 'We'll see about that.' He 'began to be a mighty one in the earth,' and took possession of the land of Shinar and all the peoples of the East.

When we read in verse 9 that 'he was a mighty hunter before the Lord,' the word 'before' would be better translated 'against'. The start of this God-hating rebel's empire was Babel. It had been at least 300 years since the Flood. The terror of God's judgement had been forgotten. The people were of one language, doing great, impressive things. Nimrod made himself powerful. The words and counsel of Eber were ignored. The gospel he learned from his grandfather, Noah, through his godly father, Shem, was held in contempt. The worship of God was trampled under foot. The sheer power of Nimrod's wealth, influence, following and terror caused the whole world, except for God's chosen remnant, to follow him and unite with him, in the name of God, in fighting against God and his people.

The Tower of Babel

The city of Babel, which Nimrod built, was more than a place of government. Babel was a religious refuge. Today, we associate the word 'Babel' with confusion. That is what the name has come to mean because it is there that God caused confusion. However, the word 'Babel' originally meant something far different. Nimrod named the city Babel because Babel meant 'the gate of God'. In the name of worshipping God, like Cain of old, Nimrod was determined to worship God only on his own terms (Gen. 11:1-4). In other words, in reality, he was worshipping himself and calling it the worship of God. This is what the Holy Spirit calls 'will worship' in Colossians 2:23. Babel was a refuge of lies, but a refuge in which men tried to secure themselves from the wrath of God and convinced themselves that they had done so.

Babel, like all false religion, was built by a confederacy of rebels: 'They said one to another...' Honest, faithful, believing men do not try to gain the approval, or amass the strength, of others in worshipping God. They just worship God, obeying his will and his Word. Rebels need the reinforcement of other rebels. They never dare to stand alone with God and for the glory of God, against the flood of human opinion.

Babel, like all false religion, was a religious refuge built according to man's wisdom. The followers of Nimrod discovered a new way of doing things. They made bricks and mixed mortar (the bricks of their self-righteous works, held together by the serpent-slime of their free will) to build a church house and a city with man-made material, for the honour of man, and called it 'the gate of God'. It was the most splendid city and the most impressive temple the world had ever seen; but God held it in utter contempt; and so did those men and women who worshipped him.

Like all false religion, the city and Tower of Babel were built by men, for men, to protect them from the judgement of God. That is the meaning of verse 4: 'Go to, let us build us a city and a tower, whose top may reach unto heaven ... lest we be scattered abroad upon the face of the whole earth.'

Obviously, the sons of Ham understood that the curse God had placed upon them meant the dispersion of their race through all the earth, the destruction of their family. They said, 'No sir. We will stay right here and protect ourselves from God's judgement, by building a house and religion which God himself will have to approve of, by which the whole world will know our names for ever.' When the Scriptures speak of this tower reaching to heaven, nothing more is implied than a very high, massive wall, a fortress (Deut. 1:28; 9:1).

It matters not what a person's refuge is, if it is not Christ and him crucified, it is a refuge of lies which will be swept away in the day of God's wrath (Isa. 28:14-21).

The religion of Babel was exactly the same as the religion of this perverse generation, the religion of the curse. False religion has always been God's curse upon men and women who refuse to worship him. All false religion is man centred, flesh pleasing, a religion of works and free will, a religion by which man attempts to make himself acceptable to God (2 Thess. 2:11-12). This was the mark of Cain. This is the mark of the beast. This is the religion of our age.

In ancient Babylon, in the days of Nimrod, in defiance to the God of Noah, men said, 'Let us build us a city and a tower, whose top may reach unto heaven, and let us make us a name.' That is the creed of all false religion. The religion of Babylon is any religion which centres on man, depends upon man, and gives him a name of honour. It matters not what name the religion wears. Any religion that makes salvation dependent upon something man does, rather than what Christ has done, is the religion of Babylon. Any religion that makes salvation something which is determined by the will of man, rather than the will of God, is the religion of Babylon. Let me be unmistakably clear.

1. Election

No one can deny that the Bible teaches the doctrine of election. But most say that election is determined by God responding to what he 'foresaw' man would do. Others say, 'God chose to save whosoever will be saved, and if a man wills to be saved, he makes himself one of the elect.' In either case, election is dependent on the will of man. The Word of God declares that election is by God's sovereign will alone (Eph. 1:3-6; 2 Tim. 1:9).

2. Redemption

All religions which claim to be Christian profess to believe in redemption by the blood of Christ. Most declare that the blood of Christ was shed to redeem those who perish, as well as those who are saved. Such doctrine means that

Christ shed his blood in vain for those who perish in hell.
It declares that it is man who makes the blood of Christ
effectual for redemption by the power of his free will. The
Word of God declares that Christ has effectually accomplished the redemption of his people (Gal. 3:13; Heb. 9:12).

3. Regeneration

Regeneration, the new birth, is declared to be the result of
man's choice. But the Word of God plainly states that man's
will has nothing to do with the accomplishment of the new
birth. It is the work of God's will and power alone (John
1:12-13; Rom. 9:16).

The cause of judgement

The cause of divine judgement was then, as it is now and
ever shall be, the wilful rejection of divine revelation (Gen.
11:5-9) The words at the end of verse 6 — 'now nothing
will be restrained from them, which they have imagined to
do' — are not a suggestion that God was fearful that these
men might actually get to heaven by their inventions. These
words are a declaration of the basis of divine judgement.
Nimrod and the sons of Ham would not, by any means, be
turned away from their delusion.

Look what happened when the Lord God came down to
Babel, to visit them with his wrath and vex them with his
sore displeasure. He confounded their language so that they
could not understand one another. He sealed them up in
confusion and reprobation. God planned it so that those
who would not believe could not believe (Prov. 1:23-33).
The sons of Ham could no longer understand the speech of
Shem's sons. The sons of God speak a language the world

cannot understand. The Lord God scattered the rebels. He scattered them from place to place over the earth. He scattered them in enmity against one another, through all the earth, so that they might serve his purpose of grace towards his elect in all places.

The purpose of God

Nothing, and no one, will ever frustrate God's purpose, destroy his church, or even slightly hinder his plan. As Satan and the demons of hell are God's unwitting vassals, so, too, the sons of Ham can do nothing but serve God's elect, exactly according to God's purpose (Gen. 9:25).

The confusion of divine judgement is ended for ever in Christ, only in Christ. The Lord God sent confusion in his wrath, to foil the schemes of hell. But when God pours upon men the Spirit of grace and supplication and turns their hearts to Christ, as he did on the Day of Pentecost (Acts 2), the confusion is over (Col. 3:10-11). All who would know, worship, and be saved by God must come out of Babel, the religion of the cursed, and flee to Christ (2 Cor. 6:14 - 7:1; Rev. 18:1-4).

16.

Abraham

Genesis 11:27 - 13:4

'And the LORD appeared unto Abram, and said, Unto thy seed will I give this land: and there builded he an altar unto the LORD, who appeared unto him' (Gen. 12:7).

Throughout the Word of God, Abraham is held up as an example of faith. The Lord God called Abraham 'My friend' (Isa. 41:8). He was 'the friend of God' (James 2:23). When Paul wanted an illustration of the believer's faith and justification, he selected Abraham as the example (Rom. 4). When he wrote to the Galatians, who were Gentiles by nature, he declared that all who believe on the Lord Jesus Christ are 'the children of Abraham' (3:7) and that we are 'blessed with faithful Abraham' (3:9). If there is any man in the Bible who should be of interest to believers, it is Abraham.

Thou art the LORD the God, who didst choose Abram, and broughtest him forth out of Ur of the Chaldees, and gavest him the name of Abraham; And foundest his heart faithful before thee, and madest a covenant with him to give the land of the Canaanites, the Hittites, the Amorites, and the Perizzites, and the

Jebusites, and the Girgashites, to give it, I say, to his
seed, and hast performed thy words; for thou art
righteous

(Neh. 9:7-8).

Consider what those Levites said about Abraham, as they
sought to worship the God of Abraham. '[Thou] didst choose
Abram' — Abraham belonged to God by God's choice in
electing love and grace. 'And broughtest him forth out of
Ur of the Chaldees' — he was brought to believe God by
God's call, by effectual, irresistible grace. 'And gavest him
the name Abraham' — Abram, the pagan, was converted to
Abraham, the believer, by a work of God's mercy. 'And
foundest his heart faithful' — God's grace in him made
Abraham faithful unto death. He persevered in faith because he was preserved by grace. 'And madest a covenant
with him' — God blessed Abraham with the blessings of
his covenant, a covenant which was a type and a foreshadowing of the covenant of grace made with all God's
elect in Christ before the world began (Jer. 31:31-34; Heb. 8).
Though this covenant was not fully revealed until the
coming of Christ and the outpouring of his Spirit upon the
Gentiles (Gal. 3:13-29), it was made before the world began.
The covenant of grace is that everlasting covenant,
according to which all who are in Christ are blessed with
all spiritual blessings from eternity (Eph. 1:3-7).

Abraham stands before us as an example of faith and a
picture of grace. Like us, Abraham was what he was by the
grace of God. All that he was and all that he experienced
throughout the days of his life show us the grace of God.
Here are seven things revealed about Abraham — or Abram
as he was then called — in Genesis 11:27 – 13:4, which are
true of all saved men and women. If we are believers,
Abraham is our father; and if Abraham is our father, we

shall both do the works of Abraham and enjoy the privileges of Abraham.

1. He was a chosen man (Gen. 11:27 - 12:1)

Terah was a man among many. He had lots of sons and daughters. There were a great many people living in Ur. But God chose Abram. The Lord appeared to him and called him. This was an act of free and sovereign grace. God's choice of Abram was the cause of Abram's faith. The Lord God is found by those who do not seek him. God's election separated Abram from other men (1 Cor. 4:7). Electing love preserved him until he was called (Jude 1). Electing grace rescued him from the idolatry of his fathers (1 Thess. 2:10-14). Let every saved sinner give thanks unceasingly to God for electing love (John 15:16). As he was a chosen man:

2. He was a called man (Gen. 12:1-4; Gal. 3:8)

The whole world around him was lying in wickedness. By this time in history, idolatry had engulfed the world. The religion of Nimrod and Babel had become the religion of the world. There were few exceptions — Job and his friends, and Melchizedek. Polytheism was rampant: 'They served other gods' (Josh. 24:2). The worship of 'saints' was common (Job 5:1). Astrology was a part of everyday life. In short, the days of Abram were much like the days in which we live. Apparently, along with the rest of the world, Abram and his family were idolaters before the Lord appeared to him.

Then, suddenly, unexpectedly, the Lord God appeared to Abram and called him. As the Lord appeared to Saul of Tarsus on the Damascus road, so the Lord took Abram by surprise. The Lord God himself appeared to Abram and preached the gospel to him, saying, 'In thee shall all families

of the earth be blessed.' Paul's inspired explanation of
Abram's call (Gal. 3) gives us the meaning of the word
'blessed,' as it is used with reference to Abram. The blessedness which God gave to him, the blessedness to which he
was called, was justification. Justification, free justification
in Christ, without works, is the blessing of the gospel. With
it come all other blessings. Without it there is no
blessedness.

When the God of glory appeared to Abram, his life was
radically changed for ever. He was converted by a particular, distinguishing call. It was an irresistible, effectual call
of almighty grace. The call by which God fetched Abram
(by which he fetches every object of his grace) to himself
was an unconditional, irrevocable call. He said, '"I," who
alone can bless, "will bless thee!"' No wonder the psalmist
sang, 'Blessed is the man whom thou choosest, and causest
to approach unto thee' (Ps. 65:4). Having been called by
God:

3. He was a believing man (Gen. 15:6)

When God called him, Abram obeyed because he believed
God (Heb. 11:8). He might have raised many questions. He
might have said, 'How can these things be? How can I, a
guilty sinner, be freely forgiven and justified? How can I
know that the Word I have heard is indeed the Word of
God?' But he did not. He simply believed God. As he walked
with God, he learned more of the details of God's promise.
But, in the beginning, he believed what God had spoken
(Gen. 22:17-18). Later, God gave him a sign (Gen. 18). But
in the beginning he had nothing but the plain Word of God,
and he believed God. Can you do that? Will you believe
God? Will you take him at his Word? If you do, your faith in
Christ will be counted to you for righteousness (Rom.
4:21-25). Believing God:

4. He was a blessed man (Gen. 12:2-3)

He was justified. He stood before God accepted in Christ, with the righteousness of Christ (the object of his faith) imputed to him. God gave him a Son in whom all the nations of the world are blessed. That Son, of whom Isaac was only a type, is Christ. Because of God's grace upon him, Abram was a blessing to all his house. God dealt with all men as they dealt with Abram, the object of his mercy, grace and love. Like Abram, all who believe are blessed by God with all spiritual blessings (Eph. 1:3). We are, in Christ, eternally, unconditionally, perpetually, universally blessed by God!

5. He was a tried man

As a believer, Abram began his pilgrimage through this world, as all believers must. His faith was constantly tried and proved by many difficulties, as all true faith is. Sarai, his wife, was still barren. He had no idea where he was going (Heb. 11:8-9). Moses tells us that God had called him to the land of Canaan. But Abram did not know it. He did not know where he was going, how he would get there, or what his place would be when he got there. Yet Abram never once asked God to show him these things. He simply committed everything to God. This was no small trial; but greater trials followed.

He had to break many earthly ties. He not only had to leave family and friends, but he also had to leave them in idolatry. When he got into the land of Canaan, new trials awaited him. The Canaanites were everywhere, troops of idolaters. Abram roamed about as a nomad, dwelling in tents. Still, he believed God (12:7). At last, his supply of daily bread began to fail and he had to go down to Egypt (12:10). Then there was trouble with Lot (Gen. 13:5-18).

Later, he was required by his God to give up Hagar and his
son, Ishmael, whom he loved dearly. Then, we are told,
'God did tempt [tried] Abraham' (Gen. 22:1-19). It is written: 'Many are the afflictions of the righteous.' Trials always
accompany faith (1 Cor. 10:13; 2 Cor. 4:17-18; Rom. 8:35-39).

6. He was a sinful man (Gen. 12:10-13)

Without question, his temptation was a severe one. Yet his
actions betrayed a lack of confidence in God. In the face of
great fear, this man of great faith displayed great unbelief,
and was willing to sacrifice his wife's honour to save his
own skin! His schemes gained him nothing, only shame.

Why is this great flaw in the life of this great man set
before us by God the Holy Spirit, without the slightest
excuse? It is set before us to teach us and remind us that
salvation is, in its totality, the work of God's free and sovereign grace in Christ. Let us ever remember that the best of
men are only men at best. True saints, all of them, are
plagued with much sin as long as they live in this body of
sin. There are no exceptions. It is not our faith that merits
our justification, but Christ, the object of our faith. Though
Abram was weak and sinful, like us:

7. He was a kept man (Gen. 12:14 - 13:4)

The Lord God would not deal with Abram according to his
sins. Instead, he intervened to deliver him. He not only
kept Sarai from Pharaoh and Abram from death, but he
also turned Abram's evil into good (Ps. 76:10). The fear of
God came upon Pharaoh. He and his house saw how blessed
the man is who is blessed by God. Abram left Egypt a richer
man. God is faithful; he will not lose his own; he will be
gracious.

17.

The God of glory appeared

to Abram

Genesis 11:27 - 13:4

'Now the LORD had said unto Abram, Get thee out of thy country, and from thy kindred, and from thy father's house, unto a land that I will show thee: And I will make of thee a great nation, and I will bless thee, and make thy name great; and thou shalt be a blessing: And I will bless them that bless thee, and curse him that curseth thee: and in thee shall all families of the earth be blessed'

(Gen. 12:1-3).

As we have said, no other man mentioned in Bible history other than our Lord himself, is set before us as a more prominent example of faith than Abraham. As we have seen, he is uniquely described as the friend of God, the father of those who believe, and the man through whom all the nations of the earth are blessed. These are the things which make Abraham a man worthy of careful study.

In fact, the book of Genesis, from chapter 11:27 to the end of the book, is taken up almost exclusively with Abraham and his seed. However, when we study the lives and experiences of men like Abel, Enoch, Noah and Abraham — men of exemplary faith and faithfulness — we must not look upon them as extraordinary men, but as men who were saved by the grace of the extraordinary God of glory. Abraham's greatness must be traced back and attributed to the greatness of God and his grace. Abraham would say concerning himself what Paul said of himself, 'By the grace of God I am what I am.' Indeed, that is the delightful confession of all who know God. Every believer delights to turn attention away from himself to the Lord God alone. It is the joy of every believing heart to sing, 'Not unto us, O Lord, not unto us, but unto thy name give glory, for thy mercy, and for thy truth's sake.' We recognize that the life we live in this body of flesh, we live by the grace of God. The life of faith is not a life of amazing will power, fortitude and self-control — far from it! The life of faith is a life of amazing grace (Eph. 2:8-9).

Faith — the gift and operation of God

Faith in Christ is the gift and operation of God in us. It begins with God, not with man. Left to ourselves, none of us would, or could, believe God. If we believe, it is because it is 'God which worketh in [us] both to will and to do of his good pleasure'. We believe 'according to the working of his mighty power'. We believe by 'the operation of God,' because he has given us faith to believe. This is exemplified in the experience of Abram.

'Now the Lord had said unto Abram, Get thee out of thy country, and from thy kindred, and from thy father's house, unto a land that I will show thee' (v. 1). Notice that Moses says, 'The Lord had said unto Abram.' We are not told exactly when the Lord first spoke to the man Abram (Abraham) until we hear Stephen's sermon in Acts 7. There we read, 'The God of glory appeared unto our father Abraham, when he was in Mesopotamia, before he dwelt in Charran' (Acts

7:2). Those words, 'the God of glory,' are used only twice in
the Bible, in Acts 7:2 and Psalm 29:3. They refer, of course,
to our Lord Jesus Christ, 'the King of glory'. It was Christ
himself who came and made himself known to Abram. What
does this teach us?

1. God gives faith to whom he will

Abram was in Ur, dwelling among the Chaldeans, living in
the midst of an idolatrous people, when God Almighty
stepped into his life. Why did the God of glory appear to
this particular man? The only answer that can be given is
this: 'It pleased the LORD.' God loved Abram; he chose him,
and was pleased to be gracious to him. Abram was one of
that great multitude whose names were written in the
Lamb's Book of Life before the world began, one of those
for whom the Lamb of God was slain from the foundation
of the world. Every sinner to whom God gives faith is, like
Abram, a monument to the sovereign will, purpose and
grace of God (Rom. 9:16).

2. Faith in the hearts of chosen, redeemed sinners

Faith is wrought in the hearts of chosen, redeemed sinners
by the revelation of Christ (Gal. 1:15). No one can, or will,
believe on the Lord Jesus Christ until Christ is revealed to
him and in him. That which is essential to faith is the knowledge of God in Christ (John 17:3). You cannot believe until
Christ, the God of glory, appears to you (2 Cor. 4:6).

Four hundred years had passed since the Flood. The
world was steeped in idolatry, much as it is today. Yet, even
in that wicked, perverse, idolatrous generation, God sent
someone to Abram who told him the story of grace, redemption and salvation. When the word was preached, 'the God

of glory appeared unto Abraham,' and he believed God.
That is always how faith comes to chosen sinners (Zech.
12:10; Rom. 10:13-17).

3. Faith is the result of the effectual call

Faith in Christ is the result of the effectual call of God the
Holy Spirit in irresistible grace. God 'called [Abraham
alone], and blessed him, and increased him' (Isa. 51:2). That
fact is revealed by God as a reason and an encouragement
to 'look unto the rock whence ye are hewn and to the hole
of the pit whence ye are digged.' Abram's call is relevant to
us because the grace of God given to him, the call by which
he was brought to life and faith in Christ, is the same grace
and call by which God saves his elect in all ages.

> Now the LORD had said unto Abram, Get thee out of
> thy country, and from thy kindred, and from thy
> father's house, unto a land that I will show thee: And
> I will make of thee a great nation, and I will bless
> thee, and make thy name great; and thou shalt be a
> blessing: And I will bless them that bless thee, and
> curse him that curseth thee: and in thee shall all fam-
> ilies of the earth be blessed
>
> (Gen. 12:1-3).

There are many things about God's calling of Abram which
must not be overlooked.

1. It was a gracious, personal, distinguishing call

God called Abram simply because he was pleased to do so.
There was nothing in him which made him the object of
God's grace. By this call, the Lord God distinguished Abram

from all those dwelling in Ur of the Chaldees. They were
left to themselves. The Lord God called Abram personally
and he called him alone. As it is written: '[The good Shep-
herd] calleth his own sheep by name.'

2. It was a separating call

The Lord God called Abram to forsake his family, his friends
and their gods. If we want to follow Christ, we must, like
him, turn from all the idolatrous gods of darkness and death
to the one true and living God (2 Cor. 6:14 - 7:1; Rev. 18:4).
All who are called by God are called to abandon self, to
yield up the rule of their lives to Christ the Lord, denying
father, mother, brother, sister, and their own lives, for the
gospel's sake (Luke 14:25-33).

3. It was a call to blessedness

The Lord God made promises of true blessedness to Abram.
These were not promises contingent upon Abram's obedience, but sure and certain promises. Abram had to obey
God's call; but his obedience as well as the blessings
following it were secured by God's purpose of grace.

The Lord promised to make of him a great nation. This
he did in both the physical nation of Israel and in that 'holy
nation' which is 'the Israel of God'. In blessing him, God
promised to make Abram's name great. Blessed indeed is
that man whose name is great before God, whose name is
written in heaven!

God promised to make Abram a blessing — wonderful
grace! God takes sinners who are corrupt and who have a
corrupting influence, and makes them a blessing. Those
who by nature defile everything and everyone they touch,
when called by God and born of his Spirit, become a

blessing everywhere they go, to all around them. Indeed,
God deals with men and nations, (providentially, in mercy
or in judgement), as they deal with his people. He says, 'I
will bless them that bless thee, and curse him that curseth
thee.'

Then, the Lord God promised Abram that he would be
the man through whom Christ, the promised Seed of the
woman (Gen. 3:15), would come, by whom redemption,
salvation and grace would come to God's elect in all nations
(Gal. 3:13-14). The word of promise was, 'In thee shall all
families of the earth be blessed.'

4. The call of God is an irresistible, effectual call

'So Abram departed, as the LORD had spoken unto him; and
Lot went with him: and Abram was seventy and five years
old when he departed out of Haran' (v. 4; Ps. 65:4; 110:3).
When God the Holy Spirit comes chosen, redeemed sinners
obey his voice.

Obedient faith

So Abram departed, as the LORD had spoken unto him;
and Lot went with him: and Abram was seventy and
five years old when he departed out of Haran. And
Abram took Sarai his wife, and Lot his brother's son,
and all their substance that they had gathered, and
the souls that they had gotten in Haran; and they went
forth to go into the land of Canaan; and into the land
of Canaan they came

(Gen. 12:4-5).

Faith in Christ is obedient; it obeys God. It is not perfectly obedient; but it is obedient. God has ordained that those who are saved by his grace walk before him in obedience (Eph. 2:10). And what God has ordained he always accomplishes. It appears that Abram's obedience was reluctant. The Lord had told him plainly to leave his kindred and his father's house and to go into the land of Canaan; but Abram and Terah left Ur together and they dwelt in the land of Haran, until Terah died (Gen. 11:31-32).

After God took his father, Terah, we read, 'So Abram departed, as the LORD had spoken unto him.' Disobedience is always costly. If we are his, the Lord God will see that we obey him. If necessary, he will take away anything and anyone hindering us, as he took Terah from Abram. Once Terah was dead, Abram went on to Canaan, as the Lord commanded him. God has his ways of making his children willingly obedient to him; and where he gives faith, he also gives obedience by the sweet discipline of his grace (Exod. 4:24-27).

Worshipping Faith

And Abram passed through the land unto the place of Sichem, unto the plain of Moreh. And the Canaanite was then in the land. And the LORD appeared unto Abram, and said, Unto thy seed will I give this land: and there builded he an altar unto the LORD, who appeared unto him. And he removed from thence unto a mountain on the east of Bethel, and pitched his tent, having Bethel on the west, and Hai on the east: and there he builded an altar unto the LORD, and called upon the name of the LORD. And Abram journeyed, going on still toward the south

(Gen. 12:6-9).

Faith, true faith, worships God. If we believe God, we shall worship him as he is, as he makes himself known to us in his Son, in his Word and in his works. If we believe God, we shall worship him at the altar he requires and in the way he prescribes. Christ is our altar of worship (Heb. 13:10). The altar at which Abram worshipped God was a type of Christ. God requires that we worship him either on an altar of earth, or an altar of unhewn stones, without steps (Exod. 20:24-26). We must worship the Lord God on the altar of his making, without any contribution from us, without any ascending steps. Christ alone is that altar. We must come to God trusting Christ alone, contributing nothing ourselves. If we make any contribution, we pollute the altar (Gal. 5:2,4). We cannot come to God by ascending degrees of a works-based sanctification, we can only come by faith in Christ alone.

If we worship God, we shall worship him in his house. 'Bethel' means the house of God. There Abram worshipped, and there God's people still worship. God reveals himself in Bethel, in his house. Bethel, the house of God, is all the more precious, because as long as we are in this world the Canaanites surround us.

Imperfect faith

In verses 10-20, the Holy Spirit shows us that faith in Christ, even the most exemplary faith, is never perfect faith. Faith must be tried. By the trial of our faith, God proves both the reality of it and the weakness of it. So the Lord sent a famine in the land of Canaan.

Abram's faith, like ours, was weak. God plainly told him to go to Canaan and promised to bless him there. But when famine came, Abram went down to Egypt. In his unbelief

and disobedience, he feared for his life and told Sarai to
tell the Egyptians that she was his sister instead of his wife.
In weakness, fear, and disobedience, Abram temporarily
forsook God for Egypt. But God abides faithful. He would
not forsake the object of his grace (2 Tim. 2:13; Mal. 3:6;
Heb. 13:5).

How gracious God is! When we would bring ourselves
to shame and misery, when we would, if left to our own
devices, destroy ourselves and all those around us, the Lord
our God graciously protects us. He will not suffer his faithfulness to fail. It is written: 'The gifts and calling of God are
without repentance.' Abram was foolish; but God is wise.
Abram was unbelieving; but God abides faithful. When
Abram chose a path of destruction, God plagued the house
of Pharaoh, kept the pagan king of Egypt from the lusts of
his own heart, and caused that pagan king to become the
protector of his erring child (Gen. 12:20).

Persevering faith

And Abram went up out of Egypt, he, and his wife,
and all that he had, and Lot with him, into the south.
And Abram was very rich in cattle, in silver, and in
gold. And he went on his journeys from the south
even to Bethel, unto the place where his tent had been
at the beginning, between Bethel and Hai; Unto the
place of the altar, which he had made there at the
first: and there Abram called on the name of the LORD'

(Gen. 13:1-4).

With all our faults, failures, failings, trials, falls and sins,
faith will never die. True faith will persevere. Faith does

not persevere because we are faithful, but because God is faithful. It does not persevere because we are strong, but because our God is strong; nor even does it persevere because of our hold on the Lord, but because of the Lord's hold upon us. This is what we see in these four verses.

God brought Abram out of Egypt (v. 1). Not only did he force Abram to leave Egypt (Gen. 12:19), but he graciously enriched him, using even his unbelief, weakness and disobedience to do so (v. 2). Abram came out of Egypt a better man. The word 'rich' means much more than wealthy. It means 'honourable'. Abram was made a better man by his failure, because God works all things together for the good of his elect, even our failures (Ps. 76:10; Rom. 8:28).

Abram pitched his tent between Bethel (the house of God) and Hai (a heap of ruins), and worshipped God at 'the place of the altar, which he had made there at the first: and there Abram called on the name of the LORD.' I can imagine the old patriarch, saying, as he kneels to worship by the heap of ruins at Bethel:

> I was glad when they said unto me, Let us go into the house of the LORD...What shall I render unto the LORD for all his benefits toward me? I will take the cup of salvation, and call upon the name of the LORD. I will pay my vows unto the LORD now in the presence of all his people... O LORD, truly I am thy servant; I am thy servant, and the son of thine handmaid: thou hast loosed my bonds. I will offer to thee the sacrifice of thanksgiving, and will call upon the name of the LORD. I will pay my vows unto the LORD now in the presence of all his people, In the courts of the LORD's house, in the midst of thee, O Jerusalem. Praise ye the LORD'

(Ps. 116:12-19).

Let us, like Abram, return to the place of the altar, to Christ our Saviour, and abide there, as sinners saved by the grace of God alone, through the merits of his blood and righteousness. 'As ye have therefore received Christ Jesus the Lord, so walk ye in him' (Col. 2:6).

18.

The strife between Abram and Lot

Genesis 13

'There was a strife between the herdmen of Abram's cattle and the herdmen of Lot's cattle: and the Canaanite and the Perizzite dwelled then in the land' (Gen. 13:7).

Genesis 13 records one of the most troubling, distressing, and most shameful experiences in the lives of God's people in this world. This chapter describes the strife between Abram and Lot, a strife which led to separation, which in turn led to even greater sorrow. This was a strife between members of the same family. Abram was Lot's uncle. This conflict arose between brethren, between two men who had enjoyed the closest possible spiritual communion and fellowship. Abram was Lot's spiritual father. He was the instrument by whom Lot had learned the gospel. It was also a strife in the church of God. The whole church in the world at this time was the family of Abram; and Lot was a member of that blessed family.

Domestic trials, family quarrels, and strife in the house of God are not easy to bear. We would all prefer to pass through this world without trouble. If we must have trouble, we would prefer to have it anywhere rather than at home. Jacob would have preferred not have had to endure the trial he had over the loss of Joseph. David would have preferred to avoid the trials he had to endure at the hand of Michal, Amnon and Absalom. And Abram would have much preferred to live out his days with Lot's constant companionship; but it was not to be. All God's people 'must through much tribulation enter into the kingdom of God'. Much of that tribulation will come from our own homes.

Why is this? Why do believers have to endure trials, particularly strife, quarrels and divisions in their homes and in their churches? There are three obvious reasons.

1. Faith must be tried in all directions

Just as silver and gold must be tried by the fire, not to destroy them, but to separate the precious metal from the dross; just as the diamond must be cut to shape it into a valuable gem, trials are intended by God to purify believers' hearts and mould them into the image of his dear Son.

2. Trials are designed to make believers long for heaven

When God permits strife to occur between believers, especially of the same family, it is to remind them that this world of sin and sorrow is not their home.

3. These troubles are permitted by God

They are brought to pass by the wise, unerring providence of a heavenly Father, so that believers may learn patience, forbearance and kindness towards one another.

God permitted the strife between Abram and Lot to come to a head, to result in permanent separation, shameful as it was, and has recorded it for us in the Holy Scriptures, so that we might learn from their mistakes.

Abram and Lot were both saved men. They were both chosen by God, redeemed by the blood of Christ and called by the Spirit. They believed God, were righteous before him, and had been made righteous by having the righteousness of God in Christ imputed to them. They are both seated now before the throne of God and of the Lamb. But, while they lived in this world, a quarrel developed between their herdsmen that brought conflict between them and separated them.

A shameful quarrel

Strife between brethren is always shameful, bringing reproach to the gospel we believe and to the God we serve. The God of glory appeared to Abram when he was in Mesopotamia. The Lord God chose Abram, called him alone, and made a covenant with him (Gen. 12:1-3).

I do not know how much Abram knew; but he was not an ignorant barbarian. He knew and believed the gospel. When he was seventy-five years old, God promised to send his Son, the Lord Jesus Christ, into this world through the loins of Abram (Gal. 3:13-16); and he believed God. By believing God, his faith was imputed to him for righteousness (Rom. 4:3,13,23-25).

After the death of Terah, his father, Abram left Haran, went into Canaan and pitched his tent at Bethel. There he built an altar and called upon the name of the Lord. Bethel was 'the house of God' to him. Yet he left Bethel because of the famine that arose in the land. He went down into Egypt for a while. And now, at the beginning of Genesis 13, Abram has returned from Egypt with his wife Sarai, all his possessions, all his servants and with Lot. They have all returned to Bethel.

Back at Bethel, Abram must have thought, 'Now my trials and troubles are all over. I am back at the place of God. It will be smooth sailing from now on.' About the time he got settled, just as he had begun to gather his family for worship again, trouble broke out between his servants and the servants of Lot. This quarrel between Abram and Lot was a shameful, needless thing.

It was particularly disgraceful because Abram and Lot had both been blessed with great wealth. They had as much of this worlds goods as they could possibly need (vv. 2,6). If one of them had been poor and needy, we could understand jealousy and strife arising between them. But both of these men were extremely wealthy. The word translated 'rich' in verse 2 has many shades of meaning. It means 'rich', as our translation indicates. But it also means 'honourable'. It could also be translated 'heavy'. Riches are a burden. Those who seek to be rich load themselves with thick clay (Hab. 2:6).

In commenting upon the fact that riches are a heavy burden, Matthew Henry wrote: 'There is a burden of care in getting them, fear in keeping them, temptation in using them, guilt in abusing them, sorrow in losing them, and a burden of account, at last, to be given up concerning them.'

Certainly, riches may be a great blessing of God's providence. Abram was a man rich in faith and rich in this world's goods. If well managed, earthly wealth is a friend to faith. It furnishes men with the opportunity to do much good. But very few men can be both wealthy and useful. I have seen a good many men make advancement in the world. But I have seen very few make advancement both in riches and in grace. How often people say, 'If I had just a little more, I could do so much more for the cause of Christ.' But, usually, the more people get the less they give, the less they attend the worship of God, and the less they do for

Christ, his people, and the furtherance of the gospel. Wise
is that man who has learned to pray, 'Give me neither pov-
erty nor riches; feed me with food convenient for me: Lest
I be full, and deny thee, and say, Who is the LORD? Or lest I
be poor, and steal, and take the name of my God in vain'
(Prov. 30:8-9). Beware of covetousness! Beware of 'the deceit-
fulness of riches'! All of Lot's woes began when his herds
and his gold began to increase!

As we have said Abram and Lot were brothers and friends
(v. 8). But more importantly, they were spiritual brethren.
Abram was Lot's spiritual father. When he left his father's
house, Abram told Lot what God had revealed to him and
urged Lot to join him. They walked together for years, in
the pursuit of God's will and glory. But now trouble arose
between them. They were both believers. They were both
heirs of eternal life. But there was conflict. There is something peculiarly sinful about strife between believers.

As we have seen, Lot owed Abram everything, both
materially and spiritually. He knew nothing, but what
Abram had taught him. He had nothing, but what Abraham
had given him. And he had for years followed Abram as
Abram followed God. But now he was willing to part company with the best friend he had in this world for a little
more property. How fickle men are, even believing men,
when left to themselves! At one time, the Galatians were
willing to pluck out their eyes and give them to Paul. But
in time, they turned against him. Paul and Barnabas
laboured together for the cause of Christ. Then, they fell
out over Mark. Strife between brethren is a disgrace. It is
always a disgrace. It is always petty too. Brethren do not
fall out over the gospel. If the gospel is at stake, we must
part company with those who oppose it. But brethren quarrel about petty things, things that really amount to nothing
but pride. What can be more shameful?

This strife between Abram and Lot was particularly shameful because 'the Canaanite and the Perizzite dwelled then in the land' (v. 7). It gave the enemies of God occasion to blaspheme. The Spirit of God indicates that this was, above all else, the great shame of this quarrel between these two men. The heathen observed it. They had seen them worshipping at the same altar. Now they saw them fighting over water and grazing rights!

Exemplary conduct

Abram had his faults. I do not suggest that he was a perfect man. We saw his weakness in chapter 12, when he was in Egypt. But in this conflict, it was Abram who moved to put it to an end. His conduct throughout the matter exemplified what believers ought to do in such matters (vv. 8-9).

Abram's behaviour was conciliatory. He was a man of peace. It was in his heart, as much as possible, to live peaceably with all men, especially with those who believe. He knew the value and blessedness of peace. He knew that 'the beginning of strife is as when one letteth out water'. Once it begins, it is almost impossible to stop. He had learned to 'leave off contention, before it be meddled with' (Prov. 17:14). Abram took the initiative (v. 8). He preferred the glory of God to his own will. He was more concerned for the gospel and the worship of God than for his own rights. The souls of men were of greater concern to Abram than cattle, water and grass. He preferred to yield to Lot's greed rather than fight with his brother and friend. He was a magnanimous man.

Lot should have yielded to Abram. God had given the land to Abram. It was all his. He was the older of the two. He was richer and stronger. Lot owed everything to Abram.

Abram was God's spokesman. But Lot was a petty, little man, obstinate and self-willed. Abram was gracious and condescended to Lot's pleasure. He was generous even to his own hurt. People of the world, looking at Abram, would say, 'You fool!' But Abram sought the glory of God. He turned the other cheek (Matt. 5:39). He accepted the wrong and allowed himself to be defrauded (1 Cor. 6:7). He made himself servant to Lot (1 Cor. 9:19; Matt. 20:26-28). Why was this? He did it for two reasons: first, to keep Lot's friendship, and second, for the honour of God.

This is exemplary Christian conduct. Christianity is more than doctrines, creeds and ordinances. Christianity is Christ in us. And if Christ is in us, he will be seen clearly in our lives.

Abram waved his rights and cheerfully gave Lot whatever he wanted. It does not appear that he was even slightly troubled by the fact that Lot took the best for himself. In fact, it seems that Abram wanted Lot to have the best. Why was this? How could he behave in this way? Abram believed God. He loved Lot. He was dead to this world!

A lamentable choice

Abram and Lot were standing on one of the high mountains of Canaan, perhaps Mount Hebron. Looking to the east, Lot beheld all the well-watered, fertile plains of Sodom and the rich hills of Moab. It reminded him of the Garden of Eden, which he had heard Abram describe; and he chose that to be his portion (vv. 10-13). He left the tents of Abram for the tents of Sodom. He left the altar of Abram for the hills of Moab. He left the worship of Bethel for the riches of the plain. He saw, he coveted, he took.

Without regard for anything spiritual, his own soul or the glory of God, Lot chose the rich plains of Sodom. His choice was sad. It tells us much about Lot. He had too much love for this world; and he had too little concern for his own soul, and the souls of those who were under his influence. There were no prophets in Sodom, only riches. There was no altar at which to worship God in Sodom, only luscious-looking grass. There was no believers in Sodom, only men and women of the world.

From the moment that Lot made his choice, he began to decline. He did not go directly into Sodom. But step by step, he hardened his heart and seared his conscience, until he convinced himself that the best thing he could do for himself, his family and his servants was to move to Sodom. He lifted up his eyes and beheld the land. Then, he chose the plains of Sodom. Soon, he separated himself from Abram. He dwelt in the cities of the plains for a while. Then, he pitched his tent towards Sodom. At last, he dwelt in Sodom. There he was elected to the city council. He became a man of great *respectability* among the Sodomites, when he had no respectability left. Do you see how lamentable Lot's choice was?

A costly choice

In the end, Lot's choice cost him everything he cherished, except his own soul. He lost all influence for God with his family, servants and neighbours. He lost all spiritual communion, fellowship and instruction. His daughters, sons-in-law and grandchildren were lost to the Sodomites. He lost all his earthly possessions, as well as his wife. Ultimately, he lost his last two daughters in his drunken incest.

He lost everything but his soul. But Abram lost nothing. He gave up everything, except the honour of God, the glory of God, and his love for Lot; but he lost nothing! (vv. 14-18).

May every child of God always endeavour to 'keep the unity of the Spirit in the bond of peace'. Avoid strife with brethren at all costs. 'Love not the world.' It is the love of the world and the love of self which lies at the root of all strife between believers. How shameful! In all our earthly decisions, we must take care not to neglect the welfare of our souls. In all things, endeavour to do that which is right: walk with God and live in peace.

The very mention of the name Lot echoes the words of Jonah: 'Salvation is of the LORD!' Lot was a saved man, a sinner saved by grace alone, through the merits of Christ's blood and righteousness, without any works of his own. Like every saved sinner, Lot was saved by God's sovereign election, blood atonement, imputed righteousness and infallible grace.

19.

Abram and Melchizedek

Genesis 14:18-20

'And Melchizedek king of Salem brought forth bread and wine: and he was the priest of the most high God. And he blessed him, and said, Blessed be Abram of the most high God, possessor of heaven and earth: And blessed be the most high God, which hath delivered thine enemies into thy hand. And he gave him tithes of all.' (Gen. 14:18-20).

Genesis 14 gives us the first account of war mentioned in Holy Scripture. When the war was over, Lot, his family and his goods had been carried away into captivity. Lot laid up treasures for himself upon the earth; and thieves broke in and took all his treasures. When Abram heard what had happened to Lot, he armed 318 of his trained servants and rescued his beloved brother, his brother's family, his goods, the king of Sodom and all his people. When Abram returned from the slaughter of the kings, Melchizedek met him and blessed him. This meeting between Abram and Melchizedek is recorded for our learning and admonition in Genesis 14:18-20.

I know that Melchizedek is a type of our Lord Jesus Christ. Hebrews 7 makes that perfectly clear. However, as I read this chapter, I am always constrained to think, 'What a blessed picture Abram is of our Saviour! What he did for Lot is exactly what Christ has done for his people.'

Because of his great love for us, our Lord Jesus Christ took us to be his brethren from eternity. We were taken into captivity and bondage by sin. We lost everything. Satan thoroughly ruined us. He held us in the dark dungeon of sin and death. When we could do nothing to help ourselves, Christ Jesus, our Elder Brother, like Abram, came to deliver us, not with 318 armed men, but by the merits of his blood and the power of his grace.

He defeated our enemies and took those captive who had held us captive (Col. 2:13-15). He ransomed us from the hands of God's offended justice (Gal. 3:15). He set us free by the power of his grace, restoring all that we had lost (Eph. 2:1-13). Christ has defeated all our adversaries, delivered us from their power for ever, and made us more than conquerors in him by the power of his grace (Rom. 8:33-39).

Yet, in this particular passage of Scripture, I am sure that the Holy Spirit has set Abram before us as a type of every believer in this world. Abraham was the father of the faithful. Allegorically, the father of all who believe on the Lord Jesus Christ. In the history of Abraham, every believer can read his own biography. His temptations, trials, tragedies and triumphs were prophetic pictures of those things that every follower of Christ must experience. Like Abraham, all the children of Abraham must, through 'much tribulation enter into the kingdom of God'. As Abram here represents the believer living in this world, Melchizedek is a type of our great King and Priest, the Lord Jesus Christ.

A warfare engaged

Abram engaged in a warfare, deliberately and purposefully. Though he was a man of peace, he lived among men of

war. In Genesis 14, we see this man who was the friend of
God taking up arms against his godless enemies, because
of the great evil they had done. Like he was, the sons and
daughters of Abraham are engaged in a warfare as long as
we live in this world.

The believer is a soldier, 'a good soldier of Jesus Christ'.
In the Word of God, the believer is compared to a soldier
engaged in warfare more often than he is compared to anything else, except perhaps a sheep. He is a man of peace.
Yet he is a man of war. We have wars within and wars without. Sometimes our wars arise, like Abram's, from erring
brethren. Sometimes they arise from providential trials.
Many times, they arise from enemies without, and more
often from enemies within. But as long as we live in this
world, we are at war. We must, as soldiers on the battlefield, carry our swords always drawn. We must protect ourselves with the shield of faith and the helmet of salvation.
We must stand fast having our feet shod with the gospel of
peace, and march onward carrying the weapon of all-prayer.
The believer must never feel himself at ease as long as he is
on this side of Jordan. Here, in this world, we are in the
enemy's land. Expect a foe behind every bush. At the end
of every day, if we have not fallen prey to some hellish foe,
let us adore God and give thanks to him for his almighty
grace which has kept us. Like Abram, we are on a battlefield. Our enemies are sin, Satan, the world and error. We
must fight the good fight of faith for ourselves, for our brethren and for the glory of God.

We fight against powerful odds. Abram had only 318
loyal servants at his command. Yet, in the name of God, he
marched against and defeated the armies of the kings of the
nations around him. He fought in God's name, for God's
cause. Therefore, he fought in God's strength. Failure was
not even a possibility.

Our warfare is one that is carried out in faith. Abram was a man of faith. The spirit of his life was simple confidence in God. Had he gone out against the kings of the nations by any other power than faith in Christ, he would have fallen. 'This is the victory that overcometh the world, even our faith.' And the weapon of faith is 'the blood of the Lamb'. We fight against our inward sins by faith in Christ, not by the resolution of our wills. We fight against the world by faith, trusting God, not by ingenuity. We fight against heresy by faith, believing the Word of God, not by logic, history, tradition and popularity polls. We fight against Satan by faith, trusting him by whose omnipotent hand the fiend of hell is bound and governed, not by the strength of our own wills. We would be wise to heed the admonition given by C. H. Spurgeon: 'Live near to Jesus, rest upon the power of his atonement and the prevalence of his plea, and then go forward against every enemy without and every foe within, and you shall be more than conquerors.'

We have the blessed consolation of knowing that our battle is right. In this great battle, carried out by faith, Abram had a God-given right to do what he did. The whole land of Canaan was his (Gen. 13:14-16). The kings of the nations had no business there. They were invaders. God, who gave him the land, promised his unfailing presence to protect him in it (Gen. 12:3; 15:1).

Is there any way we can properly apply this to ourselves? Indeed there is. If you belong to Christ, Satan has no right to keep hold on you (John 12:30-31). If you have been justified from sin, sin has no right to rule you (Rom. 6:14-18). If God is true, error (that which denies his truth) has no right to exist. If Christ is our Master, the world has no right to our hearts. God is with us, and in the name of God we shall be victorious (Ps. 118:11-12).

The warfare in which we are engaged demands diligence, and the use of all means. Abram did not sit still and say, 'Well, the Lord will deliver Lot.' That would not have been an act of faith, but presumption. Believing God, Abram called upon all his servants and went to war. We must do the same. We must engage all the servants God has given us to fight the good fight of faith. As long as we are on this battlefield, let us be engaged in prayer, skilful in the knowledge and use of God's Word, mighty in praise, and found in the company of our brethren, our comrades in grace.

This is a warfare from which there is no discharge until victory is won. Abram did not lay down his sword until he had laid hold of all that he went after and defeated every foe. Blessed is that man or woman who, believing God, follows his example (Phil. 3:4-14). We must give ourselves no rest as long as sin is in our hearts, one of God's elect is unconverted, error is found in God's earth, or one breath is left in the nostrils of that old dragon Satan. We must bring back everything that has been lost. Everything must be brought into subjection to Christ. We cannot rest until it is; and it will be. Victory will be ours (Rom. 16:20).

Visitation of grace

Abram enjoyed a visitation of grace. Many debate whether Melchizedek was Christ, or just a type of Christ. Either way, he represents Christ visiting his servant on earth. Battle-weary soldiers, engaged in the cause of Christ, may well expect and anticipate a visitation of grace. As Christ showed himself to Abram, by the appearing of Melchizedek, he will show himself to you. He knows that his warriors need strengthening, comforting and encouraging. As he came to

Shadrach, Meshach, and Abednego in the fiery furnace, the Son of God will come to you in your hour of need.

Why did the Lord Jesus appear to Abram in the type of Melchizedek? Abram was weary and needed refreshing. Being a man of sinful flesh, he may have been somewhat self-elated by his victory (Luke 10:17-20). If that were the case, the best cure for pride is the sight of Christ (Job 42:5-6). The best cure for indifference is his presence (Rev. 3:21). Perhaps the greatest reason for this gracious visitation, was the fact that Abraham was about to be tried in a far more subtle way than he had ever been tried before, and he needed to be prepared for it (vv. 21-24). The king of Sodom, a godless, reprobate man, was about to offer him great wealth and the honour of his ungodly crown. Nothing could equip Abram ,or us, to honour God and strengthen him, and us, for temptation like this than communion with Christ (S. of S. 1:2-4,12-14).

Abram had brought back the captives. He had every right to the spoils. If he had taken them, no one could charge him with any evil. What could be wrong with accepting the accolades of an ungodly king and an ungodly nation? The fact is, believers live by a higher rule than other men. Their concern is not for their rights, their own honour, or the riches of this world. The ungodly live for and seek those things (Matt. 6:32). Believers live for and seek the will and glory of God in Christ.

How did Christ appear to Abram? Melchizedek, a type of the Lord Jesus, came to Abram the way he comes to all his people, as a royal, kingly priest. He came to Abram as a king with power, a king who had power over Abram, his servant, power over his enemies, power over all things. He who is God our Saviour is the sovereign Monarch of the universe. He is also our great High Priest. Melchizedek came to Abram as a priest with a sacrifice — 'bread and wine' — tokens of our Saviour's perfect obedience and blood atonement.

What did Melchizedek do for Abram? '[He] brought forth bread and wine.' This is the food of faith (the righteousness and atonement of Christ) which we must eat (John 6:53-56). The bread and wine were a foreshadow of the elements used by our Lord in establishing the blessed ordinance of the Lord's Supper. When it is truly observed, that gospel ordinance is a spiritual feast, an act of faith. Melchizedek revealed God's greatness to his servant Abram. He conveyed God's blessing to him. As a priest, he blessed God for Abram, and taught him to bless God. In all these things, he portrayed our Lord Jesus Christ, the believer's King and Priest.

A type of Christ

Some say that Melchizedek was Noah's son Shem. Some say that he was an angelic, celestial being. Others say he was Christ. Melchizedek was a man who was a great type of our Lord Jesus Christ (Heb. 7:3-4,15). 'Consider how great this man was!' This man (both Melchizedek and Christ) was without father or mother. If Melchizedek were a mere man, no one knew his parents. Certainly, this is stated to remind us of the eternality of our Saviour. He who became a man to save us is God, the eternal Son. He was the Priest of the Most High God. He was not of the Aaronic or Levitical orders, a priest of Israel, but of God, God's special priest. He was not a priest, but the Priest. He was King. Again, he was not a king, but the King, the King of Righteousness and the King of Salem, that is to say, the King of Peace. He is called the King of Righteousness and afterwards the King of Peace, because righteousness must be established before peace can be given (Ps. 85:10; Isa. 32:17; Rom. 3:21-26; 5:1; Col. 1:20). This man was both the Priest and the King, as I said, not of Levi, but of Judah. And the Scriptures tell us that our Lord Jesus Christ is not a priest after the order of Aaron or Levi, but after the order of Melchizedek.

The Levitical priests were unclean; and therefore had to make sacrifices for their own sins and then for the peoples. Christ had no sin. The Levitical priests were mortal. Christ is a priest for ever.

The Lord Jesus Christ, God's own dear Son, is our Melchizedek. He is the great High Priest (Heb. 7:21-25). He is a priest by God's oath (Ps. 110:4). He is a surety of a better covenant. He is an unchangeable priest, a saving priest. He is an abiding, prevailing, propitiatory priest (1 John 2:1-2).

An act of consecration

Abram gave Melchizedek tithes of all that he had. We recognize that tithing was a requirement of the law; but the law had not yet been given. Like believers today, Abram made a free, voluntary gift, compelled by nothing but gratitude. It was a reasonable gift. The tithe Abram gave was an acknowledgement that all that he possessed belonged to God. By his gift, he was saying, 'I am yours.' It was a gift of faith. He gave it with confidence that the God he worshipped by his gift would supply all his needs. If we would worship God with our gifts, we must bring our gifts to him like Abram brought this gift to Melchizedek. We cannot worship God by paying a tithe. That was a legal necessity in the Mosaic age. We worship God by bringing free gifts of gratitude and faith to him (2 Cor. 9:7), voluntarily, as symbols both of our consecration to him and our faith in him, saying:

Hail, Melchizedek divine!
Christ, the Great High Priest is mine!
Here, before your throne I fall!
Take not a tithe, but take my all!

20.

Justification by faith

Genesis 15:1-6

'And he believed in the LORD; *and he counted it to him for righteousness'* (Gen. 15: 6).

Justification by faith is the great, foundation doctrine of Holy Scripture. It is beautifully illustrated in the experience of Abram in Genesis 15. In verse 6, we are told that Abram 'believed in the LORD; and he counted it to him for righteousness'. Abram's faith and his justification before God are the subject matter of this entire chapter.

Abraham is set before us in the Scriptures as the father of all who believe. He is the first man spoken of in the Word of God as a believer. Certainly, there were other believers before him. Adam, Abel, Enoch, Noah and many others also believed God. But the word 'believed' is not used with reference to any man in the Bible until we come to Genesis 15:6. Therefore, Abraham is called 'the father of all them that believe' (Rom. 4:11).

Abraham is also the father of all believers in the sense that he is held before us as the pre-eminent example of what it is for a sinner to believe God. From the time of his calling until the day of his death, the Lord God appears to have dealt with Abraham specifically to show us, by example, what the life of faith is. What is written here

concerning Abraham and his faith, is written specifically
for our instruction in the matter of faith and justification
before God. This is exactly what God the Holy Spirit tells
us in Romans 4:23-24:

> Now it was not written for his sake alone, that it was
> imputed to him; But for us also, to whom it shall be
> imputed, if we believe on him that raised up Jesus
> our Lord from the dead.

With these things in mind, let us look at Genesis 15,
beginning at verse 1.

'After these things the word of the LORD came unto Abram
in a vision, saying, Fear not, Abram: I am thy shield, and
thy exceeding great reward' (v. 1).

'After these things...' Many years had passed since the
Lord God first appeared to Abram and called him out of Ur.
Terah, his father, was now dead. It had been many years
since God first promised to make of him a great nation and
a blessing to all nations. Abram had come into the land of
Canaan. He had been tried by great famine. He went down
to Egypt. There, the Lord let him see how weak he was.
Even the father of believers was weak, when left to himself.

After he came back up to Canaan, there was a terrible
strife between Abram's herdsmen and Lot's herdsmen, and
the two parted company. Though Lot abandoned his uncle
and abandoned the land of Canaan, Abram never forgot his
erring nephew. When the kings of the land went to war,
Abram seems to have looked upon it as a matter of nothing
but casual, passing interest, at most. The fall of Sodom and
Gomorrah was of no concern to the heaven bound pilgrim.
But, when a messenger came and told him that

Chedorlaomer and the kings of the plain had taken Lot captive, Abram acted without hesitation.

Upon his return from battle, Melchizedek met Abram with bread and wine, and blessed him, as priest of the most high God. He blessed him upon the basis of that sacrifice (the sacrifice of Christ) portrayed in the bread and wine. To him, Abram gave tithes of all that he had.

The king of Sodom saw and heard all that passed between Abram and Melchizedek, but was totally unaware of what was going on and had no interest in such matters. No sooner had Melchizedek departed, than this proud man offered to give Abram the goods which Abram himself had recovered! Upon that Abram did two things, which tell us much about the kind of man he was.

1. He told the king of Sodom plainly that he would not take anything from him, because he had already sworn to his God, 'the most high God, possessor of heaven and earth,' that he would not.

2. By telling him exactly what he would do with the people and the goods, Abram pointedly told this man who wore a king's robe that the goods he was offering to give Abram were not his to give.

'After these things *the word of the LORD came unto Abram in a vision.*' The one who appeared to Abram was the Lord Jesus Christ, the eternal Word, the Son of God. God always reveals himself to men and speaks to them only through Christ, the Mediator.

'After these things the word of the LORD came unto Abram in a vision, *saying, Fear not, Abram: I am thy shield, and thy exceeding great reward.*' First, the Lord bids his servant to cease from fear. Why does he tell him not to be afraid? He had just succeeded in conquering four armies with 318 shepherds! Perhaps he feared retaliation from those who remained of the kingdoms he had conquered. That seems to be the universal opinion of the commentators. I am inclined to think otherwise. I think he was fearful simply because he was overwhelmed by the manifest presence of God. He was fearful because he knew himself to be a sinful man in the presence of the holy Lord God. Like Moses, Daniel and John after him, Abram had great reverence for God and stood in utter awe before him.

This is a blessed fear. Should a man, aware of his own corruption of heart, depravity and sin, not be overwhelmed and humbled before the Lord God? But when Christ appears to his own, he appears in perfect love, to cast out fear. Thus, he says, 'Fear not, Abram.'

Here the Lord God, our Saviour, makes two great promises to Abram, by which he quietens his fears, comforts his heart and encourages his faith.

1. '*I am thy Shield.*' Who or what will harm me, if the Lord God himself is my shield? 'Thus, in tender grace,' wrote A. W. Pink, 'did Jehovah quiet the troubled heart of the one whom he was pleased to call his "*friend*"'.

2. 'I am thy Shield, and *thy exceeding great Reward.*' After Abram had defeated the kings of the plain and had been blessed by Melchizedek, he declined to take anything from the king of Sodom, lest a heathen king should point to Abram and say, 'I made him what he is.' His refusal to be enriched by a pagan worldling is bountifully compensated here. He forsook all for the glory of God, but lost nothing. So it is to this day, and shall be for evermore. We are required to forsake all to follow Christ. Indeed, we cannot be his disciples, if we do not surrender all to him. But God will never permit his own to suffer any real loss by following him and seeking his glory. Our Lord asked his disciples,

'Lacked ye any thing?' To that question, they were compelled to answer, 'Nothing' (Luke 22:35).

3. '*I am thy Shield, and thy exceeding great Reward.*' This
great promise is applicable to all believers, to all who are
'strangers and pilgrims on the earth'. The Son of God himself is our shield of faith. He is our shield and defence.
Christ is the one behind whom faith hides, upon whom
faith leans, and in whom faith finds refuge and safety (Pss.
3:3; 5:12; 84:11; 91:4; 119:114). As he is our shield, our
Saviour is also our exceeding great reward. 'The LORD is my
portion, saith my soul; therefore will I hope in him.' 'The
LORD is the portion of mine inheritance and of my cup.'

4. '*And Abram said, Lord GOD, what wilt thou give me,
seeing I go childless, and the steward of my house is this
Eliezer of Damascus? And Abram said, Behold, to me thou
hast given no seed: and, lo, one born in my house is mine
heir.*' (vv. 2-3).

After hearing the Lord's declaration, Abram seems immediately to have thought, 'If I am to have the inheritance in
God which he has promised me, if I am to be a blessing to
all the nations of the earth, as the Lord has said, I must
have a son through whom the blessing will come.' As A. W.
Pink suggests, 'He recognized that heirship is based upon
sonship' (Rom. 8:16-17; Eph. 1:5,11).

Abram's asking God for a son, in verses 2 and 3, was not
an act of unbelief, as many suppose, but of faith. He took
God at his word. He seems to have reasoned like this: 'If
God has promised me an heritage, promised to make me a
blessing to all nations, and promised to make my seed to be
as the dust of the earth (people scattered throughout all the
earth), then he must first give me a son.' So, he asked for
one. It seems to me that that is obvious from the Lord's
response in verses 4 and 5.

5. '*And, behold, the word of the LORD came unto him,
saying, This shall not be thine heir; but he that shall come*

forth out of thine own bowels shall be thine heir. And he
brought him forth abroad, and said, Look now towards
heaven, and tell the stars, if thou be able to number them:
and he said unto him, So shall thy seed be.' (vv. 4-5).
We must remember that in Genesis 13:15-16 the Lord promised Abram that his seed would be as the dust of the earth.
Here he takes him by the hand, leads him outside, and points
him to the sky, saying, 'I shall give you a seed like the stars
of heaven.'

We need to be sure we understand the meaning of this,
as it is given in the Scriptures. Without question, his seed
has reference to the whole, innumerable multitude of God's
elect, whom he purposed to saved before the world began
(Heb. 2:16). However, the primary significance of this promise is that God promised Abram that he would send the
Seed of the woman, that great Redeemer who would crush
the serpent's head and redeem God's elect (Gen. 3:15-16)
through his loins.

6. *'And he believed in the Lord; and he counted it to him*
for righteousness.' (v. 6). When Abram heard the gospel
preached to him, as the Holy Spirit tells us he did (Gal.
3:8), he believed God. There is no other single text in the
Old Testament so thoroughly and specifically expounded
in the New Testament as Genesis 15:6. The apostle Paul
was inspired to write extensively about this text in the book
of Romans and in the book of Galatians. He uses this text as
the foundation upon which the entire house of God rests,
which is justification by faith alone.

Here the Holy Spirit gives us the first explanation of
justification found in the Bible. As we have seen previously, there were many others before Abram who were
justified in exactly the same way as he was. In fact, a careful reading of the Scriptures makes it obvious that Abram
was himself a believer, a man justified before God, before
this event.

The Scriptures tell us plainly that he was a believer when he left Ur of the Chaldees. 'By faith Abraham, when he was called to go out into a place which he should after receive for an inheritance, obeyed; and he went out, not knowing whither he went' (Heb. 11:8). Though he was then a justified man, his justification is not mentioned on that occasion because there is no connection between our experience of grace and our justification before God. Justification is the result of redemption accomplished, not redemption experienced. Therefore, the Holy Spirit speaks of Abram's justification in connection with Christ and the redemption of our souls by Christ.

That faith which was 'counted for righteousness' was, and must be, faith which believed what God had said concerning the promised Seed. Therefore, the Holy Spirit took this experience and arranged it to stand as the first and primary model and example of justification by faith.

There is no justification apart from Christ. This is the only way God has ever, will ever, or can ever justify the ungodly: 'Through this man is preached unto you the forgiveness of sins: And by him all that believe are justified from all things' (Acts 13:38-39). Justifying faith is directly connected to the person and work of Christ. Saving faith is that faith which looks to Christ crucified and trusts him. This is what is taught in Genesis 15. God made a promise and revealed to Abram that Christ, his Son, would come into the world as Abram's son and redeem him. As has been said, the gospel was preached to Abram (Gal. 3:8-16). This is not a matter of speculation on my part. This is exactly what the Holy Spirit tells us had taken place in Genesis 15:1-5. God's method of grace never changes. 'Faith cometh by hearing, and hearing by the word of God.'

But we read, too, that 'Abram believed in the LORD.' How was Abram justified? He was justified by grace alone, through faith alone, in Christ alone. He was not justified by religious ceremonies (circumcision), but by faith (Rom. 4:3-10). He was not justified by works, but by faith. Though he had done many noble, good things in the exercise of faith, though he had lived upon the Word of God, for the glory of God for many years, his works are not mentioned in connection with his justification, except as the fruit of it. He was not justified by keeping the law, but by faith in Christ. We must always distinguish between the truth — that true faith always produces good works — and the lie, the damning heresy — that our works are mixed with our faith in the matter of our acceptance with God.

We must notice this too: *'He believed* in the LORD,' not in facts about the Lord (Rom. 4:3,16-25). Christ himself is the solitary object of all true faith. Faith is not believing that there is a God. All men and women, whether they acknowledge it or not, believe there is a God, that he is holy and that they must meet him in judgement. Faith is not simply acknowledging the historic facts of Christ's incarnation, obedience, death and resurrection. You cannot be a believer and deny the historic facts of the gospel. But faith is not believing historic facts, and saving faith is not the embracing of gospel doctrine. Without question, that person is not saved and does not know God who does not believe the doctrine of the gospel. But no one has ever been justified, no sinner has ever been saved, by believing the doctrines of predestination, sovereign election, effectual atonement, irresistible grace, or any other. Saving faith does not trust facts or feelings, creeds or confessions, but a person! 'Abram believed *God!*' That is the issue, the only issue between men and God. 'Dost thou believe on the Son of God?'

Multitudes have jumped on this text, Genesis 15:6, and pointed to Abram's act of believing, saying that it was that act which was imputed to him for righteousness. Such doctrine is totally false. It makes faith a work, an act of man's will, which has merit before God. It makes justification, not a matter of righteousness and justice, but a gracious compromise, which declares that God accepts faith in the place of righteousness and satisfaction. Nothing could be further from the truth.

Justification is a legal term. It has everything to do with law, justice and righteousness, and nothing to do with compromise (Rom. 3:24-26). 'By mercy and truth iniquity is purged' (Prov. 16:6). In justification, we are declared right at law, right in the court of heaven. Our sins are all blotted out, put away and forgiven, upon the grounds of justice satisfied. We are made perfect before God, holy, blameless, utterly beyond reproof. In justification, we are accepted in the Beloved, complete in Christ, who is made the righteousness of God for us.

The act of believing has no more to do with the accomplishment of justification than the act of sinning. Our justification was accomplished by Christ, when he died at Calvary. Indeed, it was accomplished in the decree of God from eternity, and God's elect are declared to be justified from eternity (Rom. 8:28-30), justified in the Lamb slain from the foundation of the world.

We simply receive and experience the blessedness of justification by faith. Faith contributes nothing to the work of righteousness and the satisfaction of justice. Our righteousness was accomplished for us by Christ's obedience to death. It is that which was imputed to Abram, not his act of believing; and it is that which is imputed to us for righteousness, not our act of believing. Our justification is by the object of our faith — Jehovah-tsidkenu, 'The Lord our Righteousness' — not by the act of our faith (Rom. 5:19; 2 Cor. 5:21). In fact, the apostle Peter tells us plainly that our faith in Christ is the result, not the cause, of our justification (2 Peter 1:1). As C. H. Spurgeon put it:

Faith cannot be its own righteousness, for it is the very nature of faith to look out of itself to Christ... We must look altogether away from ourselves to Christ alone, or we have no true faith at all... To say that faith becomes our righteousness is to tear the very bowels out of the gospel, and to deny the faith which has been once delivered to the saints.

Christ 'was delivered for our offences, and was raised again for our justification. Therefore being justified, [the comma belongs right here, not after faith] *by faith* [this is the result], we have peace with God through our Lord Jesus Christ' (Rom. 4:25 - 5:1, italics mine). The whole work of justification was accomplished and took place outside ourselves, by Christ alone (Rom. 5:9-11).

Would you like to be justified before God? Would you like to go down to your house, like the publican, justified? Would you like to stand before God, from this day forward, in peace, for ever righteous, justified, freed from the debt of sin and the curse of God's holy law? Would you like to silence that screaming conscience that torments your soul day and night? If you would be saved, if you would be justified, you must believe on the Lord Jesus Christ, just as Abram did.

Abram believed God's promise of grace, salvation and eternal life in Christ, preached to him in the gospel. He believed God's word concerning his Son. He believed what was not possible, except by God's own work. He believed that from his dead body and Sarai's dead womb, God would raise up a Son in whom they would have life (Rom. 4:20-24). Abram believed this word from God as the word of God to him (Eph. 1:13; 1 John 5:1,10-13).

21.

Standing on justified ground

Genesis 15:6-21

'And he believed in the LORD...' (Gen. 15:6).

Abram believed God. What a tremendous declaration that is. Though faith has nothing to do with the accomplishment of justification, we cannot have justification without faith. Yet this faith which is exemplified in Abram is a thing no man can perform. It is not the result of man's will, decision, or moral and mental determination. Faith is the gift of God. No man can or will believe, except it be by the gift and operation of God in him. We believe according to the working of his mighty power. So, when the Scriptures assert that 'Abraham believed God,' the Holy Spirit is saying, 'Here is a miracle of grace. Here is a sinner doing what no sinner can do, doing what he must do, doing what only the grace of God can enable him to do.'

In chapter 15 of Genesis, when the Holy Spirit declares that Abram believed in the Lord, at least five things are evident.

1. He believed the gospel as the very word of God

He believed the gospel as a word directly from God himself. Paul tells us that the word that God spoke to him was the gospel of Christ preached to him. God had said, 'Fear not, Abram: I am thy shield, and thy exceeding great reward.' Immediately following this revelation, Abram asked the Lord to give him a son in whom all his promised mercy might be fulfilled. 'And, behold, the word of the LORD came unto him, saying, This shall not be thine heir; but he that shall come forth out of thine own bowels shall be thine heir. And he brought him forth abroad, and said, Look now towards heaven, and tell the stars, if thou be able to number them: and he said unto him, So shall thy seed be.'

Like Saul of Tarsus, Abram was a man who could declare, 'I certify you, that the gospel which was preached of me is not after man. For I neither received it of man, neither was I taught it, but by the revelation of Jesus Christ.' The gospel came to him, not as the word of man, but the word of God. His faith stood not in the words of man's wisdom, but in the power of God.

If ever a sinner believes God, it will be because the gospel has come to him in the demonstration and power of the Holy Spirit with much assurance, being assured by God himself that it is the very word of God (1 Thess. 1:5). That faith which stands in the wisdom of man is but the faith of a man. That faith which stands in the power of God is the faith of God's elect.

2. Abram believed the word of God concerning his Son

Abram believed the word of God concerning his Son, the Seed in whom and by whom redemption would be accomplished. The promise he heard from God, he recognized to be the very same as that which was made to Eve in the Garden. Abram understood that God's promise went far beyond the promise of a son. It was the promise of God concerning his Son (Gal. 3:6-16).

True faith is fixed on Christ alone. It is not the faith of this sect or that, but faith in Christ. It is not the faith of this creed or that. It is not the faith of emotion or fear. True faith looks to Christ, embracing him, his person and his work, as the God-man, our Mediator.

3. Abram believed that God could, and would, do that which was humanly impossible

Abram believed God, who gives life to the dead and calls those things which are not as though they were (Rom. 4:18-25). Faith believes that Christ is able to save. He can cause dry bones to live. He can raise the dead. He can cause the blind to see, the lame to walk, the deaf to hear and the cursed to be blessed.

4. Abram believed the promise made to him by God

Abram believed the promise made to him by God in the gospel — though vast and sublime beyond calculation — to be a matter of absolute certainty, because God had spoken it. He believed God would do all that he said he would do for him and in him by Christ Jesus (Rom. 4:8; Eph. 1:3-6).

5. Abram believed the gospel as the word of God to him

He believed God to be his shield, his exceeding great reward and his Saviour. He heard God speak the gospel to him as the word of his salvation (Eph. 1:13-14). Believing God, Abram was justified. By faith he received the blessedness of sins forgiven, righteousness imputed, and immutable, perfect acceptance with God himself through the blood and righteousness of Christ. That is what verse 6 declares: 'And he believed in the LORD; and he counted it to him for righteousness.'

From verse 7 to the end of the chapter, we see a believing sinner standing on justified ground. Oh, what a blessed place to stand! Once a man or woman believes God, he sees what he could not see before, understands things which mystified and dumbfounded him before, and rejoices in things which before were either a cause of boredom to him or stirred up his hatred of God to boiling point. Standing on justified ground, the most uneducated, illiterate believer sees with perfect clarity what the most brilliant and most educated unbeliever cannot even imagine, because faith understands all things (John 14:26; 16:13; 1 Cor. 2:9-16; Heb. 11:1-3; 1 John 2:20).

God's call

'And he said unto him, I am the LORD that brought thee out of Ur of the Chaldees, to give thee this land to inherit it' (v. 7). Standing justified before God, as a sinner accepted in Christ the beloved, faith sees the value of God's call and prizes it. Abram saw that the Lord God had called him distinctively and that it was God's call which distinguished him from all others (1 Cor. 4:7). He recognized that all the blessedness he now enjoyed and would enjoy for ever was his because the Lord had separated him from Adam's fallen race and called him to life and faith in Christ. Once he believed God, this man understood perfectly that his faith was the result, not the cause, of God's grace and the call of it. Once a sinner is made to stand before God on justified ground, he prizes the call of God, by which he has been made to believe God.

Blood atonement

'And he said, Lord GOD, whereby shall I know that I shall inherit it? And he said unto him, Take me an heifer of three years old, and a she goat of three years old, and a ram of three years old, and a turtledove, and a young pigeon. And he took unto him all these, and divided them in the midst, and laid each piece one against another: but the birds divided he not. And when the fowls came down upon the carcases, Abram drove them away' (v. 8-11).

Standing on justified ground, faith sees the glory of God in blood atonement. Every believing sinner sees clearly that the only grounds upon which God can bless and save a sinner is blood atonement: 'The precious blood of Christ.' Believers understand and rejoice in the fact that God cannot be our justifier without being just himself. He cannot be our Saviour, without being 'a just God and a Saviour'. Abram took those very sacrifices later instituted by law as types of Christ, and he seems to say, 'All the sacrifices point to one sacrifice.' He recognized that Christ alone, that promised one whom he believed, could take away sin by the shedding of his own blood. Thus, he exemplifies faith. Faith drives away every unclean foul of the air which would take away or turn it from the sacrifice. And faith sees itself involved in the sacrifice. As Abram stood in the midst of the slain animals, so the believer realizes that when Christ died, he died. Faith understands that Christ's death is the death of his people. His satisfaction is their satisfaction.

Covenant grace

'And when the sun was going down, a deep sleep fell upon Abram; and, lo, an horror of great darkness fell upon him.'

(v. 12). *'And it came to pass, that, when the sun went down, and it was dark, behold a smoking furnace, and a burning lamp that passed between those pieces. In the same day the LORD made a covenant with Abram, saying, Unto thy seed have I given this land, from the river of Egypt unto the great river, the river Euphrates'* (vv. 17-18).

Standing on justified ground, faith sees God in covenant grace, a covenant ratified by blood. Believing sinners see the connection between God's purpose, God's covenant promises, and their fulfilment and blood atonement. The blood of Christ is the blood of the everlasting covenant (Heb. 13:20). It is the blood by which the covenant has been ratified, and by which all the promises of the covenant are secured for us (Heb. 9:15-17).

Abram seems to have seen what few see today. He saw that this covenant and the promises of it involved the very glory of God. The God of glory staked, as it were, the very glory of his being, the honour of his name, and the reputation of his very throne on the fulfilment of his promises (Heb. 6:6-20). He saw himself involved in the covenant, in the sacrifice, and the very glory of God!

The trial of faith

'And he said unto Abram, Know of a surety that thy seed shall be a stranger in a land that is not theirs, and shall serve them; and they shall afflict them four hundred years' (v.13).

Standing on justified ground, faith sees that every trial, every trouble, every affliction, and every sorrow experienced in this world of woe is ordained by God in covenant mercy and comes to pass according to the purpose of God's grace in the covenant. Immediately, the Lord God caused Abram to know that while he lived in this world, and while

his seed lived in this world, faith would be tried and that
the trial of faith itself would prove to be a matter of great
blessedness. Our trials are as much a part of our blessedness as our justification. The Holy Spirit tells us this plainly
in Romans 5:1-5.

Salvation assured

*'And also that nation, whom they shall serve, will I judge:
and afterward shall they come out with great substance. And
thou shalt go to thy fathers in peace; thou shalt be buried in
a good old age. But in the fourth generation they shall come
hither again: for the iniquity of the Amorites is not yet full'*
(vv. 14-16).

Standing on justified ground, faith sees, and is assured
of, the fact that our ultimate salvation and triumph in Christ
is sure. The Lord God gave his servant, Abram, assurance
concerning all that he promised. He assured Abram that he
would both judge those who oppressed him and bless him
as the result of their oppression. He assured him that he
would die in peace. What a blessed word of grace this is.
How can a sinner be confident that he will leave this world
and go into eternity to stand before the holy Lord God in
peace? There is only one way: 'Being justified by faith, we
have peace with God through our Lord Jesus Christ!'

22.

El-Shaddai — the God of the covenant

Genesis 17:1-21

'And when Abram was ninety years old and nine, the LORD appeared to Abram, and said unto him, I am the Almighty God; walk before me, and be thou perfect. And I will make my covenant between me and thee, and will multiply thee exceedingly. And Abram fell on his face: and God talked with him' (Gen. 17:1-3).

The God of glory appeared to Abram when he was still in Ur of the Chaldees. There, the Lord God promised to make of him a great nation. After the death of his father, Terah, in Haran, the Lord appeared to Abram again, and renewed his promise. Though he was a seventy-five year old man, Abram believed God and left Haran with his wife Sarai, his nephew Lot and Lot's wife, and came into the land of Canaan. There, at Bethel, the Lord appeared to him again, and again renewed his promise.

A Son and a Saviour

In Genesis 15, after his lapse in Egypt, after the strife between his herdsmen and Lot's herdsmen, after the slaughter of the kings, after the appearance of Melchizedek, the Lord graciously appeared to Abram again, this time more fully than before, and again renewed his promise. Abram asked, and God specifically promised to give him a Son, a Son who would be his Saviour, a Son through whom he would be made righteous, a Son in whom all the world would be blessed. Then, we are told, 'And he believed in the LORD; and he counted it to him for righteousness.'

The arm of the flesh

Still, Sarai was barren. After ten long years in the land of Canaan, she devised a plan. She gave her servant, Hagar, to Abram. She seems to have thought, 'The Lord has not fulfilled his promise. He must intend for us to do something. So, it only makes sense,' she appears to have reasoned, 'if we are to have children, if God is to fulfil his promise, that it will have to be by means of a surrogate mother.' Therefore, she said to Abram, 'Behold now, the LORD hath restrained me from bearing: I pray thee, go in unto my maid; it may be that I may obtain children by her. And Abram hearkened to the voice of Sarai' (Gen. 16:2). What folly! What presumption! God does not need anything from us to accomplish his purposes. We can never do good by evil means. The arm of the flesh can never accomplish the work of the Spirit.

Yet, despite Sarai and Abram's unbelief, presumption and sin, God proved himself gracious, wise and faithful. As we have seen already (Gen. 13), our God even overrules evil for good, making all things work together for the salvation and everlasting good of his elect. The Lord used these events to reveal himself to Hagar. Though the Lord brought good our of their sin, Sarai and Abram had to live with the consequences of their actions for many years. The fruit of their unbelief and sin was Ishmael. Abram loved Ishmael, as any father loves his son; but Ishmael was the source of great, and constant, pain to him and, finally, he had to be put out of the house.[1]

Deliberate delay

When we come to Genesis 17, thirteen years have passed since the Lord last appeared to Abram. We have no record of God speaking to his servant in any way for thirteen long years. Spiritual barrenness is always the result of disobedience and unbelief. But we must never imagine that man's unbelief nullifies the purposes and promises of God. Though it often appears that the Lord God is not working, that his purpose is being hindered, that his promise has fallen to the ground, that is never the case. God's delays are always deliberate. Not only is it true that God always knows best, and does best, he always does it at precisely the best time. He always fulfils his promise in 'the fulness of time'. He is never late and he is never early. God is always on time.

Why did Abram have to wait so long for God to fulfil his promise? It was twenty-five years from the time the Lord first appeared to Abram and promised him a son, a seed in whom all the nations of the earth would be blessed, until the birth of Isaac. Why? The reason is simple. Abram had to be brought to the end of himself. He had to be brought to his wits' end. He had to be made to know that God's work is in no way dependent upon or determined by him. The simple fact is, God never acts in grace until he convinces us that our only hope is for him to act in grace. God does not show us his omnipotence until he shows us our impotence. Only when Israel was in utter desperation did the Lord speak, and say, 'Stand ye still, and see the salvation of the LORD.' It was not until Abram saw the deadness of his

own body and the deadness of Sarai's womb that God gave
him a son.

Read Genesis 17 carefully. It is a very instructive portion of Holy Scripture. In this chapter the Holy Spirit has
recorded for us the covenant God made with Abram. He
shows us that the basis upon which the covenant promises
were made to Abram and the basis upon which he believed
those promises was the omnipotence and all-sufficiency of
God our Saviour.

We do ourselves a great disservice and misinterpret the
Scriptures, if we read this (or any other passage of God's
inspired Word) as no more than an historic record. Everything in this passage is as applicable to believing sinners
today as it was to Abram (Rom. 15:4; 2 Tim. 3:15-16). The
promises made to Abram are the promises of God to all
who, believing on the Lord Jesus Christ, are his children.
With those things in mind, I want to show you four things
in this chapter. May God the Holy Spirit, whose Word we
hold before us, inscribe the lessons of this chapter upon
our hearts by his grace.

God's character

'And when Abram was ninety years old and nine, the LORD
appeared to Abram, and said unto him, I *am* the Almighty
God' (v. 1). Here the Lord God reveals himself to Abram as
El-Shaddai, 'the Almighty God'. This is the first time God
made himself known by this great name. None but the Almighty God could perform for Abram the things he promises here. This was a ninety-nine year old man. His wife
was ninety. Yet El-Shaddai promised him a son; and what
God promises he can and will perform, because he is 'the
Almighty God'. 'With God all things are possible.'

This great attribute of God's being, his absolute omnipotence, strikes terror in the hearts of the wicked; but to the believer nothing is more consoling. 'The name of the LORD is a strong tower: the righteous runneth into it, and is safe' (Prov. 18:10). Since our Saviour is the Lord Almighty, we can confidently forsake all and follow him (2 Cor. 6:17-18). Because our Saviour is El-Shaddai, 'He is able to succour them that are tempted.' Because he who loves us with an everlasting love is the Almighty, nothing can ever separate us from his love (Rom. 8:39). Seeing that our God is the Almighty God, he 'is able to do exceeding abundantly above all that we ask or think'. As he is God Almighty, the Lord Jesus Christ, our Good Shepherd, he is able to keep his sheep in his omnipotent hand (John 10:28). Because he is the Almighty God, our Saviour is able to raise our bodies from the grave in resurrection glory (Phil. 3:21). Because he is El-Shaddai, the Lord Jesus is able to keep us from falling and present us and all his own faultless before the presence of his glory in the end (Jude 24-25).

Everything in this passage is written for the edification, comfort and benefit of God's elect. It is of just as much benefit to believing sinners today as it was to that believing sinner to whom these words were first spoken. He who appeared to Abram and said, 'I am the Almighty God,' is the Lord Jesus Christ, our God and Saviour. Let believing sinners rejoice! He who is our God is El-Shaddai, 'the Almighty God'.

God's command

Look at verse 1 again. 'And when Abram ... I am the Almighty God; walk before me, and be thou perfect.' In the margin reference, our translators have told us that this word 'perfect' means 'upright' or 'sincere'. Though the word is sometimes used in that way, that is not the case here. The holy Lord God cannot and will not accept our sincerity or uprightness. He who is God indeed — perfect, holy and righteousness, the one who is light and in whom there is no darkness at all — requires and demands perfection. It is written: 'It shall be perfect to be accepted' (Lev. 22:21).

This is what God required of Abram, and what he requires of us: 'Walk before me, and be thou perfect.' This is his commandment. There is only one way in which we can walk before the Lord God in perfection. If we would walk before the holy Lord God, if we would be accepted before his august, majestic holiness, we must do so by faith in Christ, like Enoch of old (Heb. 11:5-6). This is what God requires of men (1 John 3:23).

Perfection is what God requires of sinners and what he gives to sinners in Christ (Matt. 5:20; 2 Cor. 5:21). Perfection — absolute, perfect holiness in thought, word and deed — is the standard every believer seeks, though we know it is unattainable in this life (Phil. 3:12-14). Perfection — absolute perfection of character and conduct — is what every child of God will have in heaven's glory (Ps. 17:15).

God's covenant

Abram fell on his face, fully in awe, before the Lord God, the Almighty God, who stood before him, 'And God talked with him'. I am interested in what God said to this man. We do not have to guess what it was. The Holy Spirit tells us that the Lord God, the Almighty God, El-Shaddai talked to him about a covenant (Gen. 17:2-16). In these fifteen inspired verses, the Lord God tells us six things about his covenant with Abram. Again, I remind you that these things are recorded for us. They speak to us. They speak about God's covenant, 'ordered in all things, and sure,' for us.

1. It was a covenant made for the benefit of many

We need to understand this: as it is revealed here, God's covenant with Abraham was a covenant made with one man for the benefit of many. The promised blessings of the covenant extended to all Abraham's descendants. The blessedness promised reached to the four corners of the earth. As Andrew Fuller observed, 'Surely these things were designed to familiarize us with the great principle on which our salvation should rest. It was the purpose of God to save perishing sinners. Yet his covenant is not originally with them, but with Christ. With him it stands fast; and for his sake they are accepted and blessed. Even the blessedness of Abram himself, and all the rewards conferred on him, were for his sake.'

God's covenant of grace and salvation, that covenant of which David said, 'This is all my salvation, and all my desire,' was made for us (his elect) with Christ our surety before the world began. It is this covenant of which Paul speaks in Ephesians 1:3-7.

2. A covenant of righteousness

God's covenant is a covenant of righteousness. Let it be understood that, first and foremost, God always deals with sinners upon the ground of strict, unwavering, inflexible righteousness, justice and truth. God's promised blessings of grace and everlasting salvation cannot be bestowed upon any, except those who stand perfect before him (Lev. 20:7; 1 Peter 1:15-16). The blessings of grace and salvation come to chosen sinners by the merits of a perfect surety, through

the blood of the everlasting covenant. These covenant blessings come to us on the grounds of righteousness established
and brought in by the perfect obedience of Christ in his
life. He is *'the LORD our righteousness'*; and justice is satisfied by the sin-atoning death of God's own dear Son as our
substitute (Rom. 3:24-26).

3. A covenant of grace

God's covenant with Abraham, and his covenant with Christ
as our surety, is a covenant of grace. In verse 19, the Lord
God told Abraham plainly that his covenant would be established not with Ishmael (the child of works), but with Isaac
(the child of promise and of grace). We know that this is
the meaning of the Lord's words to Abraham because the
Holy Spirit tells us so in Galatians 4:22-31.

4. A covenant of circumcision

God's covenant is a 'covenant of circumcision' (Acts 7:8).
Circumcision was instituted here by God as the outward,
ceremonial sign and seal of God's covenant with Abraham.
This Old Testament rite of circumcision was a picture of
that circumcision made without hands in the hearts of God's
elect by the Holy Spirit in regeneration (Rom. 2:29; Phil.
3:3; Col. 2:10-15).[2]

Circumcision in the flesh meant exactly the same thing
to Abraham and his descendants as the new birth means to
us. It was a mark by which God's covenant was sealed to
his people (Eph. 1:14; 4:30). It was a mark distinguishing
God's people from the rest of the world. It was a painful
mark — the experience of grace is painful to the flesh. It
was a purifying mark (Acts 15:9-11; 1 John 3:3). It was a

permanent mark. It could not be reversed (Rom. 11:29; Eccles. 3:14).

5. A covenant immutable and sure

God's covenant is a covenant immutable and sure. When the Almighty God says, 'I will,' he will. Nothing can prevent him from doing what he says he will do. All power is his. He is El-Shaddai, the almighty, all-sufficient God. Seven times in this chapter he says, 'I will.' Hear his word of promise, and rejoice (vv. 6-8,19,21). God's *shalls* and *wills* make his covenant immutable and sure (2 Sam. 23:5).

6. A covenant kept by his people

We are told that God's covenant is a covenant kept by his people. Without question, all the terms, stipulations and conditions of the covenant were kept for us by Christ our God and Saviour, the surety of the covenant. He fulfilled all for us. We could never have fulfilled God's requirements. Yet, in verse 9, the Lord God demands that we keep his covenant. 'And God said unto Abraham, Thou shalt keep my covenant therefore, thou, and thy seed after thee in their generations.' The word 'keep' does not mean to keep by fulfilling, but to keep by guarding, by holding fast. The reprobate and unbelieving despise God's covenant. Needy sinners take hold of it and hold it fast (Isa. 56:4-6).

God's child

In verses 17-27, Abraham displays the character of one who is indeed God's child. He believed God (v. 17). Abraham

prayed for his son, Ishmael (v. 18). Abraham bowed to the
will of God (vv. 20-22). Though Ishmael was his firstborn
son, though he loved him dearly, though he prayed for him
earnestly, Abraham recognized that Ishmael had no claim
upon God's grace. In humble submission, he bowed to his
God, even concerning his beloved son Ishmael. Like Eli, he
seems to have said in his heart, 'It is the LORD; let him do
what seemeth him good.'

Abraham obeyed the Lord (vv. 23-27). What an example
of obedience this old, old man sets before us. What the
Lord commanded he did. In his old age, Abraham continued
to walk before his God as an obedient child. Old men commonly talk about the things they have done, while finding
excuses to justify the neglect of present responsibilities.
This was not the case with Abraham. Until his dying day,
in keeping with the tenor of his life, he readily received
instruction from his God, and yielded implicit obedience
to him, leaving the consequences of his obedience to God
whose will he sought to obey and for whose glory he lived.

What a shining example he is. This man was justified by
faith alone, without works. But he justified his faith by his
works. His obedience was prompt — he consulted not with
flesh and blood. His obedience was precise — he did exactly
what the Lord God told him to do. His obedience was painful — obedience to God is always painful to the flesh.

Here is God's character: 'The Almighty God'. Here is
God's command: 'Walk before me, and be thou perfect.' 'This
is his commandment, That we should believe on the name
of his Son Jesus Christ,' in whom and by whom alone sinners
stand perfect before God. Here is God's covenant: '[I will]
be a God unto thee, and to thy seed after thee.' Here is
God's child: believing, obedient and blessed.

23.

Lot

Genesis 19:15-23

'And when the morning arose, then the angels hastened Lot, saying, Arise, take thy wife, and thy two daughters, which are here; lest thou be consumed in the iniquity of the city. And while he lingered, the men laid hold upon his hand, and upon the hand of his wife, and upon the hand of his two daughters; the LORD being merciful unto him: and they brought him forth, and set him without the city. And it came to pass, when they had brought them forth abroad, that he said, Escape for thy life; look not behind thee, neither stay thou in all the plain; escape to the mountain, lest thou be consumed. And Lot said unto them, Oh, not so, my Lord: Behold now, thy servant hath found grace in thy sight, and thou hast magnified thy mercy, which thou hast showed unto me in saving my life; and I cannot escape to the mountain, lest some evil take me, and I die: Behold now, this city is near to flee unto, and it is a little one: Oh, let me escape thither, (is it not a little one?) and my soul shall live. And he said unto him, See, I have accepted thee concerning this thing also, that I will not overthrow this city, for the which thou hast spoken. Haste thee, escape thither; for I cannot do any thing till thou be come thither. Therefore the name of the city was called Zoar. The sun was risen upon the earth when Lot entered into Zoar'

(Gen. 19:15-23).

The Sodomites were a reprobate people, hardened by the perverse practice of grievous, vile sin. In Sodom, homosexuality had become the normal, dominant way of life. Men with men and women with women, leaving the natural use of the body, commonly practised such wickedness that God determined he would destroy Sodom in his holy wrath.[1]

Sodom was a city under the judgement of God. However, there was one righteous man in that city; and God, who will not destroy the righteous with the wicked, would not destroy Sodom until he had delivered righteous Lot from the city. The historical record of that deliverance is found in Genesis 19.

Two angels came to Sodom to destroy the Sodomites and to deliver Lot and his family (vv. 1-3). The men of Sodom, moved by perverted lust, attempted to rape those two men (angels in human form), who had come as God's messengers, on the first night they were in town (vv. 4-11). Lot appealed to those beastly men not to commit such wicked deeds; but they paid no attention to him. Until this time, Lot had managed to get along with the Sodomites by compromise. That is the only way a righteous man can get along with godless men. So Lot, thinking that the prostitution of his daughters would be less vile than the homosexual rape of the men in his house, offered to give his virgin daughters to those desperately evil men! They laughed in his face and started to break into his house. When they did, the two men God had sent, pulled Lot inside and struck the men of Sodom with blindness. Then those messengers of mercy warned Lot to take his family and flee from the city, saying, 'The LORD hath sent us to destroy it' (vv. 12-13). Lot, being aroused with fear, went to warn his sons-in-law, but to them he seemed like one who mocked (v. 14).

What a sad, sad story. When Lot spoke for God, when he attempted to convey the message of God to his daughters and sons-in-law, they thought he was trying to play a joke on them! Having seen his life, they could not hear his words! Yet Lot stands before us in Scripture as a marvellous picture of God's grace. This is particularly illustrated for us in Genesis 19:15-23.

In verses 15 and 16, we see *the blessed violence of grace*. When the angels of God hastened Lot and commanded him to flee from Sodom, 'he lingered!' Therefore, the angels took Lot, his wife and his two daughters by the hand, and brought them out of the city. Grace snatches men and women from destruction (Jude 23; Ps. 65:4; 110:3). Lot hesitated; but grace hastened. If God had not been merciful to him, snatching him from the city, Lot's lingering would have been his ruin. The same is true of every believer. We escaped the clutches of Satan only because God our Saviour snatched us from the kingdom of darkness and translated us into his kingdom of light.

In verse 17, there is *a word of instruction for all believers*. Though he had been delivered from Sodom, Lot was still in danger. He was not to rest in the plain. He was to escape for his life to the mountain. Those of us who have been delivered by God's almighty grace from the bondage and dominion of sin are given an urgent word of instruction: 'Escape for thy life!' Ever flee from sin, Satan and the world. 'Work out your own salvation with fear and trembling.' Never imagine that you have apprehended that for which you have been apprehended by Christ, as long as you live in this world. 'Look not behind thee!' Forgetting those things which are behind, reach forward to those things which are before you. Count all things but loss for Christ. Do not hanker after the world. Flee from it. 'Escape to the mountain, lest thou be consumed.' 'Set your affection on things above.' 'Press towards the mark for the prize of the high calling of God in Christ Jesus.' Having put your hand to the plough, do not look back. It is written: 'If any man draw back, my soul shall have no pleasure in him.'

Verses 18-21 show us something about *the weakness of faith*. What a sad picture this is. It was a great weakness in Lot that he preferred Zoar, the city of his choosing, to the mountain of God's choosing. Fearing that he could not make it to the mountain, he desired to dwell in Zoar. He recognized God's grace in his deliverance from Sodom, but he did not trust God's grace to take him all the way up to the mountain. Even at this time, Lot wanted to enjoy the ease and comfort of the world. Here is a sad, painful truth, but a truth nonetheless, a truth that every child of God will learn by painful experience in this world: true faith is mixed with much unbelief.

Verses 21-23 show us *the cause of God's longsuffering*. God is longsuffering with the wicked and preserves them in life for the salvation of his own elect (2 Peter 3:9). There are some sinners in this world who must, and will, be saved. God will save his own elect. Christ will have his redeemed. The Holy Spirit will regenerate and call every sinner chosen by God in eternity and redeemed by Christ at Calvary. Until the last of God's elect is called, he will not destroy this world (Rev. 7:1-3). 'What care,' wrote Matthew Henry, 'God takes for the preservation of his people. The winds [of judgement] are held till God's servants are sealed.'

Two words found in verse 16 really summarize the life of this man Lot — 'He lingered!' The angels of God stood before him, calling him to take his family and flee from Sodom. Yet, as God was preparing to rain fire and brimstone upon the city, even then, we are told, 'He lingered!' Those two words are most solemn. They give us much food for thought. They ought to sound like the blasts of a trumpet in our ears. They should cause us all to sit up and pay attention.

Who was this man Lot?

Many seem to think that Lot was a bad man, a wicked worldling, a child of the devil, but he was not such a person. Lot was a righteous man, made righteous by the grace of God, born of God, washed in the blood of Christ, robed in his righteousness, though he often behaved in a manner not worthy of his calling in Christ.

Lot was a man with a very good beginning in the way of faith (Gen. 11:31). Very few begin as well as Abraham's nephew Lot. He clearly learned much, sacrificed much and showed great promise. If Lot had only continued as he began, we would not question the excellence of his character. He left Chaldea with his godly uncle, Abram. He forsook his youthful companions, believing the promise of God. He worshipped God with Abram. Whenever Abram built an altar to the Lord God, Lot worshipped at that altar. Whenever God spoke to Abram, Lot anxiously and carefully listened as Abram taught him the word of the Lord. Lot entered into the land of promise with Abram.

Lot was a true believer, a child of God. He was a converted man, a justified soul, or heir of heaven. Lot truly was a righteous man. The Holy Spirit places this matter beyond all controversy (2 Peter 2:7-8). God himself has given us good evidence of his grace in Lot. He was a man who lived in a wicked place, 'seeing and hearing' the evil around him. Yet he was not a wicked man. Lot had his faults, plenty of them; but he was distinctly different from the men of Sodom. '[He] vexed his righteous soul … with [the] unlawful deeds' he beheld around him. He was wounded, grieved, distressed, hurt and angered by the deeds of his neighbours. Lot had the same attitude towards the society in which he lived as David had to his (Ps. 119:136,158).

Furthermore, Peter tells us that he 'vexed his righteous soul from day to day with their unlawful deeds'. Many of us are shocked by certain acts of evil the first time we see them, but after a while we become accustomed to the abomination. That was not so with Lot. He was continually grieved by the wickedness he saw around him.

This is the thing I want you to see. God's saints in this world have many blemishes. We are sinners still. We do not despise the gold because it is mixed with dross; and we must not undervalue the grace of God in a man because it is accompanied by corruption. Lot suffered much because of his lingering, and his family suffered even more; but he was a true believer. Though he lingered in Sodom, he is seated today in the blessed circle of the redeemed around the throne of Christ. There he sits, elect, chosen by God, and precious. He is redeemed, washed and forgiven by the blood of Christ; born again, sanctified and glorified by the Spirit of grace; side by side with Abraham, and heir of the same glory.

What did Lot do?

Moses tells us, 'He lingered!' What a short sentence that is to tell us so much about this man. Consider these words in the context in which they are found, and I am sure you will agree that Lot's behaviour was shocking: 'He lingered!' It seems to me that this is the most shocking thing revealed about him. His greed and covetousness, his drunkenness, his incest are all less shocking than this: 'He lingered!' Lot knew the awful condition of the city in which he lived.

'The cry' of its abomination was 'great before the face of the LORD' (v. 13). Yet 'he lingered'! Lot knew the fearful judgement coming down upon all within the city (v. 13). Yet 'he lingered'! He knew that God is a God of righteousness, justice and truth. Yet 'he lingered'! He knew and believed that judgement was both real and imminent. He tried to persuade his sons-in-law to flee the wrath of God (v. 14). Yet 'he lingered'! Lot saw the angels of God standing by, warning him and his family to flee. Yet 'he lingered'! He heard the command of God by his messengers (v. 15). Yet 'he lingered'!

C. H. Spurgeon said, 'Lot was slow when he should have been fast, backward when he should have been forward, trifling when he should have been hastening, loitering when he should have been hurrying, cold when he should have been hot.' This seems incredible. It is shocking beyond imagination. *'He lingered!'* Lot's shocking behaviour is recorded in the Scriptures for our instruction.

There are many in the church of Christ today who are very much like Lot. We all know far more than we practise. We all linger here too much. We say we believe in heaven, but we pursue the world. We say we believe in eternal punishment, but seem to be bothered little by the fact that thousands are going to hell, even many of our own families. We know that 'the time is short,' but live as though it were long. How little we 'redeem the time'. We know that there is a war waging between light and darkness, but we appear to be at peace. We know that there is a race to run, but we seem to be content to sit still. We know that judgement is coming, but we appear to be fast asleep.

We all appear to live as though consecration to Christ is extreme and burning zeal for his glory is fanaticism. We all shrink from self-denial, personal sacrifice, and wholehearted commitment. Our Lord says, 'Take up [your] cross

and follow me.' He commands us to cut off the right hand
that hinders us and pluck out the right eye that is set upon
the world. He tells us that the gate is small and the way is
narrow that leads to life everlasting. Yet we try our best to
make the cross lighter, to nourish the hindering hand, salve
the worldly eye, widen the gate and broaden the way. Like
Lot, we linger! We try constantly to hold both the world
and Christ. We know what is right. We know the command
of Christ. We have heard our Saviour say, 'Love not the
world!' 'No man can serve two masters!' Yet we linger!

Does this apply directly to you? Be honest with yourself
before God. Perhaps you ran well at one time. But now you
linger. Once your heart burned with love for Christ. Now,
though your heart wakens, you sleep (S. of S. 5:2). Like Lot,
you linger. Like Peter, you follow the Lord afar off. Your
soul is miserable. Linger no more (Lam. 5:16-21).

Why did Lot linger?

This is an important question. If we are to learn from Lot's
lingering and be warned by it, we need to know the cause
of it. To know the cause of a problem is the first step to
finding its cure. Maybe you have no fear of lingering. Let
me remind you of Lot's history. If you choose Lot's path,
you are sure to reap his character.

The Scriptures show us several things that led to Lot's
lingering. Let me mention two things.

First, he made the wrong choice early in life. Abram and
Lot had a dispute because of Lot's greed (Gen. 13:9-10).[2]
When they parted company, Lot chose the land near the
town of Sodom. The men of Sodom who would be his neighbours were wicked beyond all thought, but the pastures
were fertile and green. He chose by sight, not by faith. Like

Eve before and Achan after, he saw, he coveted and he took. He did not seek the counsel of the Lord. He looked only upon the things of time. He seems to have thought little of eternity. He was concerned about profit, but thought little of the glory of God, the welfare of his soul and the salvation of his household. There was nothing in Sodom to help Lot or his family towards heaven. There was no prophet to minister to his soul, no place where God was worshipped and no brethren to encourage him or for him to encourage. Lot made his choice solely upon the basis of worldly desires. The move towards Sodom just seemed most profitable.

Second, Lot mixed with godless, unbelieving men when there was no need for him to do so. He chose the men of Sodom for his companions. In the first instance, we are told that he pitched his tent towards Sodom. Then we see him living in Sodom. Perhaps he moved to Sodom to please his wife, perhaps to please his daughters, perhaps to please himself. We do not know. But one thing is certain — we never lack an excuse to do what we are determined to do.

This is the cause of Lot's lingering. He made the wrong choice early in life. He chose the companionship of the ungodly. When a child of God does these two things, we are sure to hear unfavourable reports concerning his soul. There is no more sure way to danger than to make the wrong choices early in life and to engage in companionship with ungodly men and women (2 Cor. 6:14 - 7:1).

'Remember Lot' is the warning Christ gives to all who desire to follow him. Beware of Lot's choices and the consequences of them, when choosing a companion, a career, when deciding where to live and raise your family, or when thinking about taking a better position.

We have no indication that Lot approved of the Sodomites, or that he ever participated in their wickedness. He loved the riches of Sodom. Yet, in order to have the riches

of Sodom, he was willing to spend his life among the Sodomites. What a pity! If you lay your head on the lap of the
world, you need not be surprised if you awake one day like
Samson and discover that your strength has gone, that the
Spirit of God has left you!

What was the result of Lot's behaviour?

What does it matter if Lot lingered in Sodom? After all, he
was saved, he was justified, he went to heaven when he
died. Let me show you the folly of such wicked reasoning.

Though a righteous man himself, Lot did no good among
the inhabitants of Sodom. He lived in Sodom for many years.
He had great opportunity to do much good. But he had no
influence upon the men of the city for good. No one there
had any respect for him. No one respects a man who
compromises himself, his principles and his God for gain.
Not one righteous person other than Lot himself could be
found in Sodom. None of his neighbours believed his testimony. None of his friends honoured his God. None of his
servants feared their master's God. In short, his life had no
influence for good; his words carried no weight; his faith
was not followed; his God was not honoured.

Lot did not help any of his family towards heaven. Not
one person in his household believed God. He brought no
honour to Christ, his God and Saviour, in his generation. I
cannot find one large-hearted, noble-minded, or self-
sacrificing thing he ever did in his entire life. When he
died, Lot left nothing behind that would indicate that he
ever knew God at all. If we did not have Peter's record, if all
we read was the account Moses gives of his life, we would
be forced to conclude that Lot was a lost man. We should
not be surprised that Lot's life turned out as it did. Worldly,

lingering souls are never useful instruments for good to others. They have no influence for good among men. They bring no honour to Christ while they live.

What should we learn from Lot?

Lot was a sad character, a frustration and a disappointment. But, if ever there was a man who stands before us in Holy Scripture as a picture of grace, that man is Lot. His life declares, *'Salvation is of the Lord!'* The only righteousness he had was the righteousness which God, by his grace, had given him. Grace imputed the righteousness of Christ to him. Grace imparted the righteousness of Christ to him. Grace preserved righteousness in him. Lot was delivered from divine judgement, not by his free will, but by God's free grace. Truly, the Lord knows how to deliver the godly out of temptation (2 Peter 2:9).

If we are God's children, we can be assured that he will have our hearts. He may break our hearts, but have them he will. He may bring us to earthly ruin, but he will have our hearts. He may take away all earthly comfort and joy, but he will have our hearts!

Linger no more (Eph. 5:14-18). For the glory of Christ, linger no more. If you would be useful to Christ, linger no more. Oh, let us return to our God now (Jer. 3:11-14,22). Life does not linger. Death does not linger. Judgement does not linger. Hell does not linger. Let us linger no more. 'It is high time to awake out of sleep: for now is our salvation nearer than when we believed. The night is far spent, the day is at hand: let us therefore cast off the works of darkness, and let us put on the armour of light' (Rom. 13:11-12). Linger no more!

24.

Sarah and Hagar

Genesis 21:9-10 and Galatians 4:21-31

'And Sarah saw the son of Hagar the Egyptian, which she had born unto Abraham, mocking. Wherefore she said unto Abraham, Cast out this bondwoman and her son: for the son of this bondwoman shall not be heir with my son, even with Isaac' (Gen. 21:9-10).

The Bible is not just a book about history. It is a book about Christ and the redemption of sinners by Christ. However, whenever the Bible deals with historical facts, it is always accurate in every detail. The historical facts revealed in Holy Scripture are given, not just to fill in the gaps, but to convey and illustrate the message of redemption by Christ. In that sense, all of the events recorded in the Old Testament may be interpreted allegorically. An allegory, or an allegorical interpretation of Scripture, is the use of historical facts and events to portray and teach spiritual, gospel truths.[1]

Creation is an historical fact. Yet it is also a picture of grace. The Flood and Noah's ark are historical facts. Yet they are also a picture of grace, a picture of our redemption and salvation in Christ. Bible stories are much more than examples of God's miraculous power. They are examples of God's merciful acts towards the sons of men. We now have before us one story in the Scriptures that is plainly declared to be an allegory. The story of Sarah and Hagar is a beautiful and instructive picture of the grace of God. The historical facts of this story are recorded in Genesis 21:1-14. The allegorical interpretation of those facts is found in Galatians 4:21-31.

The purpose of this allegory, as Paul uses it, is to show us the believer's complete and total freedom from the law. The allegory is about two women, Sarah and Hagar, and two sons, Ishmael and Isaac. Sarah represents the covenant of grace. Her son, Isaac, represents the children of promise, all who are born again by the promise and power of God's grace. Hagar represents the covenant of works. Her son, Ishmael, represents all who go about to establish their own righteousness by the works of the law and who will not submit to the righteousness of God which is in Christ Jesus. These are children of bondage who do not know God.

No two things in all the world are more diametrically opposed to each other as law and grace. Yet all men by nature attempt to mix the two together. The mixing of law and grace is the heretical assertion that salvation is both by our works and by God's free grace through the obedience and death of the Lord Jesus Christ. We must understand the difference between these two things. Any mixture of law and grace, any intermingling of the covenant of works with the covenant of grace is deadly. Those who mix law and grace teach a doctrine that is damning to the souls of men. As we have seen previously, we must distinguish be-tween what we do in order to obtain salvation and what another does in our place for salvation. Salvation is not by something we do at all, but by the doing and dying of the Lord Jesus Christ for us! G. S. Bishop states: 'This doctrine lies at the very heart of the gospel, and is so important that he who grasps and understands it, is a master in divinity, while he who does not properly distinguish here remains in doubt and perplexity and walks in darkness, knowing not at what he stumbles.'

It is the universal assertion of Holy Scripture that all true believers are totally free from the law (Rom. 6:14-15; 7:1-4; 8:1-4; 10:4; 1 Tim. 1:9-11). It is the purpose of God the Holy Spirit to show us that fact most emphatically in the book of Galatians (Gal. 1:6-9; 2:16,21; 3:13; 19-25; 5:1,4,12; 6:14).

Two covenants

The Holy Spirit tells us plainly that the covenants which Sarah and Hagar represent are diametrically opposed to each other. (Gal. 4:24-26). God Almighty deals with men upon the basis of a covenant. A covenant is a contract made between two or more parties in which certain promises are made in the anticipation of specified conditions being fulfilled. We see this illustrated in David's covenant with Jonathan (1 Sam. 20:11-17).

Understanding the nature of a covenant, we recognize that there could only be two possible covenants between God and man. First, a covenant of works, founded upon what man would need do for his salvation; or second, a covenant of grace, founded upon what God would do for man in order to save him — a covenant of law, or a covenant of grace.

Sarah's handmaid and servant, Hagar, represents the covenant of law, works and ceremonies, revealed and given to Israel by God through his servant Moses at Mount Sinai. In the law God says to man, 'Do this and live!' John Gill asserted that the Jews in the Mosaic age were 'in bondage to the moral law, which required perfect obedience of them, but gave them no strength to perform; showed them their sin and misery, but not their remedy; demanded a complete righteousness, but did not point out where it was to be had; it spoke not one word of peace and comfort, but all the reverse; it admitted of no repentance; it accused of sin, pronounced guilty on account of it, cursed, condemned, and threatened death for it, all which kept them in continual bondage.' Hagar represents the bondage of legalism.

Abraham's true wife, Sarah, represents God's eternal covenant of grace with Christ for the salvation of his elect. G. S. Bishop says, 'The covenant of works stood between God and Adam. Adam fell, and it now lies hopelessly broken. The covenant of grace stood between God and Christ. Christ has fulfilled it, and it stands established for ever!'

The covenant of works was written out in the law in stone at Sinai. However, it was the same covenant which Adam broke in the Garden. And it is the covenant (the law) which is written upon the hearts of all men by nature, a covenant which all men constantly break (Rom. 2:14-15). But, blessed be God, the covenant of grace cannot be broken!

The covenant of grace was made long before the covenant of works (Eph. 1:3-6; 2 Tim. 1:9-10). It was made from eternity and cannot be nullified by anything done in time (Gal. 3:16-17). The covenant of grace was made between God the Father, God the Son and God the Holy Spirit, and cannot be broken by man (Heb. 7:22; 13:20; John 17:2-3). It says, 'Do this, O Christ, and thy people shall live for ever!' (Ps. 2:8; 110:3; Isa. 53:10-12). It took into consideration the failures of God's elect and made promises of grace with respect to us, even in the teeth of our sins (Ps. 89:19-37; Jer. 31:31-34; 32:37-41). This is a covenant of pure, free, immutable grace, 'ordered in all things, and sure' (2 Sam. 23:5; Rom. 8:28-34; 2 Tim. 1:9-10). Sarah represents the covenant of grace.

Though Hagar bore the first son, Sarah had a prior claim
to all the inheritance, because she was Abraham's first wife.
Sarah told Abraham to cast Hagar and Ishmael out upon
the basis of her prior claim to him. And, though the covenant of works was revealed first, the covenant of grace has a
prior claim to God's elect and to the inheritance of life.
Long before we sinned, the covenant of grace was made.
Before we became sinners, Christ stood as our surety. Before
ever we needed atonement, Christ was the Lamb of sacrifice, slain from the foundation of the world (Rev. 13:8; 17:8;
1 Peter 1:18-21). Long before we were cursed by the law,
we were blessed with God's salvation in the covenant of
grace (Eph. 1:3-6; 2 Thess. 2:13-14; 2 Tim. 1:9).

It was never intended that Hagar should be Abraham's
wife, or that Ishmael should be the promised seed of grace.
Hagar was Sarah's handmaid — nothing more! The law,
which Hagar represents, was never given, or intended to
be a means of righteousness and salvation for anyone. No
one was ever saved by keeping the law. The law was only a
handmaid to grace. The only purpose of the law is to point
men to Christ (Gal. 3:21-29). 'Christ is the end of the law
for righteousness to every one that believeth' (Rom. 10:4).
When the Word of God asserts that Christ is the end of the
law for righteousness, the Spirit of God means us to understand the following:

1. Christ is the end of the law since he is the object of it.
2. Christ is the end of the law, as he is the fulfilment of
its purpose, pictures and requirements.
3. Christ is the end of the law as he is the conclusion of it.
4. Christ is the end of the law for righteousness, both for
justification and for sanctification. We do not go to
Calvary for justification and then run back to Sinai for

sanctification. Both justification and sanctification are found in Christ (1 Cor. 1:30).

5. Christ is the end of the law in the sense that death is the end of all covenants (Rom. 7:1-4).

The law identifies sin and condemns men for sin; but it can never remove sin, justify the sinner, or sanctify a believer. The law is good, if a man uses it lawfully (1 Tim. 1:9-11); but when it is put in the place of grace, it must be cast out, like Hagar and Ishmael. The law is holy, just and good; but when it is made to be a means of winning, keeping, or improving God's favour, it is used unlawfully.

Two systems of religion

Sarah and Hagar also represent two systems of religion: grace and works (Gal. 4:25-27). There are only two religions in this world: one of grace and the other of works. These two systems mutually annihilate each other. If a person is saved in any way, either fully or in part, by his own works, then he is not saved by God's grace. If we are saved by God's grace, then we are not saved, fully or in part, by any works of our own (Rom. 11:6). There is no in-between ground where grace and works live together. Read Galatians 5:1-4. If we do anything by which we hope to gain God's favour, keep God's favour, or improve our standing in God's favour, we have missed Christ altogether.

All churches, religions, and systems of doctrine which teach salvation by the works of the law are represented by Hagar. Any teaching which says we are justified, sanctified, preserved, and gain favour with God, or inherit heavenly glory upon the basis of our own works of obedience to

God is legalism. That is contrary to Christ and damning to the souls of men. That is what Galatians. 5:1-4 declares.

Now, look at what Paul tells us about Hagar, the religion of the world, the religion of works (Gal. 4:25). She is in Arabia, outside the land of promise. She is in bondage; the law can give nothing but bondage. There is no liberty to be found at Sinai. Her children are all still in bondage. Those who live under the tyranny of the law are still wearing the iron shackles of slavery and imprisonment. They are in bondage to sin. They are still the captives of Satan. They are under the curse of the law. They are still under the sentence of death. There is nothing else to be found in the house of bondage.

Sarah represents that church, that religion, that system of doctrine which declares salvation by grace without the deeds of the law (Gal. 4:26-27). The kingdom of God is a kingdom of grace. The gospel of God is the gospel of grace. And the church of God is the true Jerusalem, the city of grace and peace. The gospel of grace is from above. The people of God are free (Rom. 6:14-15). The church of God is the mother of all who believe. The church of God, the kingdom of grace, will be triumphant and glorious in the end (Gal. 4:27; Isa. 54:1).

Hagar was never free; and Sarah was never a slave. Ishmael, being the son of a slave, could never be a free man. Isaac, being the son of a free woman, could never be a slave. All who seek salvation by their own works are for ever in bondage, and must be cast out into outer darkness. All who trust Christ alone, being saved by pure, free grace, abide in the house of grace for ever, for ever free, for ever heirs of grace. When Isaac was born, Ishmael had to go. Hagar and her son were driven out of Abraham's house, but not Sarah. So, too, as soon as the gospel of grace is revealed, the covenant of works is driven away (Heb. 10:1-10).

Two sons

The Holy Spirit uses the two sons, Ishmael and Isaac, to represent lost, religious legalists and sinners saved by the grace of God (Gal. 4:28-31). Ishmael was born after the flesh. Isaac was born after the Spirit. Legalism, all legal religion, is of the flesh, fleshly. Grace is of the Spirit, spiritual. Ishmael was the child of works, the child of unbelief. Isaac was the child of promise, born supernaturally, by a work of God. Ishmael mocked and persecuted Isaac. Ishmael was cursed; Isaac was blessed.

There is no room for legalism in the house of grace. 'We are not under the law, but under grace.' We are not justified by the law, but by grace (Rom. 3:19-24). We are not sanctified by the law, but by grace (Gal. 3:1-3). We are not ruled by the law, but by grace (Titus 2:11-14). We are not motivated by the law, but by grace (2 Cor. 5:14). The difference between the believer and the legalist is not conduct, but motive. We shall not be glorified by the law, but by grace (Jude 24-25).

Why are the Scriptures so dogmatic about this matter of the believer's freedom from the law? Legalism would rob Christ of the glory of his grace. It would rob the believer of the joy of faith, the joy of assurance and the joy of all service to Christ. It would rob the world of the hope of salvation. If salvation depends upon something done by man, then all men must for ever perish without hope. Blessed be God, that is not the case. 'Salvation is of the LORD!' 'By grace are ye saved!' 'So then it is not of him that willeth, nor of him that runneth, but of God that showeth mercy!'

'Do we then make void the law through faith? God forbid: yea, we establish the law' (Rom. 3:31). The only way any sinful man can honour the law is by faith in Christ. Christ fulfilled the law in the place of his people. Believing on him, we fulfil the law by faith.

25.

The sacrifice of Isaac

Genesis 22:1-18

'And he said, Take now thy son, thine only son Isaac, whom thou lovest, and get thee into the land of Moriah; and offer him there for a burnt offering upon one of the mountains which I will tell thee of' (Gen. 22:2).

In Hebrews 5:8 we read of our Saviour, the Lord Jesus Christ, that 'though he were a Son, yet learned he obedience by the things which he suffered.' And what was true of our Redeemer, when he walked upon this earth as a man, is true of us. If we are the children of God, as long as we live in this body of flesh, we shall be required to learn obedience. We learn obedience by the things which we suffer at the hand of God's wise and good providence.

The life of the believer is a series of trials, by which his faith is tested, proved and strengthened. Christian character is developed by discipline, and God will develop the character of his saints. It appears that frequently there is one great trial of faith, for which all other trials seem to be preparatory. Certainly, that was the case with Abraham and the great trial of his faith revealed in Genesis 22.

This is one of the great chapters of the Bible. Here, for the first time, God shows us, in a vivid picture, the necessity of a human sacrifice for the ransom of our souls. Because it was a man who brought sin into the world, sin must be removed by a man. Because man had sinned, a man must suffer the wrath of God and die. The blood of bulls and goats could never take away sin. But the Man, Christ Jesus, 'after he had offered one sacrifice for sins for ever, sat down on the right hand of God... For by one offering he hath perfected for ever them that are sanctified' (Heb. 10:4,12,14).

Genesis 22 records Abraham's greatest trial and the greatest revelation of the gospel which God made to Abraham. I am sure our Lord was referring to this chapter when he said, 'Your father Abraham rejoiced to see my day: and he saw it, and was glad' (John 8:56). This chapter is full of Christ and full of redemption. Someone suggested, 'It could rightly be called "The Gospel of Moriah"'. Many, with good reason, believe that Mount Moriah and Mount Calvary were the same place.

Everything in this chapter portrays God's great sacrifice of his dear Son, the Lord Jesus Christ, in the place of sinners. We have examples of great faith in Abraham and in Isaac. God's great purpose of grace in Christ is displayed in Abraham's confident declaration, 'God will provide himself a lamb,' and in his calling the name of the place 'Jehovah-jireh'. However, the dominant theme of the chapter is the picture of substitutionary redemption and God's great provision for his people in Christ. As the ram caught in the thicket was sacrificed in Isaac's place, and God provided in that ram everything Isaac needed, so Christ died in the place of his people, and God has given his elect all they need for time and eternity in Christ (Eph. 1:3).

The time

First of all, we should notice the time of this trial: 'And it came to pass after these things' (v. 1). After all the other trials, hardships, heartaches, and difficulties he had already endured, perhaps Abraham had begun to think, 'At last, the storms are over.' He had left his home and family, buried his father, endured family strife, waited twenty-five years for God to fulfil his promise in giving him a son, had been required to cast his son, Ishmael, out of his house, and much more.

Abraham must have thought to himself, after all he had been through, 'Now the worst is over. Now I shall live in peace. Ishmael is gone. Hagar is gone. Lot is gone. I have just Sarah and Isaac. All is well.' But it was not so. 'It came to pass after these things that God did tempt Abraham.' Abraham had been tested again and again. But now the Lord seems to say, 'My son, give me thine heart' (Prov. 23:26).

The Tempter

The one who brought this trial upon Abraham was the Lord his God: 'God did tempt Abraham' (v. 1). Here the word tempt means 'to try,' 'to test,' or 'to prove' (James 1:2,3,12). God brought this trial upon Abraham, not because he was angry with him, but because he loved him. The purpose of the trial was to prove to Abraham the reality of his faith and to reveal to him the glory of God's grace in Christ. When the trial was over, Abraham knew himself better than he did before; and he knew Christ better than he did before.

All through his life, God had been preparing Abraham for this event. Now, 'it came to pass after these things'. Our great, sovereign God does all things 'in due time' (Rom. 5:6), '[in] the fulness of time' (Gal. 4:4). 'After these things' — after the fall, the flood, the exodus, the tabernacle, the law, the prophets, the kings, and the priests had all run their course, it pleased God to fulfil every prophecy, pattern and promise of Holy Scripture by the sacrifice of his only begotten Son. What came before were preparatory events, picturing and pointing to the hour when Christ would die (Acts 10:43; Luke 24:27,44-46).

God's providence is always on time: 'All things are of God' (2 Cor. 5:18). God does all things well. If we learn these three things, we shall learn to live in peace:

1. Our trials always come from our heavenly Father.
2. Our trials are brought upon us by God to prove and improve our faith.
3. Our trials reveal Christ and make him more precious.

Read verse 2 and try to grasp something of the magnitude of this great trial, which God's friend and faithful servant was called upon to endure. 'And he said, Take now thy son, thine only son Isaac, whom thou lovest, and get thee into the land of Moriah; and offer him there for a burnt offering upon one of the mountains which I will tell thee of.'

The words of this verse, taken one by one, reveal the greatness of Abraham's sacrifice, the love behind it and the agony he endured through it. Can you imagine Abraham's grief when he received this command? Who can enter into the sorrow he suffered as he contemplated the death of his son by his own hand? What great love he must have had for God to sacrifice willingly his darling Isaac? No mere man ever made such a supreme sacrifice to God.

Every word in this verse must have been like a sword in his heart! Yet there is a greater Sacrifice than that of Abraham. Here the Lord God himself is telling us what he has done for us. 'Take now thy son' — the Lord Jesus Christ, whom God sacrificed for us, is himself the Son of God. 'Thine only son' — our Saviour, whom God gave for the ransom of our souls, is God's 'only begotten Son' (John 3:16). 'Isaac' — Isaac means 'laughter', or 'delight.' And Christ is the one, the only one, in whom God is well pleased. 'Whom thou lovest' — God said, 'This is my beloved Son.' Yet he sacrificed his darling for us, the very chief of sinners! 'And offer him ... for a burnt offering' — not just a sacrifice, 'a burnt offering!' The Lord Jesus Christ is our burnt offering, our sin-offering, sacrificed for us by the hand of God, according to the will of God (Isa. 53:10; Heb. 10:9-10). 'Thanks be unto God for his unspeakable gift!' (2 Cor. 9:15).

Try to imagine the difficulties Abraham had to overcome to obey God's command. There were many things he might have put forward as reasons for disobedience; but he 'conferred not with flesh and blood'. God called Abraham to sacrifice his son, but gave him no reason for requiring such a sacrifice. All Abraham had was God's command. The commandment was contrary to nature, reason and love; but it was crystal clear. This commandment appeared to be contrary to the promise of God; but it came from God who made the promise. If Abraham obeyed God, as he knew he must, he would be sure to suffer much ridicule, persecution and reproach for it. What would he tell Sarah? What would he say to the Egyptians?

Matthew Henry correctly informs us that 'God's commands must not be disputed, but obeyed. We must not consult with flesh and blood about them (Gal. 1:15-16), but with a gracious obstinacy persist in our obedience to them.' 'Whatsoever he saith unto you, do it!' (John 2:5).

When we read verses 3-10, we should turn our thoughts away from Abraham. This is a picture of God's whole purpose of grace and his work of redemption by the sacrifice of Christ. 'Abraham rose up early in the morning,' and prepared everything with great care (vv. 3-4).

He had three long days to think about what must be done. As they journeyed those days and slept through those nights, the burden and sacrifice constantly lay upon his heart. But our heavenly Father planned, purposed and ordained the sacrifice of his Son for us, not three days, nor three thousand days, but from eternity, before ever the world was made (Rev. 13:8; Eph. 1:3-4). And he never thought about altering his purpose!

Abraham carefully prepared everything for the sacrifice. And our great God carefully prepared everything for the sacrifice of his darling Son for us (Acts 2:23; 4:27-28). '[Abraham] saw the place afar off.' So, from everlasting, the Lord God set his heart and mind upon the place of sacrifice, Mount Calvary.

Abraham and Isaac went to the mountain of sacrifice together, but alone (vv. 5-8). Redemption was the work of God alone, a transaction between God the Father and God the Son. 'God was in Christ, reconciling the world unto himself' (2 Cor. 5:19). Twelve went with the Son of God to the Passover. Eleven went with him to the garden. Three went with him to pray. But when he went to the cross, our Saviour was alone (Heb. 1:3). The wood was laid upon Isaac's back. Christ carried his cross. The instruments of death were in the Father's hands.

In verse 7, Isaac asked, 'Where is the Lamb for a burnt offering?' He knew that God could not be worshipped without a blood sacrifice (Exod. 12:13; Lev. 17:11; Heb. 9:22). His father answered, 'God will provide himself a lamb for a burnt offering' (v. 8). This is clearly a prophecy of Christ, the Lamb of God. Christ is the sacrifice for God. He is the sacrifice from God. God requires only what he gives; and he will always accept that which he has given. Jesus Christ is described here as that sacrifice who is God!

At last, Abraham and Isaac came to the place of sacrifice (vv. 9-10). Abraham built the altar and laid the wood upon it. He bound his son and laid him on the altar. Isaac willingly submitted to his father's will. Abraham stretched forth

his hand to kill his Son. No explanation is needed. This is
a picture of our great Saviour, the Lord Jesus Christ. He
was delivered to death by the will of God, and put to death
as our substitute by the hand of divine justice (Acts 2:23;
Isa. 53:8-10; Zech. 13:7). Yet he freely volunteered to be
our sin-atoning sacrifice (John 10:17-18; Heb. 10:5-14;
1 Peter 2:24).

Once Abraham's faith was proved, God intervened to
save Isaac, and the type changes. Verses 11-13 reveal the
beautiful, blessed picture of substitutionary redemption.
When God spoke, Abraham looked. When he looked, he
saw a ram caught in the thicket, which he offered 'in the
stead of his Son!' (2 Cor. 5:21). That ram represents Christ.

'Abraham called the name of that place, Jehovah-jireh'
(v. 14). That name might be properly translated in three
ways. Each translation reveals blessed, soul-cheering, gospel
truths by which the believer's heart is encouraged and comforted throughout his earthly pilgrimage. Jehovah-jireh
means 'The Lord will see.' He sees all our needs. In particular, he sees our need for righteousness and atonement. It
also means 'The Lord will provide.' He who is our God provides all that we need in his dear Son, the Lord Jesus Christ,
who is made by God wisdom, righteousness, sanctification
and redemption for us (1 Cor. 1:30). And it means 'The Lord
will be seen'. In the provision he makes for his people, in
the substitutionary sacrifice of his dear Son for the salvation
of his people, the Lord God reveals the glory of his great
being (2 Cor. 4:4-6; Rom. 3:24-26; Ps. 108:6; Eph. 2:7).

When the work had been done, Isaac, the object of his
father's love, was exalted (vv. 15-18). He was promised a
great posterity: 'I will multiply thy seed!' He was made to
be a great ruler: '...[possessing] the gate of his enemies.' He
became the source of universal blessedness. In all these
things, Isaac portrays that greatness, glory and exaltation

given to our Lord Jesus Christ as our Mediator, when he had finished his work of redemption upon the earth and put away the sins of his people (Phil. 2:9-11; Heb. 10:10-14; John 17:2; Ps. 2:8; Eph. 1:3).

In the light of these things, as we consider what the Lord God has done for chosen sinners in the sacrifice of Christ for the ransom of our souls, let us take to heart the following three questions:

1. What trial is too great for me to endure for him, who endured such great agony for me?
2. What sacrifice is too costly for me, a sinner redeemed by the precious blood of Christ,to make for my Saviour?
3. What work is too demeaning or too demanding for one, who has been purchased by a Saviour so demeaned in obedience which demanded his death as my substitute under the wrath of God?

26.

Jehovah-jireh

Genesis 22:14

'And Abraham called the name of that place Jehovah-jireh: as it is said to this day, In the mount of the LORD it shall be seen' (Gen. 22:14).

Pay no attention to those who teach that it is never God's will for his children to suffer, or that all suffering is an indication of God's displeasure. As we saw in the previous chapter, Genesis 22 writes this message in bold letters: true faith must be proved by trials. Here the Holy Spirit has recorded Abraham's most severe trial. Abraham was the friend of God. But, in God's wise and good providence, Abraham was called upon to endure the most heart-rending trial any man ever had to face in this world, other than the Man of Sorrows. Faith must be proved; and it is proved only when it is put to the test.

However, the primary thing to be seen in this chapter is not Abraham's trial, but God's provision for Abraham and his son upon the mount. The Lord God provided a ram as a substitute to die in the place of Isaac. There Abraham raised up an everlasting memorial to his God. It has already been mentioned that the name by which God revealed himself to Abraham, 'Jehovah-jireh,' may be translated in three ways: 'The LORD will see,' or 'The LORD will provide,' or 'The LORD will be seen.' However we translate this one of God's names, Jehovah-jireh expresses the idea of God seeing and being seen. For God, to see is to provide. We sometimes say, 'I shall see to it,' when we mean, 'I shall take care of it,' or 'I shall provide for it.' That is the meaning here.

The truth contained in the name, Jehovah-jireh, ruled Abraham's heart even before he uttered it and established it as a memorial in the place where God provided a substitute for Isaac. It was faith in Jehovah-jireh that sustained the old patriarch's heart throughout this ordeal. Faith in Jehovah-jireh, the Lord who will provide, enabled Abraham to render the prompt and unswerving obedience that is recorded in this chapter. Many things must have crossed Abraham's mind which could have caused him to disobey his God. As he took that painful journey to Moriah, he must have had many perplexing questions about Sarah, his relationship with her, the promises of God that were bound up in Isaac, Isaac himself, and the response of his friends and neighbours to this act of slaying his son in the name of God. Yet the old man strengthened his heart, as he went up to Moriah. Determined to obey God, regardless of cost or consequence, Abraham said to himself, 'The Lord will see and the Lord will provide. God will not break his promise. He will not change his word. Perhaps he will raise Isaac from the dead. But even if he is not pleased to do so, by one means or another, my God will justify my obedience and vindicate his command. His name is Jehovah-jireh.' This name of God, Jehovah-jireh, silenced every unbelieving thought and objection of human reasoning.

Do not miss the practical application of this to your own heart. If you believe God, if you follow the Lord's commands, he will see to it that you are not ashamed or confounded (Rom. 10:11). If you come into great need by following his command, the Lord will see to it that you lose

nothing by your obedience. If difficulties rise like mountains before you, so that your way seems to be completely
blocked up, your God will see to it that the way is cleared.
Walk in the way of obedience and, as you walk, every obs-
tacle will fall before you: 'Whatsoever he saith unto you,
do it' (John 2:5). Confer not with flesh and blood, and the
Lord will make a way for you to do his will (Gal. 1:16). If
we are willing to walk in the way of faith and obedience,
the Lord will see us through. He will see to our way, if we
dare to walk in his way (Prov. 3:5-6).

The Lord will see and the Lord will provide. We should
not be surprised to find Abraham declaring this truth and
attaching it to the spot that was to be famous for ever. His
whole heart was saturated with it. His soul was sustained
by it. His trial taught him more of his God than he knew
before, or could have known in any other way. In fact, it
gave him a new name for his God. And Abraham's grateful
heart desired to keep this as a memorial to all future generations, to encourage all who believe God to obey his will
and persevere in his ways. Abraham says to all, 'The name
of our God is *Jehovah-jireh*, the Lord will see and the Lord
will provide.'

This was not the first time Abraham had used such language in speaking of God. In verse 14, 'Abraham called the
name of that place Jehovah-jireh,' because he had seen it to
be the truth. This was something he had experienced for
himself. The ram caught in the thicket had been provided
as a substitute for Isaac. Not only had the Lord seen, but
according to the promise made to Abraham's faith, the Lord
had provided as well. Even before he knew how this trial
would end, Abraham confidently believed God, trusting
him to provide what was needed (Rom 4:20). In verse 7,
Isaac said, 'Behold the fire and the wood: but where is the
lamb for a burnt offering?' Abraham answered with

confident faith in his God, 'My son, God will provide!' And in due time, God did provide. In verse 14, Abraham honoured God, repeating the words he had spoken to his son, with only one change. Instead of using the ordinary name for God, he used his special covenant name, Jehovah. He said, 'Jehovah will provide.'

As these words were spoken prophetically by Abraham concerning Isaac and his substitute, they were also a direct prophecy of our Lord Jesus Christ, the Substitute whom God has provided for sinners. By the Spirit of prophecy, he was saying to us, 'As God provided a substitute for Isaac, so he will provide a substitute for all his covenant people in whom the Lord will be seen.' That substitute is the Lord Jesus Christ, the Lamb of God. He was also saying, 'As God provided for him in his time of extremity, so he will provide for all who trust him.' The God of Abraham lives today! He is the same today as he was in Abraham's day. In the hour of Abraham's great need, when there seemed to be no possible way of escape, the Lord appeared for him and was seen on the Mount. So it will be with all the children of Abraham. We shall be tried and tested, but in the hour of our utmost need, our God will see us. In seeing our need, he will make provision for it; and he will be seen in the provision he makes.

The name of our God is Jehovah-jireh. He is worthy of absolute trust and confidence. The Lord, Jehovah, is the one who preserves us and provides for us. Let this truth take root in our hearts. God's provision for Abraham and Isaac was a type of the far greater provision of his grace, by which all believing sinners are delivered from sin and death. God's provision for us in Christ, by his death at Mount Calvary, has given us the guarantee that all our needs, both physical and spiritual, will be provided by him for both time and eternity. A careful examination of the three translations of this name, Jehovah-jireh, by which God revealed himself to Abraham will clearly demonstrate that this name reveals God's glorious saving purpose towards his people.

The LORD will see

The first meaning of Jehovah-jireh is 'The LORD will see. God constantly sees the needs of his children and provides for them. The provision of the ram was the type, a significant type, which Abraham's saw when he called the name of the place Jehovah-jireh. Our Lord tells us that 'Abraham rejoiced to see my day: and he saw it, and was glad' (John 8:56). Surely, if ever Abraham saw Christ's day and rejoiced because of it, it was at that moment when the Lord provided a substitute for Isaac. Whether he understood the full meaning of what he said is not important. He spoke by the inspiration of the Holy Spirit, not for himself, but for us. (2 Tim. 3:16-17; Rom. 15:4; 1 Cor. 10:11).

The teaching is clear. In the gift of his Son, the Lord Jesus Christ, God made full provision for all the needs of his people. The Lord graciously beheld the needs of his sinful people long before they were even aware that they had any needs before him. The law of God demanded our punishment (Gal. 3:10). The gates of hell were opened wide, ready to swallow us up into perdition. We were all perishing, dead spiritually and condemned to die eternally. But our great and merciful God beheld our need and intervened to save us by his free grace (Eph. 2:5-9; Ezek. 16:6-8).

Just when Isaac was in imminent danger of death, the Lord stepped in to deliver him. The knife was lifted up by the resolute hand. Isaac was but a second from death, when the angelic voice was heard, saying, 'Lay not thine hand

upon the lad' (v. 12). God provided when the need was press-
ing. So it was with us. When God saw that the world had
come into a state of great danger and misery, he sent forth
his Son, born of a woman, born under the law, to redeem
those that were under the law. God sent his Son into the
world that the world through him might be saved (John
3:17). 'In due time Christ died for the ungodly' (Rom. 5:6).
'When the fulness of time was come, God sent forth his
Son' (Gal. 4:4).

The same thing is true in the experience of grace in conversion. It is not until men and women feel themselves lying
at hell's door, with the anguish of their guilt and sin crushing them down into eternal ruin, that God the Holy Spirit
reveals Christ, the sinner's substitute. No man will ever be
saved until he is lost. No one will ever be clothed until he
is stripped. No one will ever be filled until he is empty.
Christ comes *only* to those who need him. But he *always*
comes to those who need him.

The LORD will provide

Secondly, Jehovah-jireh means 'the LORD will provide'. If
God sees our need, his provision is sure. Jehovah-jireh was
Abraham's testimony to the goodness and grace of God in
providing a ram to take the place of his son, Isaac, upon the
altar of sacrifice. This is the testimony of every sinner who
sees Christ, as his substitute, sacrificed upon the altar of
divine justice at Mount Calvary.

God's provision upon the Mount was voluntary and free.
And the provision God displayed in the fulness of time at
Calvary, when he gave his Son to die in the place of sinners,
was also voluntary and free. Christ died for us freely —
unsought, undesired and unwanted by us. God sent his Son

to redeem us and Christ came to redeem us by his death, simply because he loved us (John 10:15-18; 1 John 3:16; 4:9-10).

The provision God makes is always the very thing needed — 'a ram!' Here is a substitute to take Isaac's place. This is just what was needed, a bloody sacrifice to die in the place of Isaac upon the altar. God knew what we needed, and only he could provide the needed Sacrifice. We needed a substitute; and Christ our passover was sacrificed for us (1 Cor. 5:8; 2 Cor. 5:21).

This provision for our need was made by God himself. Where will a redemption be found by which it will be possible for the vast multitude of God's elect to be effactually redeemed from death and hell? Such a ransom could only be found by God himself, and he could find it only in himself. Since no one else could provide a ransom for our souls, God provided it and said, 'Deliver [them] from going down to the pit: I have found a ransom' (Job 33:24).

One other thing that must be noted is this: God's provision is gloriously effective. Isaac did not die! Like the ram that was slain for Isaac, our Lord Jesus Christ is a burnt offering, acceptable and well pleasing to God on our behalf (Eph. 5:2). By his one sacrifice, Christ put away our sins. Therefore God's elect, for whom he was slain, cannot die (Rom. 8:1).

The LORD will be seen

Thirdly, Jehovah-jireh means 'the LORD will be seen'. He will be seen in the mount of sacrifice. He will be seen in the gospel of Christ, our crucified Saviour. Go often to Calvary, for there the Lord will be seen. He will be seen in the mount of trial. Your trials may seem severe, but do not despair. In your greatest extremity, the Lord will be seen. He will be seen in Mount Zion. Look up to heaven, there the Lord will be seen in the person of Jesus Christ our substitute. Would you know God? Then study Christ. Learn of him. Know him.

Soon all who are born of God, all who believe, all for whom the Son of God died upon the cursed tree, will see him as he is, and will be seen with him (Heb. 9:28). Jehovah-jireh will see us with satisfaction; and we shall see him with satisfaction. Jehovah-jireh will provide us with glory; and we shall provide him with pleasure. Jehovah-jireh will be seen with us; and we shall be seen with him. The gift of the Lord Jesus Christ as our substitute is a provision that secures all other provisions. 'He that spared not his own Son, but delivered him up for us all, how shall he not with him also freely give us all things?' He will give us all things in providence. He will give us all things promised in the covenant. He will give us all things in heaven.

27.

Isaac

Genesis 25:5

'And Abraham gave all that he had unto Isaac' (Gen. 25:5).

Isaac is presented to us in the Scriptures both as a type of Christ and as a type of the believer in this world. In Genesis 22, Isaac represents Christ in yielding himself up as a voluntary sacrifice to God upon the altar. He also represents God's elect for whom the Lord God provided a Lamb of sacrifice, even his own dear Son, the Lord Jesus Christ, as a substitute to die in our place under the wrath of God.

In Genesis 24, Isaac is a picture of Christ for whom an appointed bride is sought. Christ is our bridegroom. God's elect people are his bride, the church, sought out from among men by the preaching of the gospel. Isaac is also a picture of a believer waiting upon God to give him his chosen bride, the life-long companion of God's choice, from among his own people.

Again, in Genesis 25, Isaac stands before us as a type both of Christ and the believer: 'And Abraham gave all that he had unto Isaac' (Gen. 25:5). Without question, this text speaks of Abraham's greater Son, the Lord Jesus Christ, 'whom [God] hath appointed heir of all things' (Heb. 1:2). Yet the text also speaks of all who are the sons of God by electing love, adopting grace and saving faith. Like Isaac, God's elect are possessors of all the wealth and privileges of the Father's house (Rom. 8:17,21). As Isaac represents our sonship and our privileges as the heirs of God, so he also represents our heavenly calling (Phil. 3:20).

Canaan represents both the believer's life of faith in this world and the heavenly glory and rest that awaits him. Isaac is never seen anywhere except in the land of Canaan. Abraham, Jacob and Joseph all left the land, at least for a season; but Isaac never did. Every time you see Isaac, he is in the land of Canaan. So, too, the believer is always in the grace of God, the land of rest. We often fall; but the believer never leaves the land of grace and is never expelled from it. 'Our conversation is in heaven.' God's elect are a people who have been called with a heavenly calling, and they live accordingly.

Yet, as we have seen, the believer's life is a life of trial, conflict and struggle. Isaac illustrates that too. Though he lived in the land of Canaan, like us, Isaac had a war to wage (Eph. 6:12) against the world, the flesh and the devil. That war is recorded in Genesis 26. Isaac was pre-eminently the man of the well. His life revolved around five wells. These five wells are specifically named because they stand as types of the experiences of every believer in this world. Here are five wells from which all believers drink:

1. The well called 'Lahairoi' (Gen. 24:62) means 'The living one who sees me'. What joy and comfort we have in the midst of our trials, when we realize that he who is the living God has his eye upon us at all times!

2. Esek (Gen. 26:20) means 'strife'. In this world, every child of God lives in unceasing strife, strife from the world without and from his own flesh within.

3. Sitnah (Gen. 26:21) means 'hatred'. It may well represent the world's hatred for Christ and his people.

4. Rehoboth (Gen. 26:22) means 'spaciousness and abundance'. 'Where sin abounded, grace did much more abound.'

5. Shebah (Gen. 26:33) means 'good fortune'. All things are ours in Christ, and all things work together for our good in him and by him.

The first thing we are told about Isaac, after his redemption which stands as a type, is this: 'Isaac came from the way of the well Lahairoi' (Gen. 24:62). This well is intended to draw our attention to God the Holy Spirit and his gracious operations in the hearts of men (John 7:37-39). In God's works of grace, election is followed by predestination, predestination is followed by redemption, and redemption is followed by regeneration (Gal. 3:13-14). Redemption is portrayed in Isaac on Mount Moriah. The sure result of redemption is regeneration, the washing of the Holy Spirit. In the Holy Scriptures, the Holy Spirit is symbolized by a dove, by oil and by water. As Isaac's well was 'a well of springing water' (Gen. 26:19), 'living water,' so the Holy Spirit springs up in the hearts of God's elect as a well of living water.

As water is necessary for all natural life, so the 'living water', the Spirit of God operating through the Word, is necessary for our spiritual life. Without water any plant will wither and die, even if it has the best food packed around its roots. So, too, without the operations of God the Holy Spirit in our hearts, we would wither and die. We must have the food of gospel doctrine. But doctrine alone is not enough. We must have the living Spirit of Christ. Like Isaac, God's saints are people of the well, people who live and walk in the Spirit (Rom. 8:5-17). Isaac's experiences provide us with some very important lessons about ourselves, about the life of faith and about the grace of God.

The blessedness of divine worship

The first well with which Isaac was associated was Lahairoi — 'the well of the living one who sees me' (Gen. 24:62; 25:11). That well represents the unfailing care of our ever-living, ever-present God. At the well Lahairoi, Isaac dwelt in the presence of God!

Where can we find such a well today? Where is 'the living one who sees me' to be found? The well of Lahairoi is the house of God, where his Word is opened, his ordinances are kept, his praises are sung and his presence is promised.

The first thing we see in the life of Isaac is the blessedness of worshipping the living God. As long as Isaac dwelt at Lahairoi, all was well. His trouble did not begin until he left the place of God's manifest presence, Lahairoi. The same is true of us (Heb. 10:25). The assembled church of God is the house and temple of God (1 Cor. 3:16-17; 1 Tim. 3:15-16). God promises his presence in his house, where Christ is found at the mercy-seat, (Matt. 18:20; Exod. 25:22). The church of God is the believer's home. It is the place of refreshing, refuge, safety and instruction (Eph. 4:11-16).

Those who engage in religious rituals make too much of mere attendance at the house of God. They make worship idolatry. However, most people make far too little of public worship. The local church (a true, gospel church) is the place from which God sends out his Word, and the place where he pours out his blessings upon his people. I am sure that Isaac often wished he had never left Lahairoi, 'the well of the living one who sees me'; but he did.

The weakness of the flesh

When a time of famine came, Isaac departed from Lahairoi and went down to the land of the Philistines in Gerar (Gen. 26:1). Here is a sad, but common picture. When Isaac was in a difficult situation, instead of continuing in the presence of God at Lahairoi, instead of abiding in the worship of God, he worked out a scheme to improve his circumstances; but his cunning cost him dearly.

Obviously, Isaac was on his way down to Egypt; but God intervened and stopped him (Gen. 26:2). God's saints in this world (all of them!) are sinners still, sinners kept and preserved by the power and grace of God in Christ (1 Peter 1:5). Verses 3-5 show us this. God's blessings of grace do not depend upon our obedience. Our obedience depends upon God's blessings of grace.

The consequence of unbelief

Next, we read, 'And Isaac dwelt in Gerar' (v. 6). Gerar was the borderland, midway between Canaan and Egypt. God told Isaac to 'sojourn in this land;' but Isaac dwelt there for 'a long time' (v. 8). In Gerar, Isaac is a believer who has lost the blessed joy of communion with God by his unbelief. This is ever the consequence of unbelief. Unbelief is the cause of disobedience to God; and disobedience breaks communion. Unbelief caused Isaac to leave Lahairoi. It caused him to dwell in Gerar, and to lie to his neighbours (compare. Gen. 20:1-2 and 26:7)[1]. Horrible as Isaac's actions were, when we consider what he was prepared to do, we have to see that what Isaac was, we are. There is nothing we shall not do if God leaves us to ourselves, even for a moment.

The faithfulness of God

Let saved sinners ever rejoice and give thanks to God for his great faithfulness (vv. 12-14). Those who do not understand the character of God and the sovereignty of his grace have a very difficult time understanding these verses. They say, 'How could God bless Isaac so, when he was behaving in such a manner?'

The blessings of God upon Isaac were unconditional, covenant blessings (Gen. 22:17-18; 26:3-5; Eph. 1:3-7). 'The gifts and calling of God are without repentance' (Rom. 11:29). Our God rules and overrules all things, sovereignly making all things work together for the good of his elect, even our miserable failures (Rom. 8:28). God is faithful (Lam. 3:26; 2 Tim. 2:13; Heb. 10:23). Because Isaac would not leave Gerar, God arranged to have him cast out of the land (v. 16). When Isaac was cast out into a dry valley, God sweetly forced him to dig again the wells of water which he had dug with his father Abraham (vv. 17-19). When God's providence appeared to turn against him, it was working for him, bringing him again to the 'wells of living water'!

The life of faith

In verses 19-22, we are taught what it is to live by faith. Instead of standing up for his rights and contending for himself against his enemies, Isaac chose the path of peace, trusting God to provide for him. True faith makes men and women content and peaceful in the midst of difficulty (1 Peter 2:19-20). Nothing was at stake but water, and he could easily get more. It was not God's truth, his glory, or the welfare of his people that were at stake. The only thing at stake here was water. It was not worth needless aggravation.

The restoration of grace

God brought Isaac to Beersheba, 'the well of good fortune'
(vv. 23-25, 32-33). Beersheba was also 'the well of the oath'.
Look what happened when Isaac returned to the place of
his oath and allegiance to God. He found good fortune
indeed. On the very night that Isaac returned to Beersheba,
'the LORD appeared unto him' (v. 24). There Isaac built an
altar and called upon the name of the Lord. He came back
to the house of God, the place of worship, and the place of
sacrifice (v. 25). There, at Beersheba, he found water — life
refreshing, cleansing, reviving, soul-cheering water (v. 32).
Isaac pitched his tent at Beersheba, to dwell in the presence of God (v. 25). There God made Isaac's enemies to be
at peace with him (vv. 26-31; Prov. 16:7).

The grief of disobedience

In verses 34-35, we see the sad consequence of Isaac's disobedience. May God give us grace and wisdom to learn by
his grief. It is true that the Lord God forgave Isaac for his
sin, and even overruled his sin to do him good. Yet Isaac
saw and felt the grief of his own disobedience in his son
Esau, who married a Hittite.

'God is not mocked; for whatsoever a man soweth, that
shall he also reap!' As Isaac went down to the world for
help in time of famine, Esau, following his father's example,
went down to the world to find himself a bride; and Esau
never knew God. This was a grief to Isaac. But it was, in
great measure, a grief he brought upon himself by disobedience to the will of God. When he should have been
careful, Isaac was careless, and it brought grief to his soul.
It always does.

28.

Jacob

Genesis 28:10-22

'And Jacob went out from Beersheba, and went towards Haran'
(Gen. 28:10).

Blessed is that man who possesses the key with which to open the treasure chest of Holy Scripture. That key is Christ. No one understands the Word of God, the whole or in part, who does not understand that the Book of God is all about the Son of God (Luke 24:27,44-47). In our Lord's days upon this earth, those who claimed to believe the Word of God, kept sabbath days, and zealously defended their religious traditions, doctrines, and practices, were totally ignorant of the message of the Old Testament Scriptures which they claimed to believe. When he who is the Truth stood before them and told them the truth about God and themselves, they hated him, persecuted him and ultimately crucified him. Why was this? The Lord Jesus himself tells us, and you will see the reason: 'Had ye believed Moses, ye would have believed me: for he wrote of me. But if ye believe not his writings, how shall ye believe my words?' (John 5:46-47).

Things have not changed in the least. Like the Pharisees of old, the religious multitudes of our day, standing upon the Book, the blood and the blessed hope, have missed the message of the Word of God. The message of the Bible is

Jesus Christ himself. Every word written in Holy Scripture is inspired of God and intended by him to reveal who Christ is and what he did.

Our Saviour said, 'Moses wrote of me.' The history, laws, types and pictures, visions and dreams of which Moses wrote in the first five books of the Bible, were designed to reveal the redemptive purpose and work of God's grace in Jesus Christ. The events in the life of Jacob illustrate this beautifully. I grant that there are many things about Jacob which are difficult to understand; but the one thing we do know about him is the fact that he is a picture of God's grace. Jacob was a man loved by God and chosen by God to be an heir of eternal life (Gen. 25:21-23; 35:9-13; Rom. 9:10-13).

His name means 'supplanter,' one who takes the place of another by force or by scheming (Gen. 27:35-36). That well describes Jacob. He tricked his brother Esau into selling him the birthright (Gen. 25:29-34). Then, through his mother's influence and help, he deceived his father Isaac, and tricked him into giving him the blessing reserved for the firstborn (Gen. 27:19-24). He supplanted his brother Esau. After such wicked, deceitful behaviour, being a coward by nature, Jacob took the birthright and the blessing and fled from his father's house, hoping to escape the wrath of his brother (Gen. 27:41-44).

As he fled from Esau, when he was alone in the desert, God met Jacob in grace. What a night that must have been! There, in the desert, God spoke to Jacob, promised him his presence and his covenant mercies, and revealed to him the Lord Jesus Christ as the only way to God, the only way of salvation, grace and eternal life. Everything Jacob experienced that night in the desert, between Beersheba and Haran, portrayed the work of God's sovereign, saving grace in chosen sinners.

A lost sinner

Verses 10-11 reveal Jacob's lost condition. There was Jacob, alone in the desert, afraid and helpless. He had no pillow upon which to lay his head, but the cold, hard rocks of the earth. There was no more time for plotting, scheming against others, manipulating and supplanting others. He was alone, isolated and weary. There are two reasons why Jacob was in such a horrible condition.

First, Jacob was in this mess because of his sin. The same is true of all the sons of Adam. We are what we are — proud, covetous, unhappy and depressed — because of our sin; and we are where we are — separated from God, under the curse of the law, without help, without strength and without hope — because of our sins. Lost man has no one to blame for his lost condition, but himself! 'Your iniquities have separated between you and your God, and your sins have hid his face from you' (Isa. 59:2). Like us, Jacob was completely unworthy and utterly undeserving of God's grace. God is just in condemning sinful men. He is altogether clear when he judges us (Ps. 51:3-4). Do you understand this? It is essential that you do. God will never save a man until he brings him to recognize his lost condition, until he stops his mouth and causes him to take sides with God against himself, justifying God in his own condemnation.

Second, Jacob was brought into this lowly, hopeless condition because God was about to be gracious to him. The time of love had come, and God was about to speak to his heart (Hosea 2:14). Therefore, he brought Jacob down. God knows how to bring sinners down (Ps. 107). Like the prodigal, Jacob came to the end of himself. Blessed is the man whom God brings down. If he abases, he will exalt. But he will exalt none, except those who are abased by him. He strips and he clothes. But he will clothe none with the righteousness of Christ, except those whom he strips of self-righteousness. He kills and he makes alive. But he will make none alive in Christ, except those whom he slays by his law.

A saving revelation

The Lord revealed his mercy to Jacob in a dream (vv. 12-14). When it pleases God, he reveals his Son, the Lord Jesus Christ, in his people. In his Son, he reveals his mercy, love and grace (Rom. 5:6-8); and that revelation brings life to chosen sinners (Eph. 2:1-7). Here is Jacob, the sinner, quiet and still, at last subdued by sovereign grace. God deals with him. There is nothing for him to say or do. As God spoke, he revealed a ladder set up upon the earth, reaching into heaven. That ladder is Christ.

First, the ladder was set up upon the earth, but the top of it reached into heaven. So the Lord Jesus Christ, although he stood upon the earth in the flesh, never left the bosom of the Father. He became a man. But he never ceased to be the most high God (John 1:14,18,33-34; Phil. 2:6-8).

Second, the angels of God went up and down on the ladder. As the ladder represents Christ our Mediator, so the angels of God, ascending and descending upon it, tell us that the only way sinful men and women can ascend to God and find acceptance with him is by Christ the Mediator (John 14:6); and it is only by, and through, Christ that God comes to us. 'God was in Christ, reconciling the world unto himself.'

Third, the Lord God stood above the ladder and made all his rich promises of grace to Jacob (v. 14). All the blessings and promises of grace, eternal life and heavenly glory are made and given to sinners in Christ and for Christ's sake

(Eph. 1:3-7; 4:32; 2 Tim. 1:9). As all the blessings of God come down to us by Christ, so all our praise goes up to, and is accepted by, God through Christ (1 Peter 2:5).

Grace promised

Those promises which God made to Jacob (v. 15) are the promises of God to all the sons of Jacob, to every believer; and the promises of God are all yea and amen in Christ Jesus. Here are four things promised to God's elect, four things every believer can be assured of by faith in Christ.

1. 'I am with thee'

God is with us, always with us, in covenant mercy, redemptive grace and constant love (Phil. 3:3-4). He is with us to save us, protect us, and do us good in all things (Rom. 8:28-39).

2. 'I will keep thee'

Not one of those sinners chosen by God in eternity, redeemed by Christ at Calvary, and called by the Spirit in grace will ever perish. We are kept by the power of God (Mal. 3:6; John 6:37-45; 10:24-30).

3. 'I will bring thee again into this land'

Canaan was a type of heaven. Christ, our surety and good Shepherd, will bring God's sheep home to glory (John 10:16). There is plenty of room in heaven for all who desire to enter in by Christ Jesus. But when all things are finished and time will be no more, there will be no vacancies. Every place prepared by Christ will be occupied by the one for whom it has been prepared (John 14:1-3).

4. 'I will not leave thee until I have done that which I have spoken to thee of'

Of Christ it is written: 'He shall not fail...' (Isa. 42:4); 'The pleasure of the LORD shall prosper in his hand' (53:10-11); 'He shall save his people!' (Matt. 1:21). (See Phil. 1:6; 1 Thess. 5:24). God's elect are secure in Christ, as secure as the very throne and veracity of God himself!

Conversion at Bethel

Verses 16-19 describe Jacob's awakening and conversion by the grace of God. As soon as Jacob was awakened, he sensed the presence of God and was filled with the fear of God. He found himself in the house of God, at the gate of heaven. There he built an altar for the glory of God and worshipped.

Jacob called the place where he was Bethel, though the name of the place had previously been Luz. Luz means 'separation'. Bethel means 'house of God'. God calls us to separation from the world, but as we leave the world we enter the house of God (2 Cor. 6:14 - 7:1). That is a blessed separation, a separation by which we lose nothing and gain everything.

The house of God is the place of God's presence. It is not brick and mortar stacked together in ornate, stately buildings. The house of God is God meeting with his people in any place. The church of the living God is the assembly of Christ with his people. Our Lord prayed and preached in private homes, in the open air, on the mountain side, by the seashore, and in a fishing boat, as well as in the temple and synagogue.

Today, we place far too much emphasis upon the place of worship and far too little emphasis upon the presence of God. Until the third century, there was no such thing as a 'church building'. God's saints gathered wherever they could, and God met with them. Nothing makes any place sacred but God's presence. Wherever God is present with his people, that is the house of God! In the days of its apostasy, God brought this indictment against Israel: 'Israel hath forgotten his Maker, and buildeth temples' (Hosea 8:14). It is an indictment which might well be brought against the church of our day. The house of God is the place of God's presence. If we have that, we have everything! If we miss that, we have nothing. The house of God, the assembly of his saints, is the place of worship. It is a place of reverence for him. It is the very gate of heaven!

A vow made

Jacob's vow of consecration (vv. 20-22) is the first time in Scripture we read of a vow being made to God. It is worthy of our attention. This vow of consecration was made by Jacob in response to what he had seen, heard and experienced in his soul of God's sovereign, saving grace in Christ. Believer's baptism is a good parallel to this. Symbolically, when the believer rises up from the watery grave, he consecrates himself to walk with Christ in the newness of life (Rom. 6:4-6).

The word 'if' is a poor translation in verse 20. Jacob is not laying down mercenary, legal conditions upon which he is consecrating himself to God. The word should be translated 'since'. This is a word of argument or reason. He is saying, 'Since God has promised such grace to me, I'll live for him' (1 Cor. 6:19-20). His vow of consecration was remarkable (v. 22).

'This stone, which I have set for a pillar, shall be God's house' (v.22). He was saying, 'I shall worship the Lord God of this house and him only' (Gen. 35:1-7). He had many faults, but Jacob kept his vow.

'Of all that thou shall give me I will surely give the tenth unto thee.' He vowed to honour God with the substance of his increase. It is written: 'Honour the LORD with thy substance, and with the firstfruits of all thine increase' (Prov. 3:9). The law of tithing had not yet been instituted. Jacob was under no obligation to give a tithe, except the obligation of love and gratitude. This was a voluntary act of his heart (2 Cor. 9:7). It was directly connected with the worship of God and the house of God. Here God's servant, Jacob, teaches us some very important, needful lessons about giving.

1. By this promise of the tithe, Jacob acknowledged that all he had came from God and belonged to God.
2. In giving the tithe, he demonstrated his faith in God to supply his needs.
3. The tithe was given to maintain the worship of God wherever he went.
4. What he gave, Jacob gave for the glory of God, the God of Bethel.

Jacob stands before us as a picture of grace. What a good picture he is. He was lost by nature. Christ was revealed to him and in him. He possessed all blessedness by the promise of God. This lost sinner was converted by the grace of God. Being converted by the grace of God, Jacob consecrated himself to the Son of God.

29.

Jacob's ladder

Genesis 28:12-13

'And he dreamed, and behold a ladder set up on the earth, and the top of it reached to heaven: and behold the angels of God ascending and descending on it. And, behold, the LORD stood above it, and said, I am the LORD God of Abraham thy father, and the God of Isaac: the land whereon thou liest, to thee will I give it, and to thy seed' (Gen. 28:12-13).

The ladder Jacob saw in his dream was our Saviour, the Lord Jesus Christ. We know that this is the true and proper interpretation of this text, because our Lord himself gave this interpretation of it (John 1:51). When the Lord God revealed his Son to Jacob, he revealed him as a ladder. What an instructive and helpful representation that is of our Saviour. The Lord Jesus Christ is made a ladder for us by God!

We all know what a ladder is and how it is used. When you need to get from a low place to a high place, or you need to move something from a high place to a low place, you need a ladder to do it. Nothing will serve your purpose so well as a ladder. Everyone knows how to use a ladder. In spiritual things, Christ is a ladder. Blessed are those who learn to use him as a ladder. Take careful note of what the Book of God says about Christ our ladder in Genesis 28. I mention again the three points made in the previous chapter.

First, this ladder stood upon the earth, but the top reached into heaven. So Christ, the Son of God, who is the most high God, never ceased to be God even though he stood upon the earth as a man. He never left the bosom of the Father (John 1:18; 3:13).

Second, the angels of God went up and down on the ladder which Jacob saw. So, we are able to ascend to God in heaven only by the Lord Jesus Christ (John 14:6); and it is by and through Christ that God comes down to us. God Almighty meets with, deals with, and blesses sinners only in Christ.

Third, the Lord God stood above the ladder and made all his promises of grace to Jacob. This shows us that all the promises of God's grace come to sinners through Christ. All spiritual blessings, all the promises of eternal life, all the glory of heaven are in Christ. All things come to chosen sinners through Christ, the Mediator, our ladder (Eph. 1:3-14).

What kind of ladder is the Lord Jesus Christ?

There are many kinds of ladders for many different uses: step ladders, long ladders, extension ladders, strong ladders, and shaky ladders; but Christ is in all respects an extra ordinary ladder. There is none other like him. Phillip Henry[1] gave the following sixfold description of Christ as a ladder:

1. He is a living ladder

As he is called 'a new and living way' (Heb. 10:20), so, he is a new and living ladder. Other ladders are dead things, but this ladder lives. It is true, he once died, but he is alive again and lives for evermore (Rev. 1:18). Because he lives, all who are in him live also.

2. He is a long ladder

Here is a ladder that reaches from earth to heaven. Jacob saw the foot of it upon the earth, 'and the top of it reached to heaven'! This represents the two natures of our Redeemer. He is both God and man in one glorious person, as fully God as though he were not man and as fully man as though he were not God.

As a man, he was set upon the earth (Gal. 4:4-5). As God, he was always in heaven, the eternally begotten Son of God, infinite, eternal, incomprehensible and unchange-able (John 1:14; 1:18; 3:13). The union of these two natures, God and man, in one person is the mystery of all mysteries (1 Tim. 3:16). That the glory of Christ's Godhead did not destroy the weakness of his manhood, nor the weakness of his manhood destroy the glory of his Godhead is incomprehensibly mysterious. The incarnation of Christ is like the bush Moses saw, burning with the glory of God, but not consumed with the fire.

Why was the foot of the ladder upon the earth? Why was it necessary for the Son of God, our Redeemer to become a man? If Christ was to redeem us, he had to have a body in which to bear our sins, to suffer and die as our substitute. He had to have a body and nature like ours. He had to be a man to redeem man, because it was man who sinned. Because man sinned, man must suffer for sin. For this reason, God the Holy Spirit prepared a body in the womb of the virgin for God the Son (Heb. 10:5).

Why was it necessary that the top of the ladder reached into heaven? Why must our Saviour be God as well as man? It is the fact that he is God which gives infinite merit, virtue, and efficacy to the sufferings of his manhood. Someone said, 'Christ is both God and man, because God could not suffer and man could not satisfy; but the God-man both suffered the wrath of God and satisfied the justice of God when he bled and died as the sinners' substitute upon the cursed tree.' Moreover, it was Christ's being God that supported and sustained his manhood in all his sufferings. Manhood could never have borne the agony of Gethsemane and the torments of Calvary had it not been that the man who suffered was also the eternal God.

In addition to these things, it was necessary that our Mediator be both God and man so that he might bring God and man together. He must be God so that he can deal with God, which man, as man, is not fit to do. He must be man that he might deal with man, which God in his holiness cannot do without consuming the sinful creature. 'Thanks be unto God for his unspeakable gift!' This is the meaning of our Saviour's incarnation. Immanuel is God with us, God in our nature. Were he not both God and man, he could not be Jesus, our Saviour (Matt. 1:21-23).

3. He is a lasting ladder

Other ladders wear out with use; but here is a ladder which lasts for ever. Christ himself is immutable (Heb. 13:8), the immutable God (Mal 3:6). The righteousness he brought in, by his obedience to God as our representative and covenant surety, is everlasting righteousness (Dan. 9:24). The redemption he accomplished, by his sin-atoning death at Calvary as our substitute, is eternal redemption (Heb. 9:12). From the beginning of time, sinners have made use of this ladder. It has never failed anyone who used it, and it never will. 'He is able also to save them to the uttermost that come unto God by him' (Heb. 7:25); and the salvation he gives is eternal salvation (Heb. 5:9).

4. He is a free ladder

He is open to all who come to him; and whosoever will, may come to this ladder and make use of it. The promise of the gospel is proclaimed in broad, general terms (Isa. 55:1; Matt. 11:28; John 7:37; Rev. 22:17). Christ is the fountain opened, not the fountain shut (Zech. 13:1). He is the door opened, not the door closed (Rev. 4:1). If you do not exclude yourself by unbelief, God has not excluded you. Predestination does not shut sinners out of heaven. Predestination threw open the door for sinners and built a ladder for sinners, by which men and women who would never have been able to come to God may now come to him. The door is Christ. The ladder is Christ.

5. He is a firm ladder

Steady and strong, Jacob's ladder was seen standing upon the earth, unshaken, unmoved, immovable. That is a good picture of our great Saviour. Christ Jesus is God almighty to save. He is that God who saves his people from their sins. He saves all his people from all their sins, completely. He saves from the guilt of sin, the dominion, the penalty, the consequence of sin, and ultimately from the very being of sin.

6. Christ is a fitted ladder

He is a Saviour suited to every purpose for which he is intended and for every need his people have. Christ is the only ladder there is which reaches from earth to heaven. There is no other way to God. Some vainly imagine that there are many ladders, many mediators, many ways to God. There are others who believe in a free will, and those who worship the will convince themselves that they need no ladder. Still others think that they can earn their salvation. Like Nimrod, they foolishly imagine that they can build a ladder for themselves. God declares, 'Christ is the ladder!' (see 2 Tim. 2:5).

How are we to use Christ as a ladder?

Christ is a ladder suited to every purpose for which he is intended. Let us ever use him as such. All the blessings of God descend from heaven to poor, needy sinners upon Christ the ladder (Eph. 1:3-7; 2 Tim. 1:9). It is written: 'God shall supply all your need according to his riches in glory by Christ Jesus' (Phil. 4:19). All grace comes (John 1:16), all pardon (1 John 1:7), all providence (John 17:2), and all the answers to our prayer come down this ladder (John 16:23).

It is by Christ the ladder, only by Christ the ladder, that believing sinners ascend to heaven and find acceptance with the holy Lord God (John 14:6). The distance between earth and heaven is infinite; and it is an uphill climb. How can we possibly get there? 'Behold, a ladder!' How am I to climb such a ladder? It can only be climbed by faith. Faith is the hand by which we take hold of the ladder and the foot by which we climb. 'Reach hither thy hand' and climb (Heb. 11:6). The only way we can come to God is by Christ. 'No man cometh to the Father' but by him. We cannot come to God's kingdom, his presence, or his glory, except by Christ. His blood purchased salvation for his elect, and obtained it (Eph. 1:11; Heb. 9:12). His Spirit makes chosen, redeemed sinners fit for glory in sanctification, and his inter-cession brings us there at last (1 John 2:1-2). The only way any of our performances can ascend to God is upon Christ the ladder (1 Peter 2:5; Matt. 17:5). God bathes our prayers, our praise and our works in the blood of Christ, and accepts both us and what we do for him for Christ's sake.

Why did Jacob see the angels of God ascending and descending upon him?

The angels of God are 'ministering spirits sent forth to minister for them who shall be heirs of salvation' (Heb. 1:14). The purpose of this vision was to comfort Jacob and all God's elect (the sons of Jacob), in the face of danger. The angels of God ascend to heaven by Christ to get fresh orders from him (Zech. 1:10-17), to give account of what they have done (Job 1:6), and to carry the departed souls of God's saints into Abraham's bosom (Luke 16:22). Those angels descend upon Christ the ladder, too, to surround and protect, to provide for and preserve, and watch over God's Jacobs and bring them safely home.

What are the rungs of the ladder?

There are two ways to count the rungs of a ladder, from the top down, or from the bottom up. First, we must count the rungs of the ladder from the top down, as we think of Christ coming down to us. The rungs of the ladder are our Lord's covenant engagements from eternity: the prophecies and promises, types and pictures of the Old Testament, his incarnation, his obedience in life, and his sin-atoning death. Then, we must count the rungs of the ladder from the bottom up as we find them in experience. First, we are given faith in Christ. Believing on him, we know that we are born of

God and have been effectually called by his Spirit. We make our calling and election sure by believing on the Son of God. All who are born again and have faith in Christ, have been called. All who have been called have been redeemed and justified by the blood of Christ. And these will be glorified by his grace, according to the purpose of God (Rom. 8:28-30). It is no fanaticism to carry the type a little further. Every ladder has two side pieces to which the rounds are connected, giving it strength and stability. So does this one. On one side, there is God's eternal purpose of grace. On the other side, there is God's immutable, preserving grace.

Why is the word 'behold' used in connection with this ladder?

It is common, in both the Old and the New Testament, when Christ is spoken of, to use the word 'behold' (Isa. 7:14; 42:1; John 1:29). This word, 'behold,' indicates what we are responsible to do. We are to admire and wonder as we think of him whose very name is 'Wonderful' (Isa. 9:6). Behold the ladder and bless God for it (2 Cor. 9:15). To behold Christ is to believe him (Isa. 65:1; 45:22). That is what we must do. We must believe on the Son of God. As the Israelites bitten by the fiery serpents were instructed to look to the serpent of brass held up upon the pole, so are we commanded to look to Christ crucified. Life begins with looking to Christ (John 12:32). We persevere in life by looking to him (Heb. 12:2). Our spiritual, eternal life will be consummated in looking upon the Son of God (1 John 3:2). Blessed, blessed day it will be when we see him face to face!

Here are four special times when we are to behold Christ our ladder:

1. When we attempt to do anything for God, behold the ladder. Christ is our strength, our guide and our acceptance.

2. When we have done anything against our God, let us still behold the ladder (1 John 2:1-2). When guilt stares us in the face, when we need pardon, cleansing and reviving, let us ever look to Christ: 'Behold, a ladder!'

3. When distress, trouble and danger are before us, behold the ladder. When the Esaus of the world surround us and we have no earthly comfort, when we need peace for our hearts and a pillow for our aching heads, let us lie down upon God's promises, look up to heaven, and 'Behold, a ladder'. See the angels ascending and descending.

4. When death is near, when the cold sweat of death is on our brows and the rattle is in our throats, 'Behold, a ladder!' (Acts 7:56).

30.

Jacob — an object of grace

Genesis 28:15; 31:3,5; 48:21

'And, behold, I am with thee, and will keep thee in all places whither thou goest, and will bring thee again into this land; for I will not leave thee, until I have done that which I have spoken to thee of' (Gen. 28:15).

Here are four passages of Scripture, each revealing a specific aspect of the grace of God in the life of Jacob. However, if all we see in these texts is the history of God's dealings with Jacob, we miss the purpose of God the Holy Spirit in giving us the inspired volume of Holy Scripture. These things were written for our spiritual learning, for our comfort, and to encourage our hope in Christ (Rom. 15:4). Believers should always apply the Word of God to themselves. We should never look upon the Book of God as a mere record of historical, doctrinal, or prophetic facts. Therefore, as we look at these four passages of Holy Scripture and see the grace of God in the life of Jacob, the sons of Jacob ought to apply each text to themselves and see the hand of God's grace in their own lives.

Present grace

In Genesis 28:15, God's grace is set before us as grace for the present. The Lord God says to his servant Jacob, 'Behold, I am with thee,' right now, presently. Grace is the present heritage of every believer. We rejoice to know that grace is eternal (Eph. 1:3-6; 2 Tim. 1:9). Our hearts delight in the fact that the Lord Jesus Christ has purchased by his blood all the inheritance of grace and glory for his people. In Christ, grace is our purchased possession (Eph. 1:11); and we thank God for past experiences of grace. Grace experienced in the past fills our hearts with sweet memories of God's goodness to us. Grace sought us out of a fallen race. It called us from death to life. It revealed Christ in us and gave us faith in him. It caused us to come to Christ in the beginning; and it has kept us coming to him. But living bodies cannot live on yesterday's bread. We must have some bread today. Neither can we feed our souls on yesterday's grace. We must have grace today. Child of God, I want you to see that grace is yours this very hour. God says to Jacob, 'Behold, I am with thee!'

Jacob was part of a long line of men chosen by God; and he, too, was chosen as the object of God's grace (v. 13). Grace does not run in blood lines; but sometimes God does call many from the same family. That was the case with Jacob. His father Isaac and his mother Rebecca were believers. His grandfather Abraham and his grandmother Sarah were believers. What a blessing! To have for your father and mother, for your grandfather and grandmother, men and women who walked with God is the most

distinguished hereditary honour in the world. Well might
Jacob rejoice to hear the God of his fathers say to him, as he
had said to his fathers, 'Behold, I am with thee.' The believing sons and daughters of believing parents are possessors of an indescribably rich heritage. Yet none should
foolishly imagine that grace is a matter of heredity, passed
on from father to son (John 1:11-13). Grace comes to chosen
sinners according to the sovereign will and pleasure of God
alone (Rom. 9:16).

This word of grace, 'Behold, I am with thee,' came to
Jacob at a time when he greatly needed it. He had just left
his father's house. He was about to be faced with a great
trial. Nothing could have so effectually prepared him for
twenty years in Laban's house as this promise from God.

This word came to him when he needed it most. It was
at the time when he was totally alone, a family outcast,
without friends, and a pilgrim in a strange land, that God
Almighty spoke to him and said, 'Behold, I am with thee!' I
defy anyone to measure the height or depth, length or
breadth of that infinite blessing. What more could God say
than this: 'I am with thee'?

It is a guarantee of infinite love, mercy and grace, when
God is with you. God will not dwell with those he hates.
He is not with those to whom he is not merciful. He does
not abide where he does not dispense grace. But to each of
his people, he says, 'Fear not: for I have redeemed thee, I
have called thee by thy name; thou art mine... I have loved
thee... Fear not: for I am with thee' (Isa. 43:1-5). As a man
delights to be with his friends, so our God and Saviour, the
Lord Jesus Christ, delights to be with those whom he has
chosen, redeemed and called.

'I am with thee' means I shall help you (Isa. 41:10). C. H.
Spurgeon said, 'Whatever we undertake, God is with us in

the undertaking; whatever we endure, God is with us in the enduring; whithersoever we wander, God is with us in our wandering.' 'If God be for us, who can be against us?' If God is with us, what can we not do, or endure, or overcome? This is what Paul meant when he wrote, 'I can do all things through Christ which strengtheneth me.' Let every son of Jacob, every believer, hear the promise as a promise coming directly from God himself to you. God is with you, so completely with you that he is in you. The whole Godhead is with you, in the entirety of his being!

When God says, 'I am with thee,' he promises, along with his presence, his sympathy. Our Saviour is so touched with the feeling of our infirmities that he feels what we feel, suffers what we suffer, and endures what we endure. If we have a load to bear, he is with us. If we have a work to do, he is with us.

How precious, rich and full this word of grace must have seemed to Jacob as he lay under the stars in the wilderness. His bed was the cold earth. His curtains were the bushes around him. The heavens were his canopy. His pillow was a rock. He was alone, afraid and helpless, until the Lord God appeared to him and said, 'Behold, I am with thee!' If you are a believer, if you are washed in the blood of Christ and born again by the Spirit of God, you are one of Jacob's sons; and God says, 'Behold, I am with thee.' That is God's present assurance of grace.

Future grace

In Genesis 31:3, we read God's promise of future grace. He says, 'I will be with thee.' Whatever the future holds for us, let every believer be assured of this: it holds grace, rich, free, abundant grace in Christ.

Were it not for the weakness of our flesh, this promise
would be unnecessary. When God says, 'I am with thee,'
we can count on it, he will be with us. God does not change.
He will never forsake his people (Heb. 13:5). Some people
believe in a god who loves today and hates tomorrow, who
pardons one day and condemns the next. Such a god is no
God at all. Our God is the God of Jacob, who changes not
(Mal. 3:6).

Jacob had lived with Laban for twenty years. In those
years he endured many troubles. It was now time for him
to leave Laban and return to his home in Canaan. The word
of grace needed to be renewed to his heart, so the Lord God
said to him, 'I will be with thee.'

Jacob began to settle down among the worldlings. So
God called him away. Then he forced him to obey. Laban
had begun to despise Jacob (31:2). Laban's sons were envi-
ous of him (v. 1). Those upon whom he had relied turned
against him. Those whose good he had served opposed him.
Those who were most indebted to him were envious of him.
So it is with God's elect in every age. Therefore, the Lord
God said, 'I will be with thee!'

The journey Jacob was about to take was a dangerous
one, and he knew it. Laban would not willingly let him go.
Esau had sworn to kill him. Such a journey with such a
large family would be very difficult. But God called, and
Jacob had to obey. Therefore, the Lord God said to him, no
matter what you have to face, 'I will be with thee.' Your
future is full of grace!

Acknowledged grace

In Genesis 31:5, we see the grace of God experienced and
acknowledged by Jacob. 'The God of my father hath been

with me.' Every believer's life is, from beginning to end, an unceasing experience of God's grace. Right up to the time that he left Laban's house, Jacob said, 'The God of my father hath been with me.'

He had not been a very gracious man; but God was with him nonetheless (Ps. 89:30-33). The Lord chastened and corrected him; and the Lord protected and blessed him. Though Laban cheated him out of his wages ten times, God blessed Jacob! Everything done against him only worked for his good. Our great God is a God who ought to be trusted with implicit confidence. He is faithful. His grace and his faithfulness are unconditional.

Though he was a believer, though he had experienced so much grace, when he was fleeing from Laban and he heard that Esau was coming after him, poor Jacob was distressed and full of fear. But, the Lord was with him (Gen. 35:3). Thank God, he does not leave his people because of their fears. If he did, we would all have been castaways long ago.

On the night of his wrestling with the Lord, when he was humbled, broken, and made to confess his name, the Lord God was with him. He says, '[God] was with me in the way which I went!' Jacob was the object of God's everlasting love, the eternally chosen object of his grace (Rom. 9:11-13). God was with him in his mother's womb. He was with him in his youth. He was with him when he fled from his father's house; and when he broke his thigh and broke his spirit. God was with him in Laban's house and when he returned home again. On his death bed, old Jacob confessed more fully than ever that the Lord God had been with him all his days (Gen. 48:15-16). He had lost Rachel, but God was with him. He had endured famine, but God fed him. He had lost Joseph, but the Lord God was with him. At the time he said, 'All these things are against me;' but now he has to take back his words. He realized that God had never been more fully for him! Now he says, '[The Lord God] redeemed me from all evil.' If you are a believer, this will be your verdict upon your life at the end of your days: 'God was with me!' He has 'redeemed me from all evil'. Every believer's life is, from beginning to end, an unceasing experience of God's grace!

Transmitted grace

In Genesis 48:21, we see the grace of God transmitted from one generation to another. 'Behold, I die; but God shall be with you.' Those were Jacob's dying words to Joseph. He was saying, 'God will yet be gracious.' So it will be, from generation to generation, as long as the world exists. The grace we have received and experienced at the hand of our God will be transmitted to the generation that succeeds us.

We all tend to worry needlessly about the future. We fret about our children. We worry about the future of God's church. We concern ourselves too much with what will become of those who depend upon us. God will not cease to be gracious when we die. He still has an elect remnant. He will be gracious to them. He will be with them as he has been with us.

This has special application to every believer's family. We can and must entrust our sons and daughters to the sovereign goodness of our God. God's grace does not run in bloodlines. We cannot save our children, or make God obliged to save them. But we can believe God. Long before my only child was born, I gave her to my God. On the night she was born, as I gave thanks to God for her, I gave her back to him. On the day my wife and I brought her home from the hospital, together we dedicated that child to our

God and committed her to his hands. We trained her in the nurture and admonition of the Lord. What is the significance of that? Just this: God has never yet rejected a child given to him in faith. Samuel, Samson, Solomon and John the Baptist are all testimonies to God's faithfulness in this regard. I do not suggest that God has not cast away the children of believing parents. Eli's sons and David's children tell us otherwise. But I do say that God has never cast away any child given to him in faith.

This is what I am saying: I believe God. Anything we refuse to give to him, he will take from us. Anything we give him for the honour of his name, he will receive. Does the Word of God confirm this, or does it deny it? Let no one misunderstand. The Book of God does not teach faith by proxy. We cannot believe God for someone else, not even for our children. Each one must personally trust the Son of God for himself. But God honours and uses the faith of others to bring chosen sinners to himself. The Canaanite woman's faith had something to do with her daughter's healing (Matt. 15:22-28). Jairus' faith had something to do with his daughter's resurrection from the dead (Luke 8:41-42, 49-56). When the Lord Jesus saw the faith of four men who carried a desperately needy soul to him, he said to the palsied man, 'Man, thy sins are forgiven thee' (Luke 5:20).

This also has special application to every gospel church. The time will come when the pastor will be taken away from his flock; but God will be with his church. The church of God does not depend upon the preacher. God's cause, his truth and his kingdom do not depend upon any preacher, or any man, no matter how great, how gifted, or how useful he is in his day.

Someone once asked Mr. Spurgeon, 'What will become of the Tabernacle when you are gone?' He replied, 'It will probably be the greatest of blessings when it happens.' Many good men have clung to their places longer than they should have done, and have pulled down much that they have built up. It is well when the Lord says to such, 'Friend, come up higher.' George Müller was once asked what would become of the great orphanage he had built for homeless children, when he was gone. Müller replied, 'God will use George Müller as long as he likes, and when he chooses to put him aside, he will use somebody else.' When Abraham dies, God will be with Isaac. When Isaac dies, God will be with Jacob. When Jacob dies, God will be with Joseph. When Joseph dies, God will be with Ephraim and Manasseh. And when we die, God will have those who bear his name; and he will never lack a champion to bear his banner among them. The Lord will be with them. When Elijah was taken up, Elisha picked up his mantle and cried, 'Where is the LORD God of Elijah?' And God was with him.

1. Grace is ours now. God says, 'I am with you!'

2. Grace will be ours in the future. The Lord's promise is: 'I will be with you!'

3. Grace has been ours all the days of our lives. With Jacob, we look over the days of our lives and say, 'The God of our fathers hath been with us.'

4. And the grace of God will be with those who follow us in faith: 'God shall be with you.'

31.

Jacob at Peniel

Genesis 32:24-32

'And Jacob was left alone; and there wrestled a man with him until the breaking of the day. And when he saw that he prevailed not against him, he touched the hollow of his thigh; and the hollow of Jacob's thigh was out of joint, as he wrestled with him. And he said, Let me go, for the day breaketh. And he said, I will not let thee go, except thou bless me. And he said unto him, What is thy name? And he said, Jacob. And he said, Thy name shall be called no more Jacob, but Israel: for as a prince hast thou power with God and with men, and hast prevailed. And Jacob asked him, and said, Tell me, I pray thee, thy name. And he said, Wherefore is it that thou dost ask after my name? And he blessed him there. And Jacob called the name of the place Peniel: for I have seen God face to face, and my life is preserved. And as he passed over Penuel the sun rose upon him, and he halted upon his thigh. Therefore the children of Israel eat not of the sinew which shrank, which is upon the hollow of the thigh, unto this day: because he touched the hollow of Jacob's thigh in the sinew that shrank'

(Gen. 32:24-32).

Though this passage of scripture is often used as a picture of conversion, this was not Jacob's conversion experience.

It teaches us many things about conversion, as we shall see. We know that conversion to Christ is a lifelong experience. We are continually coming to him (1 Peter 2:4). Yet this was not the point in Jacob's history when he first came to know the Saviour. Christ was revealed to him twenty years earlier at Bethel, as the only ladder by which God could come down to man and upon which man must ascend to God. At Bethel, Jacob met Christ the Mediator and learned to worship him (Gen. 28:10-22). This is the Mediator who had been presented as a type in all those blood sacrifices he had seen offered by his father, Isaac, as he worshipped God.

Frequently, this passage is also used as a picture of a man wrestling with God in fervent prayer. But that, too, is a mistake. In our text, it is not Jacob who wrestles with God, but God who wrestles with Jacob. Genesis 32:24-32 sets before us a picture of the Lord God subduing the proud, sinful flesh of his believing people by his almighty grace.

Left alone

'And Jacob was left alone' (v. 24). Was there ever a man more alone than Jacob? His whole life had been filled with trouble and disappointment. Now, as he was returning home, he feared for his life. When he heard that Esau was coming to meet him with four hundred men, he was confused, frightened and alone.

All his life, he had played second fiddle to his brother Esau. He was born second to Esau. He was, by all measures, an inferior man to Esau. His father, Isaac, preferred Esau, and Jacob knew it. Instigated by his mother, Jacob deceived his father on his deathbed and stole the birthright. He had lived in exile with the guilt of his deeds for twenty years.

When Esau threatened to kill him, Jacob fled into exile. As he fled from Esau, God met him at Bethel, promised his covenant blessings to him, and confirmed what, I am sure, his mother had told him from his youth (Gen. 25:22-23; Rom. 9:10-13). God himself caused Jacob to know that he was loved and chosen by him from eternity. God saved him, blessed him with his grace and assured him that he was yet to be greatly blessed.

As he had deceived his father Isaac, so he had been deceived by his uncle Laban and tricked into marrying a woman whom he did not want (Gen. 29:16-26). Then, the Lord God appeared to him and told him to return home with this promise: 'I will be with thee' (Gen. 31:3).

No sooner did he start home in obedience to God's command than he discovered that Esau was coming to meet him with four hundred men (Gen. 32:6-8). Earlier in the day, he kissed his wives and his children good-bye, took them across the brook Jabbok out of harm's way and waited to die by the hand of his angry brother. Now, we read, 'And Jacob was left alone.' He was now more alone than ever.

Alone, confused, helpless and afraid, Jacob sat down and waited for death. His plotting, scheming and manipulating was over. He was shut up to the sovereign power and will of God. Like Israel at the Red Sea and Jonah in the whale's belly, Jacob was totally dependent upon God to deliver him, and he now knew it (Exod. 14:13; Jonah 2:9).

God knows how to bring his Jacobs down; and he always does. Those whom he is pleased to save, to whom he will reveal his mercy and grace in Christ, must be brought down and made to know their utter helplessness and inability. God's grace and his work leave no room for boasting and glorying in the flesh (Ps. 107:1-6,11-13; 1 Cor. 1:26-31). 'Jacob was left alone.' He seemed to be in a miserable condition, helpless and alone; but he was truly in a most blessed condition.

'To be left alone with God is the only true way of arriving at a just knowledge of ourselves and our ways. We can never get a true estimate of nature and all its actings until we have weighed it in the balances of the sanctuary, and have there ascertained its real worth. No matter what we may think about ourselves, or what man may think about us, the great question is: what does God think about us? The answer to this can only be learned when we are 'left alone'. As C. H. MacIntosh has said, 'Away from the world, away from self, away from the thoughts, reasonings, imaginings, and emotions of mere nature, and "alone with God," — thus and thus alone, can we get a correct judgement about ourselves.'

Isolation is always the forerunner of revelation, grace, salvation and blessing. Before God saves, he separates (Hosea 2:14; John 8:9; Acts 9:3-8).

Wrestling

'And there wrestled a man with him until the breaking of the day' (v. 24). About the time the sun went down, suddenly a man appeared out of nowhere, laid hold of Jacob, and wrestled with him until the morning sun began to rise. This was not a vision or a dream, but a real struggle, both physical and spiritual. It was not a brief encounter, but one that lasted all night long.

There is no question at all about the fact that this man was also God (v. 30). This man who wrestled with Jacob was the Lord Jesus Christ, the God-man, the angel of the covenant (Hosea 12:4), through whom all the blessings of covenant grace come to God's elect.[1]

This man, the Lord Jesus Christ, the Son of God, wrestled with Jacob. We are not told that Jacob wrestled with the man, but rather, 'there wrestled a man with him.' Those who use this story as an example of importunate prayer miss the mark. Jacob was not wrestling with this man to obtain the blessing. The man was wrestling with Jacob to give the blessing.

It is the object of a wrestler to bring his opponent down, to pin him to the ground, to render him helpless; and that was the object of our Lord here. He wrestled with Jacob to pin him down, to conquer his spirit, to subdue his flesh, to render him helpless. The Lord wrestled with Jacob to reduce him to a sense of his own nothingness, to make him see what a poor, helpless, worthless creature he was. God's purpose in all our trials is to make us strong in grace and strong in faith; and the way he makes us strong is to make us know, recognize and acknowledge our weakness: 'When I am weak, then am I strong' (2 Cor. 12:7-10).

This man wrestled with Jacob 'until the breaking of the day'. There were issues involved which had to be resolved permanently in Jacob's heart and at this time. This was not a brief, passing encounter. It was not an indifferent decision made on the spur of the moment. Great issues were at stake. Eternal matters had to be settled. What were the issues? Jacob had to acknowledge Christ as his Lord (Rom. 10:9-10). He had to bow to the will of God. Jacob had to lose his life to Christ. He had to surrender to Christ in all things, in his heart, willingly (Ps. 110:3).

God was determined to bless and use Jacob. His purpose could not be defeated. But he would not grant his blessing and he would not use him until Jacob had been conquered, broken and subdued by his almighty grace. This conquering of the flesh, this breaking and subduing is not a once-for-all experience. It is a lifelong battle. It continues throughout the night of our sojourn upon this earth. It is a warfare in our hearts (Rom. 7:14; Gal. 5:17). If we are his, our Lord

will conquer us; and he will make us willing to be conquered. If we are his, Christ will prevail over us (Rom. 7:25).

Made willing

*'And when he saw that he prevailed not against him, he
touched the hollow of his thigh; and the hollow of Jacob's
thigh was out of joint, as he wrestled with him'* (v. 25). Without question, God could have easily subdued Jacob. This
conflict was ordered and instigated by God. The outcome
was never in doubt; but God's people are not puppets or
robots. We must be made to see, feel and experience the
frailty of our flesh, the emptiness of this world, and the
glory of God in Christ, so that we desire his presence and
his salvation above all things. 'Thy people shall be willing!' Grace makes God's elect willing to bow to him in the
day of his power. This is the purpose of all that God reveals
to us, of all the trials we endure and of all God's dealings
with us. Let us ever thank God for the sharp, painful blows
of providence and grace that bring us down before him. At
last, Jacob was brought to the end of his own resources.
One swift stroke from the hand of God rendered him utterly powerless. As A. W. Pink states:

> This is the purpose God has before him in his deal-
> ings with us. One of the principal designs of our gra-
> cious heavenly Father in the ordering of our path, in
> the appointing of our testings and trials, in the discip-
> line of his love, is to bring us to the end of ourselves,
> to show us our own powerlessness, to teach us to have
> no confidence in the flesh, that his strength may be
> made perfect in our conscious and realized weakness.

Favour sought

'And he said, Let me go, for the day breaketh. And he said, I will not let thee go, except thou bless me' (v. 26). Now, the Lord had accomplished his goal. Jacob was helpless. With his leg out of joint, he could no longer wrestle. All he could do was cling to his Master. Until now, Jacob had tried to order his own life: planning, scheming, devising and deceiving to get what he wanted. Now, he is rendered helpless. All his strength is taken away; and he clings to Christ, saying, 'I will not let thee go, except thou bless me.'

> Other refuge have I none,
> Hangs my helpless soul on thee!

He did not only say, 'I will not let thee go;' he also said, 'I will not let thee go, except thou bless me.' Henry Mahan comments:

> The battle is not over for Jacob until he is assured of the Lord's permanent blessing upon him and his peace within him. This was a life or death struggle for Jacob, a battle that would not be fought again. He had heard the promises of God's blessings. Now, he wanted them in truth. He was still Jacob, his past clouded with sin. He was a wanderer in a strange country and must still face Esau, his angry brother. He knew he was no better off for this experience unless the Lord gave him his approval, acceptance, and presence.

The one great blessing Jacob sought from Christ was the assurance of God's favour!

Thou, O Christ, art all I want!
More than all in Thee I find.

A new name

*'And he said unto him, What is thy name? And he said, Jacob.
And he said, Thy name shall be called no more Jacob, but
Israel: for as a prince thou hast power with God and with
men, and hast prevailed'* (vv. 27-28). Jacob was compelled
to confess his name. When the Lord said, 'What is thy
name?', it was not for his information, but for Jacob's humiliation and instruction. God forced Jacob to acknowledge who
and what he was. 'My name is Jacob.' I am a cheat, a supplanter, a deceiver. I hold the birthright by my own efforts,
and all my efforts are sin. I am Jacob, the sinner.

God gave him a new name: 'Israel'. This name, Israel,
implies royalty, sonship, acceptance and favour with God.
It means 'Prince with God'. Israel is one who has power
with God, because he has favour with God. This was not
the result of Jacob's will, his works, or his worth. It was the
gift of God's free grace (John 1:11-13; Rom. 9:15-16; Eph.
1:3-7). The name Israel also means 'God commands'. Israel
is one whose life is commanded and ruled not by self, or by
Satan, or by the world, or by circumstances, but by God.

As a prince, Jacob had power with God and with men,
and prevailed. His new name, Israel, was a constant reminder to Jacob that his success, his strength, his blessings, indeed, all that he had and experienced, which made
him differ from and prevail over men, was the gift of God's
grace, the result of God's command, not the result of his
own excellence (1 Cor. 4:7).

'And Jacob asked him, and said, Tell me, I pray thee, thy
name. And he said, Wherefore is it that thou dost ask after
my name? And he blessed him there' (v. 29). Jacob was a

subdued man; but his flesh was not yet destroyed. In curiosity, he asked and tried to pry into that which was not yet revealed. Pride dared to seek familiarity with the Almighty. God refused to tell him his name. Jacob must believe God within the scope of his revelation. Faith demands no more than God reveals. Yet, in spite of this sinful curiosity, the Lord confirmed his blessing to Jacob — the blessings of grace are unconditional and free!

Face to face

'And Jacob called the name of the place Peniel: for I have seen God face to face, and my life is preserved' (v. 30). Jacob had met the living God. The hand of God had touched him. He had personally encountered his Redeemer. And God, who might have justly killed him, blessed him with life (Rom. 8:33-34). What a small thing it would be for him to meet Esau now! He who has met God and lived has no need to fear anything or anyone!

'And as he passed over Penuel the sun rose upon him, and he halted upon his thigh' (v. 31). As Jacob left Penuel 'the sun rose upon him'. This was a token of God's favour. 'The Sun of Righteousness' rises and shines upon those whom God has blessed (Mal. 4:2). 'The path of the just ... shineth more and more unto the perfect day' (Prov. 4:18). Yet, while Jacob walked with God, he 'halted upon his thigh'. The sinew of his thigh 'shrank', but it was not removed. Though God, by his grace, subdues our flesh, he does not remove it while we live in this world. We shall go halting through this world, forced to lean upon Christ. God will not allow us to trust ourselves!

The chapter closes with a sad, sad fact. Religious men and women who never experience God's grace will always substitute idolatrous superstition and works for the knowledge of Christ and his grace (v. 32). John Gill informs us that the Jews have an entire chapter in the Misnah, giving rules concerning the eating of the sinew of any animal which is upon the hollow of the thigh, telling men how to cut it out, and demanding that any who eat a piece, even the size of an olive, are to be beaten with forty stripes. 'Keep yourselves from idols' (1 John 5:21).

32.

Joseph — a type of Christ

Genesis 37:1-11

'And Jacob dwelt in the land wherein his father was a stranger, in the land of Canaan. These are the generations of Jacob. Joseph, being seventeen years old, was feeding the flock with his brethren; and the lad was with the sons of Bilhah, and with the sons of Zilpah, his father's wives: and Joseph brought unto his father their evil report. Now Israel loved Joseph more than all his children, because he was the son of his old age: and he made him a coat of many colours. And when his brethren saw that their father loved him more than all his brethren, they hated him, and could not speak peaceably unto him. And Joseph dreamed a dream, and he told it his brethren: and they hated him yet the more. And he said unto them, Hear, I pray you, this dream which I have dreamed: For, behold, we were binding sheaves in the field, and, lo, my sheaf arose, and also stood upright; and, behold, your sheaves stood round about, and made obeisance to my sheaf. And his brethren said to him, Shalt thou indeed reign over us? or shalt thou indeed have dominion over us? And they hated him yet the more for his dreams, and for his words. And he dreamed yet another dream, and told it his brethren, and said, Behold, I have dreamed a dream more; and, behold, the sun and the moon and the eleven stars made obeisance to me. And he told it to his father, and to his brethren: and

his father rebuked him, and said unto him, What is this dream
that thou hast dreamed? Shall I and thy mother and thy breth-
ren indeed come to bow down ourselves to thee to the earth?
And his brethren envied him; but his father observed the
saying'

(Gen. 37:1-11).

There is hardly a child who has been to Sunday School
who has not heard the story of Joseph and his brothers many,
many times. Who does not know about Joseph's coat of many
colours? Who is unaware of the fact that his brothers hated
him and sold him into slavery? There are numerous moral
lessons and warnings to be drawn from the story.

In his character and conduct, Joseph shows us how we
ought to live in this world for the glory of God, and how
God honours those that honour him. In their character and
conduct, Joseph's wicked brothers represent everything that
is base, vile and malicious. They were wicked, covetous,
self-centred, self-serving men. Obviously, Joseph represents
all that we should be and do. His brothers represent all that
we should avoid.

These lessons might be readily perceived by any natural moralist. Yet there is much more here than lessons
about moral conduct. In fact, if that is all we learn from the
story of Joseph and his brothers, we have not understood
the last fourteen chapters of Genesis. Like everything else
in the Old Testament Scriptures, this story is intended to
be a revelation of the Lord Jesus Christ in type and picture.

1. As our covenant head, Adam was a type of Christ.
2. Abel showed forth the death of Christ as our sacrifice.
3. Noah represented Christ in the saving of his
household.

4. Abraham and Isaac portrayed the substitutionary sacrifice of Christ on Mount Moriah.

5. Melchizedek revealed Christ as our great High Priest.

6. Isaac pictured Christ the promised seed, in whom all the nations of the earth are blessed.

7. Jacob saw Christ as a ladder, the only Mediator between God and men.

However, the fullest, most complete and striking type of Christ to be seen in the book of Genesis is Joseph. A. W. Pink, in his *Gleanings in Genesis*, lists 100 ways in which Joseph is a picture of our Saviour. Looking at just a few of the highlights of Joseph's life, we see him as a beautifully, instructive type of the Lord Jesus Christ. As we have observed, the book of Genesis is the book of Beginnings. Here, God revealed his purpose of grace in the salvation of sinners, and showed fallen men how he would save his elect by the sacrifice of his own dear Son. Joseph is one of the many illustrations we are given of God's grace and salvation in Christ.

1. His name

Joseph's name makes him a type of Christ. Actually, he was given two names —Joseph and Zaphnathpaaneah (41:45). Zaphnathpaaneah is the name which Pharaoh gave him when he made him Lord over all of Egypt. In this he was like our Saviour who has two names, a divine name and a human name. His divine name is Christ, which means 'Anointed of God'. His human name is Jesus, which means 'Saviour'. He has two names because he is both the Son of God and the Son of Man.

The names given to Joseph are significant as a type of our Saviour. Joseph means 'adding' (30:24). Adam was one who subtracted. We lost everything in Adam. But Christ, the Second Adam, is the one who adds to heaven the sons of God. To this end, he came into this world, lived in righteousness, and died upon the cursed tree (John 12:24; 14:3).

Joseph's second name, Zaphnathpaaneah, has a double meaning. It means 'revealer'; Christ is the one who reveals God to us (John 1:18). It also means 'provider', and Christ is our great provider. He is Jehovah-jireh, the Lord who provides. He provides his people with all things temporal and physical, as well as all things eternal and spiritual.

2. His relationship

In his relationship to his father, Joseph is a type of Christ: 'Israel loved Joseph more than all his children' (v. 3). How Jacob loved Joseph! All his life long, his happiness was bound up in this son. He rejoiced when he was born. He distinguished him from the sons of Leah, by making a coat of many colours for him. His heart broke when he thought he was dead. He took a long journey in his old age to see Joseph's face. He committed himself to Joseph (47:29-31).

As Joseph was the object of his father's love, so the Lord Jesus Christ is the object of his Father's love (John 3:35). The Lord God delights in his Son (Prov. 8:22,30; Matt. 3:17; 17:5). God has placed all things in his hands (John 3:35). Christ has pre-eminence over all things and in all things (Col. 1:18).

Joseph was the object of Israel's love, because he was the child of Israel's old age (v. 3). Here again is a picture of Christ. From all eternity, he is the Son of God. He was not born in time. He is the eternally begotten Son of the eternal Father, very God of very God, equal with and of the same substance as the Father (John 1:1-3). The Lord Jesus Christ is not a creature of God. He is God the Creator. He is not a mere emanation of God. He is God, the one in whom all the fulness of the Godhead dwells (Col. 2:9). He is infinitely more than a manifestation of God. He is 'God ... manifest in the flesh' (1 Tim. 3:16).

3. His occupation

Joseph represents the Lord Jesus Christ in his occupation. He was a shepherd, 'feeding the flock' (v. 2). No representation of Christ is more beautiful than that of a shepherd. 'The LORD is my Shepherd' (Ps. 23:1). He is set before us as the good Shepherd in his sin-atoning death (John 10:11-16; 1 Peter 2:21-25). He is the great Shepherd in his resurrection glory (Heb. 13:20-21). He is the chief Shepherd in his glorious second advent (1 Peter 5:4). What can be more beautiful than the comparison of Christ to a shepherd? The figure suggests his tender care, his unceasing devotion, his constant provision, his watchful protection, his blessed patience, his peaceful presence and his matchless love. Our Joseph is our Shepherd, the 'Shepherd of Israel' (Ps. 80:1).

4. His coat

In his coat of many colours, Joseph is a picture of Christ (v. 3). There has been much debate about this coat of many colours. Some find fault with Jacob for making it, and some find fault with Joseph for wearing it. Yet it cannot be denied that this coat was providentially and prophetically significant. It was not, as Dolly Parton's song implies, a coat of many rags. It was made with great care and given to him by his father as a mark of distinction and honour. It separated

Joseph, the son of Rachel, from his brothers, his half-brothers, the sons of Leah. It identified him as one of noble birth, distinct from all others (Judg. 5:30; 2 Sam. 13:18).

Did not the Lord God so distinguish his Son, the Lord Jesus Christ, from all other men? At his birth the angels sang and a star appeared. Never was there such a birth. At his baptism heaven opened, God spoke, and the Holy Spirit appeared in the form of a dove. This had never happened before, nor since. Our Lord washed his disciples feet with water; but his feet were anointed with precious ointment. When he died upon the cursed tree, the Lord God made it clear to all that he was no ordinary man. The three hours of darkness covered the earth. The earth itself shook and quaked at the death of the God-man. The veil in the temple was rent from top to bottom when, by his blood, the Lord Jesus opened the way for sinners to draw near to and be accepted by the holy Lord God. After the Lord Jesus died, one of the Roman soldiers, who had observed the whole day's infamy, declared, 'Truly this was the Son of God!' And, after he arose from the dead, many of the saints arose with him. Throughout his life and ministry, God the Father put on his Son a coat of many colours.

5. His character

Joseph was an eminent type of Christ in his character. As he excelled his brothers in every aspect of his character, so Christ excels all the sons of men in the infinite excellence of his character. Joseph was obedient to his father, righteous in his behaviour, faithful to God, kind to men, and patient in suffering. In all these things, Joseph was a type of the Lord Jesus Christ, who, because of his great love for us, was obedient to death, even the death of the cross, that he might glorify God, his Father and our Father, in redeeming and saving his people from their sins.

6. His actions

Joseph presents a type of Christ in his actions. If we simply changed Joseph's name to Christ as we read about his life, we might be tempted to think we were reading one of the four Gospels instead of the book of Genesis. As Joseph was sent by his father into the wilderness to visit his brothers who treated him contemptuously, so the Lord Jesus Christ came into this dark wilderness, being sent by his Father, to visit and redeem his people. When he came here, our Saviour, like Joseph, was hated without a cause. His own kinsmen conspired and plotted to kill him (John 1:11). As Joseph secretly fed and cared for his brothers in their time of need, though they knew him not, so the Lord Jesus secretly cared for, fed, and protected us when we knew him not (Hosea 2:8). Joseph suffered much at the hands of his brothers. They betrayed him. They sold him into bondage. It was as a result of his brother's actions that he was imprisoned in Egypt. His own brothers delivered him up to die. So far as they knew, Joseph was dead; and so it was with our Saviour.

As Joseph did nothing but good to his brothers, though they fully deserved his wrath, so Christ, who was and is so greatly abused by us, does nothing but good for his elect (Rom. 8:28). In the time of love, Joseph revealed himself to his brothers (45:1-3). So, at the time of love, Christ reveals himself to God's elect (Ezek. 16:8; Gal. 1:15-16). As Joseph forgave his brothers for all the crimes they had committed against him and assured them that he was in God's place for the salvation of his household (Gen. 50:19-21), so Christ forgives us and assures us of God's purpose of grace. Though we killed the Lord of glory, he is in God's place to save his people. As Joseph taught his brothers to love one another — 'See that ye fall not out by the way' (Gen. 45:24) — so the Lord Jesus, above all else, teaches his disciples to love one another.

7. His exaltation

Joseph was an eminent type of Christ in his exaltation. His two dreams, described in Genesis 37, prophetically made him as lord over the earth (vv. 5-8), lord over heaven (vv. 9-11), and thus lord over his brothers, just as the Old Testament Scriptures prophesied that, as a man, Christ would be made Lord over all things, as the result of his accomplishments as our God-man Mediator (Isa. 53:10-12). After much humiliation and suffering, Joseph was highly exalted by Pharaoh (Gen. 41:39-41,53-57). He was given the place of highest honour in the land. He was made to have dominion over all Egypt and all its stores. Everyone in Egypt was required to bow before him, and anyone who wanted anything from Pharaoh's bountiful store was required to 'go unto Joseph'.

So it is that the Lord God has highly exalted his Son as our Mediator (John 17:2; Rom. 14:9; Phil. 2:8-11). Of what do you stand in need? What is it that you want from God? Is it grace, forgiveness, righteousness, peace, eternal life, strength, comfort, or direction? Go to Christ. He is all; he has all; and he gives all. Christ is our Joseph. He is in the place of God; he rules all things; he possesses all things. If we would live, we must 'go unto Joseph'. We must go to Christ.

33.

Joseph brought down to Egypt

Genesis 39

'And Joseph was brought down to Egypt; and Potiphar, an officer of Pharaoh, captain of the guard, an Egyptian, bought him of the hands of the Ishmeelites, which had brought him down thither' (Gen. 39:1).

As Joseph was brought down to Egypt to save his people, so the Son of God was brought down to this earth as a man to save his people. This is the picture drawn by the Holy Spirit in Genesis 39. Certainly, there are other things taught in this chapter. There are other moral and spiritual lessons to be learned from these twenty-three verses. But the primary purpose of the Holy Spirit in giving us this piece of history is to show us a picture of Christ, our Redeemer. In chapter 39 of Genesis, the Holy Spirit continues with the history of Joseph, giving us several more aspects of his life in which he is a type of our blessed Saviour.

Joseph was a servant

'And Joseph was brought ... down thither' (v. 1)

He who was the beloved son of his father's house was brought down to Egypt as a lowly servant. Here Joseph portrays Jehovah's righteous servant, the Lord Jesus Christ (Exod. 21:5-6; Isa. 50:5-7; Ps. 40:6-10; Heb. 10:5-14; Phil. 2:5-11).

> Behold my servant, whom I uphold; mine elect, in whom my soul delighteth; I have put my spirit upon him: he shall bring forth judgement to the Gentiles. He shall not cry, nor lift up, nor cause his voice to be heard in the street. A bruised reed shall he not break, and the smoking flax shall he not quench: he shall bring forth judgement unto truth. He shall not fail nor be discouraged, till he have set judgement in the earth: and the isles shall wait for his law
>
> (Isa. 42:1-4).

The Lord Jesus Christ voluntarily became his Father's Servant to redeem and save his people (Isa. 50:5-7). He is that one to whom the law of God referred in Exodus 21:5-6. The bondslave who refused his freedom because he loved his master, his wife, and his children was a type of our Saviour. In the covenant of grace, before the world began, the Son of God voluntarily made himself his Father's Servant because he loved his Father and his chosen family.

It was in this capacity that he spoke in Psalm 40:6-10. Hebrews 10:5-14 explains that the words of our Lord in Psalm 40 referred to his obedience unto death as our substitute, by which the Lord of glory obtained the everlasting salvation of his chosen. Our great Saviour came into the world in the fulness of time to fulfil his covenant engagements as Jehovah's Servant. When he had fulfilled those engagements his people were redeemed, sanctified and perfected for ever by his finished work.

Wherefore when he cometh into the world, he saith, Sacrifice and offering thou wouldest not, but a body hast thou prepared me: In burnt offerings and sacrifices for sin thou hast had no pleasure. Then said I, Lo, I come (in the volume of the book it is written of me,) to do thy will, O God. Above when he said, Sacrifice and offering and burnt offerings and offering for sin thou wouldest not, neither hadst pleasure therein; which are offered by the law; Then said he, Lo, I come to do thy will, O God. He taketh away the first, that he may establish the second. By the which will we are sanctified through the offering of the body of Jesus Christ once for all. And every priest standeth daily ministering and offering oftentimes the same sacrifices, which can never take away sins: But this man, after he had offered one sacrifice for sins for ever, sat down on the right hand of God; From henceforth expecting till his enemies be made his footstool. For by one offering he hath perfected for ever them that are sanctified

(Heb. 10:5-14).

The basis of our Lord's exaltation and glory, the means by which the God-man, our Mediator, obtained the monarchy of the universe was his accomplishments as Jehovah's Servant (Ps. 2:8; John 17:1-5; Rom. 14:9; Phil. 2:5-11; Heb. 1:1-3).

'The Lord was with Joseph' (v. 2)

Behold, a greater than Joseph is here. Our Lord Jesus Christ is that man who is God Almighty, Immanuel, the incarnate

God, one with the Father, full of grace and truth (John
1:1-3,10-11,16-17). Not only was God with him and he with
God, the incarnate Christ is God with us. 'The Word was
made flesh, and dwelt among us, (and we beheld his glory,
the glory as of the only begotten of the Father,) full of grace
and truth... And of his fulness have all we received, and
grace for grace. For the law was given by Moses, but grace
and truth came by Jesus Christ' (John 1:14,16).

'The LORD *made all that he did to prosper in his hand'* (v. 3)

Again, Joseph portrayed our Lord Jesus Christ. As Jehovah's
Servant, Christ is that truly blessed man: the man who
walked not in the counsel of the ungodly, who stood not in
the way of sinners, who sat not in the seat of the scornful,
and whose delight was in the law of the Lord. What does
the Lord God tell us about that blessed man?

> And he shall be like a tree planted by the rivers of
> water, that bringeth forth his fruit in his season; his
> leaf also shall not wither; and whatsoever he doeth
> shall prosper
>
> (Ps. 1:3).

> Behold, my servant shall deal prudently, he shall be
> exalted and extolled, and be very high
>
> (Isa. 52:13).

> Yet it pleased the LORD to bruise him; he hath put him
> to grief: when thou shalt make his soul an offering for
> sin, he shall see his seed, he shall prolong his days,
> and the pleasure of the LORD shall prosper in his hand
>
> (Isa. 53:10).

Joseph was a trusted servant

'And Joseph found grace in his sight, and he served him: and he made him overseer over his house, and all that he had he put into his hand' (v. 4)

Potiphar trusted Joseph with everything he had and put everything into his hands. The Lord Jesus Christ is that servant whom the Father has trusted with everything, into whose hands he has put everything he has. The Father trusted the Son as his Servant, putting his glory, his people, the world and all things in it into his hands (Eph. 1:12; John 17:2).

'The Lord blessed the Egyptian's house for Joseph's sake' (v. 5)

Egypt was altogether insignificant, except for the fact that Joseph was there, his people were to sojourn there, and redemption was to be accomplished there. Therefore, for Joseph's sake, God blessed the Egyptians in providence. So, this world, all its nations and all its people, are altogether insignificant, except for the fact that Christ has his people here. Redemption and grace must be performed here. Therefore, God blesses the world and preserves it for Christ's sake (Isa. 65:8-9; 2 Peter 3:9). But his object is the salvation of his people. He does not hesitate to sacrifice men and nations for the people of his love (Isa. 43:3-4).

Joseph was a faithful servant

When he was tempted to sin, Joseph proved himself a faithful man, true to his master in all things (vv. 6-12). The Lord

Jesus Christ, our Saviour, was tempted in all points just as we are, yet without sin. He who was made to be sin for us, that we might be made the righteousness of God in him, knew no sin. He was holy, harmless, undelfiled, and separate from sinners.

He was falsely accused of evil

'*And she laid up his garment by her, until his lord came home. And she spake unto him according to these words, saying, The Hebrew servant, which thou hast brought unto us, came in unto me to mock me: And it came to pass, as I lifted up my voice and cried, that he left his garment with me, and fled out*' (vv. 16-18).

Joseph was accused of crimes he did not commit. When the chief priests, elders and all the Jewish council did their best to find some charge against our Saviour, they found none. At last, they hired two false witnesses to perjure themselves by bringing false charges against him, and they accused the Lamb of God of insurrection (Matt. 26:59-61).

He was numbered with trangressors

And it came to pass, when his master heard the words of his wife, which she spake unto him, saying, After this manner did thy servant to me; that his wrath was kindled. And Joseph's master took him, and put him into the prison, a place where the king's prisoners were bound: and he was there in the prison. But the LORD was with Joseph, and showed him mercy, and gave him favour in the sight of the keeper of the prison. And the keeper of the prison committed to Joseph's hand all the prisoners that were in the prison; and whatsoever they did there, he was the doer of it. The

keeper of the prison looked not to any thing that was
under his hand; because the Lord was with him, and
that which he did, the Lord made it to prosper

(vv. 19-23).

It is obvious that Potiphar did not believe his wife's accus-
ations. Had he believed her, he would probably have had
Joseph executed for attempting to rape his wife. Yet to save
face before men, he delivered Joseph to prison. That is
exactly what happened in the case of our Lord Jesus Christ.
Pilate knew that our Master was totally innocent of the
charges trumped up against him. He knew that the Jews
wanted him crucified simply because of their spiteful envy.
Yet to save face with men, he delivered the Son of God up
to the hands of the soldiers to crucify him as a common
criminal. Not only was our Lord Jesus Christ numbered
with transgressors, he died in the transgressors' place, as
their substitute (Isa. 53:7-12).

In all these things, Joseph was a type of our Saviour, the
man whom the Lord God sent to save us, whom he has
made Lord of his house and ruler of all his substance.

He sent a man before them, even Joseph, who was
sold for a servant: Whose feet they hurt with fetters:
he was laid in iron: Until the time that his word came:
the word of the Lord tried him. The king sent and
loosed him; even the ruler of the people, and let him
go free. He made him lord of his house, and ruler of
all his substance

(Ps. 105:17-21).

34.

Joseph opens the storehouses

Genesis 41:55-57

'And when all the land of Egypt was famished, the people cried to Pharaoh for bread: and Pharaoh said unto all the Egyptians, Go unto Joseph; what he saith to you, do. And the famine was over all the face of the earth: and Joseph opened all the storehouses, and sold unto the Egyptians; and the famine waxed sore in the land of Egypt. And all countries came into Egypt to Joseph for to buy corn; because that the famine was so sore in all lands' (Gen. 41:55-57).

Joseph was so hated by his brothers that they 'could not speak peaceably unto him' (Gen. 37:4). Because he was so greatly loved by Jacob, they envied him; and because God revealed to him that he would one day rule over them, his brothers were filled with jealousy. Therefore, his brothers sold him into slavery. But God was with Joseph. By several acts of divine providence, he was thrown into prison in Egypt.

It was in prison that he met the chief butler of Pharaoh's court and interpreted his dream. Later, when Pharaoh had a dream which none of the magicians of Egypt could interpret, the chief butler remembered Joseph and told Pharaoh about him (Gen. 41:1-14). Pharaoh called for Joseph and asked him to interpret his troubling dreams, and Joseph did so. God revealed to Joseph that there would be seven years of great abundance in the land of Egypt, followed by seven years of great famine (Gen. 41:28-32). Then, Pharaoh appointed Joseph to be ruler over all the land of Egypt, second only to himself (Gen. 41:39-46). The seven years of great abundance came, then the seven years of great famine. We pick up the story at Genesis 41:55-57.

As we read chapter 41 of Genesis, there are numerous texts of scripture which come to mind. The spiritual lessons to be gleaned from this chapter must not go unnoticed.

1. Divine sovereignty

Here is an example of God's glorious sovereignty. It is written, 'The king's heart is in the hand of the LORD, as the rivers of waters: he turneth it withersoever he will' (Prov. 21:1). It was no accident that Pharaoh dreamed what he did when he did. God's time had come for Joseph to be delivered from prison and exalted to a position of great honour. Pharaoh's dreams were merely the instrument employed by God to accomplish his purpose.

The hand of God is manifest in the whole history of Joseph's life. God was behind the scenes, secretly, sovereignly accomplishing his own purpose. Nothing happened by accident. God who is above all, ruled and overruled all the events recorded in Genesis 37 - 50. All the people, and all their actions, good and bad, were ruled by God to accomplish his will and purpose concerning Joseph and his chosen people (Gen. 45:5; 50:20; Isa. 46:9-11; Acts 4:26-28; John 6:37-39).

As it is revealed in the life of Joseph, God's sovereignty extends to all men and women, righteous and unrighteous, to all the elements of nature, the weather, the crops of the field, and the cattle, all the nations of the world, and even to the dreams of men! 'Our God is in the heavens: he hath done whatsoever he hath pleased' (Ps. 115:3). 'Whatsoever the LORD pleased, that did he in heaven, and in earth, in the seas, and all deep places' (Ps. 135:6).

2. Foolishness

The story of Joseph also shows us that the wisdom of this world is foolishness. 'Hath not God made foolish the wisdom of this world?' (1 Cor. 1:20). 'For the wisdom of this world is foolishness with God' (1 Cor. 3:19).

In Joseph's time, Egypt, the land of the Pharaohs, was the most advanced civilization of the world. It was the centre of learning, science, education, culture and philosophy. But the Egyptians were idolaters. Therefore, they had no true wisdom. The light they had was darkness. The magicians of Egypt were impotent. All their wise men could not decipher the meaning of Pharaoh's dream and tell him what God was about to do. So Pharaoh had to turn to Joseph, the only man in the land who knew God, for instruction.

3. Faith's wisdom

Does this not demonstrate something of the wisdom of faith? Psalm 25:14 declares, 'The secret of the LORD is with them that fear him.' God makes known his counsels, his purposes and his truth, not to the wise, the mighty, the noble and the great people of the world, but to them who believe him. 'The fear of the LORD is the beginning of knowledge.' All true knowledge begins with faith in Christ.

4. The mystery of providence

Joseph certainly demonstrates the fact that 'all things work together for good to them that love God, to them who are the called according to his purpose' (Rom. 8:28). How this story of Joseph demonstrates the goodness of God's providence towards his elect! How we need to take this to heart. Too often, we become so occupied with our present circumstances that we forget the promise of God. That should never happen.

> Judge not the Lord by feeble sense,
> But trust him for His grace;
> Behind the frowning providence
> He hides a smiling face.

Remember, 'Better is the end of a thing than the beginning thereof' (Eccles. 7:8). Believers should ever be of good cheer and not faint. Sorrow may endure for a night, but joy 'cometh in the morning'. So it was for Joseph. For a season he suffered wrongfully, but in the end God vindicated him and exalted him, so that he said, 'God ... hath made me forget all my toil,' (Gen 41:51) and 'hath caused me to be fruitful in the land of my affliction' (v. 52).

5. Faithfulness

Certainly, Joseph stands before us as an example of faithfulness to God. In the greatest trials, adversities and most difficult surroundings, Joseph walked with God. Though he had no godly companions and lived in a heathen land among idolaters, he never became one of them. He maintained a strong testimony to the truth and the grace of God. Even in Egypt, Joseph glorified God, and there God honoured him. As it is written: 'Them that honour me I will honour' (1 Sam. 2:30).

Let us take these five lessons to heart. Our God sovereignly rules all things. The wisdom of this world is foolishness. 'The secret of the LORD is with them that fear him.' 'All things work together for good' to God's elect. God honours those who honour him.

Joseph and Christ

The story of Joseph opening the storehouses is intended to reveal and magnify the Lord Jesus Christ, our Saviour, and to show us the glory and grace of God in him. The parallels between Joseph and Christ that are to be found in this chapter are numerous.

1. As Joseph was delivered from prison in due time, so Christ was raised from the dead at God's appointed time (Ps. 16:9-11).
2. As Joseph was the revealer of secrets, so Christ reveals the things of God to his people (John 15:15).
3. As Joseph warned of coming danger, and urged men to make provision for it, so Christ warned sinners of the wrath of God and urged them to come to him for salvation (Mark 16:16).
4. As Joseph was wise and skilled in counsel, so our Saviour's name is Wonderful Counsellor (Isa. 9:6).
5. As Joseph was exalted over all of Egypt, so Christ has been exalted over all things (Rom. 14:9).
6. As Joseph was worthy of his exaltation, so Christ is worthy of his (Heb. 10:11-14)).
7. As, upon his exaltation, Joseph was invested with the glorious apparel of Pharaoh, so the exalted man Christ Jesus is clothed with the glory which he had with the Father before the world was made (John 17:1-5).
8. As Joseph's power and authority were publicly owned and acknowledged by all men, so all men will one day

publicly own and acknowledge Christ as Lord (Phil. 2:9-11).

9. As Joseph was given a wife by Pharaoh, so God the Father has given his Son, the Lord Jesus Christ, a bride (John 6:37-40).

10. As Joseph's marriage was planned and arranged by Pharaoh, so the marriage of the Lamb was planned and arranged by the Lord God in eternity (Eph. 1:3-6).

11. As Joseph was thirty years old when he began his life's work, so the Lord Jesus Christ began his public ministry when he was thirty years old (Luke 3:23).

12. As Joseph went out on a mission from Pharaoh's presence, so Christ came into this world to do his Father's will (Heb. 10:5-10).

13. As Joseph's exaltation was followed by a season of great plenty, so Christ's exaltation was followed by a time of great grace, poured out upon the earth (Acts 2:16-21).

14. As the years of plenty were followed by years of famine, though Joseph was still on the throne, so these last days, these perilous times, are years of great famine, though Christ is still on his throne (Amos 8:11-12; Rev. 5:6; 10).

15. As in the days of famine, Joseph opened the storehouses of Egypt to all who came to him, so now the Lord Jesus Christ opens the storehouses of God's abundant grace to all who come to him (John 4:10; 7:37-38).

Opening the storehouses

Joseph opened the storehouses in Egypt by royal authority (41:41,44-45). Pharaoh placed all things into Joseph's hands: all food, authority and power. When the people came to Pharaoh for anything, he said, 'Go unto Joseph!' In the same way, by God's royal design and decree, all things pertaining to life and godliness: all grace, mercy, salvation, life and heaven have been given into the hands of the Lord Jesus Christ. God the Father has vested all things in him (John 3:35-36). All power and authority belong to him (John 17:3). All the fulness of the Godhead and of grace and glory is in him (Col. 2:9-10; John 1:16; Col. 1:19). The only way any sinner can get anything from God is to go to Christ. He has everything (Eph. 1:3-4). Why is this so? 'For it pleased God!' God is determined 'that in all things [Christ] might have the pre-eminence!'

Joseph was the only fit person to open the storehouses (41:53-55). He was the only one who understood what was going on and what must be done. He had prophesied that the famine would come. No one else knew about it. He had planned the crops, built the storehouses and had them filled before the famine came (41:35-36,49).

So our Lord Jesus Christ is the only fit person to open the storehouse of God's mercy, love and grace to needy sinners. As Joseph foreknew the famine in Egypt, though he did not cause it, our Lord Jesus Christ foreordained the fall and famine of humanity, though he did not cause it. (Gen. 2:17). As Joseph built the storehouses and filled them in anticipation of the famine, so, in the covenant of grace, Christ provided for the needs of his people before the world began. The storehouse of grace is God's covenant (Eph. 1:3; 2 Tim. 1:9). The provision is Christ, the Lamb slain from the foundation of the world (Rev. 13:8).

Christ filled the storehouse. In the fulness of time the Son of God came to this earth in human flesh. He obeyed the law in order that his people might have perfect righteousness before God. He died on the cross that we might be justified through his blood. The storehouse is full. Let all who are hungry come. Sinners find grace abundant and free in Christ. He alone has the capacity to contain all fulness. He alone has the wisdom to distribute all fulness. He alone has all fulness for ever, immutable and un-diminished, though all his people draw upon it continu-ally (2 Tim. 1:12; Phil. 3:20-21).

'And Joseph opened all the storehouses' (41:56). Joseph became the Saviour of all people: Jews and Gentiles. He opened the storehouses and dispensed the bread of life to the perishing multitudes. His resources to do so were immeasurable (41:49). What joy it must have given him to see the people coming to him and to give them the bread they needed. That is why he built the storehouses in the first place and filled them, so that the people might eat and live. Christ became our surety, substitute and sin-offering, so that sinners might be saved by him (Matt. 1:21; 1 Tim. 1:15; Luke 19:10).

Though the storehouses were filled, they would have brought no glory to Joseph and would have done no good for the people, if he had not opened them. Joseph's glory was not that he had plenty, but that he delighted to distrib-ute it. This is the glory of our Redeemer: 'He delighteth in mercy!' He has plenty, and he delights to distribute it. His chief glory is his goodness (Exod. 33:18-19). Our Saviour cries to men, 'Ho, everyone that thirsteth, come ye to the waters!' Christ is the bread of life: he invites hungry sinners to eat and live. Christ is the water of life: he calls thirsty souls to come and drink.

Then, we are specifically told that Joseph opened the storehouses 'when ... the people cried ... for bread' (41:55-56). When hungry sinners cry for bread, Christ opens the storehouse and feeds them (Matt. 7:9-11; Luke 11:5-13). Lost sinners who cry to him will be heard (Rom. 10:13). Needy believers who cry to him will be heard (Heb. 4:16).

As often as we cry to him for the bread of his grace, he gives it.

Joseph opened the storehouses to all who came (41:57). They were opened not only to the Egyptians, but to all nations. All who came to Joseph got bread. In just the same way, our Lord Jesus Christ opens the storehouse of grace to all who come to him, Jew and Gentile, black and white, rich and poor, male and female, old and young (Matt. 11:28). 'Whosoever will, let him take the water of life freely' (Rev. 22:17). Jesus Christ is the mighty Saviour, able and willing to save to the uttermost all who come to God by him (Heb. 7:25).

As Pharaoh said to the people, 'Go unto Joseph', so I say to you, whatever your soul's need is, 'Go to Christ!' He has all power and authority. He alone can open the storehouse of heaven. He will open the storehouse to all who come to him. Eat the bread he gives, and you will never hunger again. Drink the water he gives, and you will never thirst again.

35.

Joseph and his brothers

Genesis 42:2-3

'And he said, Behold, I have heard that there is corn in Egypt: get you down thither, and buy for us from thence; that we may live, and not die. And Joseph's ten brethren went down to buy corn in Egypt' (Gen. 42:2-3).

God in his wisdom uses the natural world, creatures and events to illustrate spiritual truths and make known his saving grace and redemptive work in Christ Jesus. Henry Mahan wrote, 'The wonders which God performs in the heart can be seen in the wonders God performs on earth and records in his Word.' The smitten rock (1 Cor. 10:4), the brazen serpent (John 3:14), and Jonah in the whale's belly (Matt. 12:40) are all examples of this fact.

Joseph's dealings with his brothers in Genesis 42 - 45 present a type of the way in which the Lord Jesus Christ deals with his erring brothers, who were given to him by God the Father before the world began, and who were redeemed by his own precious blood at Calvary.

I cannot fully expound this type of Christ in these chapters. If you read the history of Joseph twenty times, each time you read it you will see the type more clearly and fully. Then, when you read it again, you will still find some fresh parallels between the son of Rachel and the Son of

Mary, who is God over all and blessed for ever. The story of
Joseph and his brothers beautifully portrays the experiences
of sinners, awakened by the grace of God, as they come to
Christ and have him revealed to them and in them in saving
mercy.

Famine

God sent a very great famine; it was the work of God
(41:32,57). This famine was not only in the land of Egypt,
but in all the lands, even in Canaan where the chosen family
dwelt (42:5). Certainly, there is a sense in which this famine
is a picture of the sin and spiritual death which is spread
over all Adam's race, even over those who are chosen by
God for salvation. God's elect are born into this world in
the same state as all other men: fallen, depraved and under
the curse of the law. It is written: 'Death passed upon all
men, for that all have sinned' (Rom. 5:12). 'All have sinned,
and come short of the glory of God' (Rom. 3:23). We were
by nature 'children of wrath, even as others' (Eph. 2:3).
Before God saved us, we were, like all other people, 'without Christ ... having no hope, and without God' (Eph. 2:12).
This is the condition of all men by nature, lost alienated
from God, without life and without hope. But this famine
cannot be said to be the work of God. It is the fruit of sin.

  The famine spoken of in this chapter was sent and caused
by God to bring his chosen ones to Joseph. When God brings
his elect to Christ, he does so by causing a famine in their
souls (Ps. 107:4-6,17-21). No man will ever come to Christ
until he is made to see that, by reason of his own sin, he is
altogether void of life. Then, 'hungry and thirsty,' fainting
and drawing near to death, 'they [cry] unto the LORD in their
trouble'. Joseph's brothers came to him, because God sent

famine upon them. Had there been no famine, they would not have come. And so, no sinner will ever come to Christ, the bread of life, until God the Holy Spirit sends a famine in his soul and makes him hungry for that living bread.

Good news

When the famine came, when they were perishing, they heard some good news (42:2). Jacob called his sons together and said, 'Boys, we don't have to die. I have heard that there is corn in Egypt!' This is the good news of the gospel, preached to hungry, weary, dying sinners. We do not have to continue in our famine. Poor, hungry, dying sinners do not have to perish. There is life, mercy and grace abundant in Christ. The Son of God calls thirsty sinners to come to him and drink (John 7:37). He fills the hungry soul with good things (Luke 1:53). He, who is the Saviour of the world, says to hungry souls, 'I am the bread of life' (John 6:48-50).

Jacob could not be sure that the rumour he heard about corn in Egypt was true. But we are sure that Christ is the bread and the water of life, because we have the sure Word of God (1 John 5:9-11). Jacob did not know that Joseph was on the throne in Egypt. He very likely had doubts about whether the ruler in Egypt would let him have the corn he so desperately needed. But we are sure that all who come to Christ for mercy and grace will obtain the grace they need. We have God's Word for it (Heb. 4:16). Our heavenly Father has given all things to Christ, our Saviour; and Christ is the friend of sinners. He loved us and gave himself for us. He possesses all things in order that he might save his people.

Jacob could not be sure that he could get enough food for his whole family. There were seventy of them in total.

But we are assured that God's grace is abundantly sufficient in Christ Jesus to save to the uttermost all those who come to God by him (Isa. 1:18; Matt. 11:28; 1 John 1:7-9).

A command

An urgent command was given (42:1-2). Jacob said to his sons, 'Do not hesitate. Do not stand here looking at one another. There is corn in Egypt. Go down there and buy food that we may live and not die!' The command of the gospel is urgent. It calls for immediate response. If you are without Christ, you must not delay. 'Today is the day of salvation.' You are a sinner, without life, without hope before God. If you remain where you are, you will perish for ever. There is life in Christ, who has been made by God all that sinners need (1 Cor. 1:30; Col. 2:9-10). Come to Christ. Flee to Christ. Believe on the Lord Jesus Christ (Isa. 45:20-25; John 5:39-40). Without Christ you are lost for ever.

Down to Egypt

Hearing the urgent command of their father and knowing their desperate need, Joseph's brothers 'went down to buy corn in Egypt' (42:3). Chapters 42 - 44 are very instructive. 'Joseph knew his brethren, but they knew not him.' Even though Joseph knew what he would do for them before he revealed himself to them, his brothers had to learn some things. As I set the primary events of these chapters before you, you will see that Joseph's dealings with his brothers are a picture of our Lord's gracious dealings with us in saving grace.

First, Joseph's brothers tried to pay for what they received from him (42:3). The word 'buy' occurs five times in the first ten verses of this chapter. These poor men had no thought of securing corn except by paying for it. How foolish! What could they give to Joseph? Yet all men by nature, when first awakened to a sense of need, foolishly imagine that they can earn God's approval, win his favour and merit his acceptance. When Naaman came to Elisha for healing, he brought gifts to pay for mercy (2 Kings 5:5). When the prodigal first came to himself, he thought he would ask his father to make him a 'hired' servant (Luke 15:19). The rich young ruler thought he could do something to obtain eternal life (Luke 18:18). The Philippian jailer thought he had to do something to be saved (Acts 16:30). By nature, all men presume that they can, and should, do something to cause God to favour them, just as Joseph's brothers thought they could, and should, offer some payment for the corn Joseph possessed.

Second, these men knew they were perishing. Yet they clung to their own righteousness before Joseph who knew them (42:11). They said, 'We are true men.' When Joseph spoke roughly to them (42:7,9), they resented it and defended themselves. It is ever the nature of fallen man to justify himself.

Third, Joseph put his brothers into prison for three days (42:17). This is exactly what they deserved. Joseph had no intention of destroying them. He put them in their proper place, the place of shame and condemnation, so that they would know their guilt and acknowledge their sin. He abased them because he was determined to exalt them. So it is with our Saviour. He always abases before he exalts. He shuts us up before he sets us free. He slays before he makes alive. As we have seen before, he will never save a sinner until he gets him lost and makes him know that he needs saving.

Fourth, when they were shut up under the law, Joseph's brothers began to remember their sin (42:21). The terrors of hell are the terrors of an awakened conscience without repentance. The first terrors of a soul under conviction are the terrors of an awakened, guilty conscience (Rom. 3:19). This is the law's purpose. It identifies sin and condemns the sinner, shutting us up to Christ.

Fifth, when they began to know and acknowledge their guilt and their desperate need, Joseph began to show his brothers that deliverance is by grace alone (42:25-26). The bread of life cannot be purchased. It must be accepted as a free gift, if it is received at all (Eph. 2:8-9).

Sixth, Joseph's brothers found a brief satisfaction and reprieve (42:26). They got their corn and went home. They enjoyed a time of peace. But Joseph was still unknown. This is what religion gives sinners — peace without Christ. But God will not allow his people to rest until they rest upon Christ.

Seventh, Joseph's brothers soon had their superficial peace shattered (42:27-28). Their hearts failed them and they were filled with fear. When they had eaten their corn, the famine was still there (43:1-2). This was all by Joseph's wise arrangement. What wisdom and grace! So it is with Christ our Saviour. He so arranges all the affairs of chosen sinners that they are both compelled and fully willing to come to him at the appointed hour. (Ps. 65:4; 110:3).

Eighth, Joseph's brothers still retained their legal spirit (43:11,15). They doubled their efforts to please Joseph. How little they knew him. He prepared a feast for them. He said, 'These men shall dine with me' (43:16). He provided everything. Is not this the word of the gospel? 'Come, for all things are now ready!' Christ is the provider; we only receive.

Ninth, Joseph graciously forced his brothers to take their proper place before him and confess their sin to God. There could be no fellowship between him and his brothers until they fully confessed their sin and guilt; and he graciously forced them to do it (Ps. 65:4; 110:3). He arranged everything to secure his purpose (44:1-2; Rom. 8:28-30). He sent his steward to bring them to him (44:4), just as our Lord sends his Spirit to call chosen, redeemed sinners in the time of love. His brothers came fearful, broken, helpless, and bowed before him (44:13-14). Standing is over. These once proud, boasting men now bow in terror before Joseph. Speaking for the rest, Judah acknowledged that God had found out their iniquity, and they sought mercy (44:16).

Joseph

When his brothers confessed their sin and sought mercy, bowing before his feet, Joseph could not restrain himself. 'Joseph made himself known unto his brethren' (45:1-3). What a touching scene this is. It was Joseph who made himself known to his brothers. He cleared the room. The Lord Jesus always gets the chosen sinner alone with himself when he is about to make himself known (Hosea 2:14; John 8:9). He spoke personally to his brothers. No priests, personal workers, or mediators were used. When Christ makes himself known to chosen sinners, he does so by his Spirit, through the Word of his grace, without the witchcraft of religious inventions.

There is a wealth of instruction in the way Joseph made himself known to his brothers. In everything he did, he was a type of Christ. If you did not know better, you would think he had already read the New Testament, and was deliberately acting as a type of Christ. The fact is, though he knew it not, that is exactly the case. God raised him up specifically to portray redemption and grace to sinners in Christ. First, he declared his name: 'I am Joseph.' Then, he invited them to come near to him (45:4) and declared his relationship to them: 'I am Joseph your brother!' (45:4). At last, he comforted them.

Look at the way he comforted them. He assured them of forgiveness (45:5). He explained what God had done (45:7-8). He told them of the provision he had made for them (45:10-11). He promised them all the fulness of his grace. He said, 'You will always be near me. I shall sustain you and nourish you. No evil will befall you. You have my word for it.' Then Joseph kissed his brothers (45:15). His kiss was the assurance of his love, his forgiveness and of complete reconciliation. The fame of this was heard throughout all of Pharaoh's house (45:16). The day will soon come when the fame of God's goodness and grace to chosen sinners will for ever reverberate through all creation (Eph. 2:7).

Joseph, who represents our Saviour, was pleased. His brothers, who represent all saved sinners, were pleased. Pharaoh, who (at least, in the picture given here) represents God the Father, was pleased. This thing even pleased all the servants of Pharaoh's palace, just as the salvation of God's elect and the glory of Christ revealed in saving them pleases the Spirit of God, all the servants of God, all the heavenly angels, every faithful gospel preacher and all the affairs of providence.

Then, Joseph sent his brothers on an urgent mission to bring all the chosen family to him (45:18). The mission was simple. His brothers were to go and tell all the family that Joseph was alive, that he was lord over all, that everything they needed was in his hands, and that he bade them all come to him. That is exactly the mission our Lord has given us (Matt. 28:18-20). As he sent them out on their mission, knowing the depravity of their hearts, Joseph gave his brothers one word of admonition. He said, 'See that ye fall not out by the way' (45:24). It is a sad fact, but a fact, nonetheless, that saved sinners, sent as we are to carry the gospel of God's free and sovereign grace in Christ to other sinners, still need this admonition (Eph. 4:1-7). Joseph's brothers were faithful to their commission. Let us ever be faithful to ours. They did not invent a message of their own, or alter the message Joseph gave them. They just told others what Joseph told them and did for them. Good preaching and good witnessing are simply telling sinners what the Lord Jesus Christ has done for you and taught you by his grace. As God owned and honoured their message, for the salvation of all Israel, he will own and honour the gospel today; and by it, all Israel, that is to say all God's elect, will be saved (Isa. 55:11).

36.

A surety for Benjamin

Genesis 43:8-9

'And Judah said unto Israel his father, Send the lad with me, and we will arise and go; that we may live, and not die, both we, and thou, and also our little ones. I will be surety for him; of my hand shalt thou require him: if I bring him not unto thee, and set him before thee, then let me bear the blame for ever' (Gen. 43:8-9).

God the Holy Spirit is anxious for every believer to enjoy the comforting assurance of salvation in Christ. He is our comforter. That is the work he was sent to perform. His method of comfort is to take the things of Christ and to show them to us (John 16:7,13-14). He knows that the more fully we know Christ, and the more clearly we see him, the more we shall enjoy the comfort and assurance of our salvation in him.

Therefore, the Spirit of God always points us to Christ, especially in the inspired volume of Holy Scripture. He not only tells us who Christ is, what he has done, and what he is doing for us, but he also uses metaphor after metaphor to show us pictures of our great Saviour, pictures designed to assure God's believing people that all is well between them and God. We have seen this repeatedly throughout the book of Genesis.

Here, in Genesis 43:8-9, the Spirit of God gives us another beautiful and instructive picture of the Lord Jesus

Christ and of the grace of God in him. As Judah became surety for Benjamin, assuming all responsibility for him, so the Lord Jesus Christ, who came from the tribe of Judah, became surety for God's elect before the worlds were made, in the covenant of grace, assuming total, absolute responsibility for the salvation of his people (Heb. 7:22). In this study, I shall try to explain what a surety is and how the Lord Jesus Christ performs this work on our behalf.

What is it to stand surety?

A person who stands surety for another is someone who commits himself to making good for another. He approaches one person on behalf of another person and acts as a representative who places himself under obligation to the person he approaches for the one he represents. In this sense, Christ is our surety. He drew near to God the Father on our behalf, before the world began, and laid himself under obligation to God for us (Ps. 40:7-8; John 10:16-18).

To stand surety for someone is to strike hands with another in solemn agreement. To a man of honour, suretyship is a voluntary bondage (Prov. 6:1-2). When Christ became our surety, he voluntarily placed himself in bondage to his Father until his service had been performed (Isa. 50:5-7; John 10:16-18; Heb. 10:5-14).

This is what the Lord Jesus Christ did as the surety for God's elect, in the everlasting covenant of grace, before the world began. He drew near to God the Father on behalf of his elect (Prov. 8:30-31). Because justice had to be maintained, even in the exercise of mercy (Prov. 17:15), our great Surety promised to perform faithfully all that God required for the salvation of his people. Our Saviour pledged himself, according to the will of God, to bring in an everlasting righteousness for us, to satisfy all God's law and justice on our behalf, to put away our sins by the sacrifice of himself, to give the chosen a new, holy nature in the new birth, to raise them up in glorification and perfection, and, at last, to present them to the Father in the perfection of holiness, to the praise of the glory of his grace.

Upon this pledge of suretyship, our Saviour struck hands with his Father in solemn agreement. These three texts — Ephesians 1:3-14, Romans 8:28-30 and 2 Timothy 1:9-10 — simply cannot be understood except in the light of this fact. God the Father trusted his Son to fulfil his suretyship engagements (Eph. 1:12). He entrusted his elect into the hands of his dear Son as their surety, as a man entrusts sheep to the care of a shepherd (John 10:14-18). As Israel said to Judah, so God the Father said to our Surety, 'Take them, and go! Bring them again to me in the perfection of holiness' (John 6:39). The matter of our salvation was then and there settled for ever (2 Tim. 1:9). The experience of salvation is the reception of the promise of eternal life which God, who cannot lie, promised and gave his elect in Christ before the world began (2 Tim. 1:10; Heb. 9:14-17). All the blessings of grace come to chosen, redeemed sinners in the form of a testament or a will; but they were promised as the reward of Christ's obedience as our covenant surety.

How did Christ become our surety?

With men, a surety is a mere guarantor, one who is jointly responsible with the principal debtor for the payment of a debt. This is not the kind of surety Christ is. He did not merely agree to meet our obligations to God's law if, by some circumstance or condition, we became incapable of meeting our own obligations. As our surety, Christ took upon himself all responsibility for the totality of our obligation to God's holy law and justice.

With men, a man may be legally forced into suretyship. A father is legally responsible for the debts and liabilities of his minor children. A husband is legally responsible for the debts and liabilities of his wife. But willingly, voluntarily, cheerfully, Christ placed himself in servitude to God the Father, to obey his will and fulfil his law, as the surety of his elect. At the moment he became our surety, he became servant to God his Father (Isa. 42:1; 49:3; John 10:17-18). Our Saviour's subordination to the Father as our surety does not imply any lack of equality between the Father and the Son in the Godhead. It is a voluntary subordination. The Lord Jesus Christ is an absolute surety by voluntary consent.

When Christ became our surety, he took the whole of our debt upon himself. He became responsible for our obligations to God. As soon as he was accepted as our surety, we were released from all our debts and obligations to God's holy law; he set us free. God ceased looking to us for satisfaction. He freed us from all the curse, penalty and obligation we would incur by reason of sin, and looked to his Son alone for the satisfaction of our debts (Job 33:24). This is beautifully illustrated for us in the case of the apostle Paul and Onesimus (Philem. 8).

When Christ became surety for us, all the sins of God's elect were imputed to him in the mind and purpose of God. By divine imputation, our sins were placed to his account. He became responsible for them. Christ was made to be sin for us when he hung upon the cursed tree; but he became responsible and accountable to God for our sins when he became our surety. They were laid to his account from eternity (Isa. 53:6; Ps. 40:12; 69:5; 2 Cor. 5:19).

When Christ became our surety, we were redeemed, justified, pardoned and made righteous in the sight of God. God's forbearance, patience and longsuffering with this world are due to the suretyship engagements of Christ. God's eye has always been upon the blood. It is the blood of Christ, our surety, that held back the hand of God's judgement when Adam sinned. The Old Testament saints were pardoned and justified upon the basis of Christ's obedience as our surety, though he had not yet actually rendered that obedience (Isa. 43:25; 45:22-25; Rom. 3:24-26). Those men and women had knowledge of and faith in Christ as their surety (Job 19:25-27; Ps. 32:1-4; 119:122; Isa. 38:14).

The Lord Jesus Christ became our surety by his own voluntary will. He was accepted as such in the covenant of grace before the world began; and we were accepted by God in him (Eph. 1:6).

What did the Lord Jesus Christ agree to as our surety?

When Christ became our surety, he made certain promises to God the Father in the name of his covenant people which he is honour bound to perform. The promises were made voluntarily, without any constraint or force, except the constraint of his love and the force of his grace. But now, having made the promises, he is bound, bound by his own honour, to perform them. What are those promises? What did Christ agree to do as our surety? He agreed and promised to do two things.

First, he agreed to fulfil all our responsibilities to God. Standing as our surety, in an absolute sense, Christ did not simply assume part of our responsibility in a given area, leaving us to make up the balance. He willingly became absolutely responsible for his people in all things.

He agreed to render that perfect obedience to the law of God, which we were obliged to do, establishing perfect righteousness for us. He worked out and brought in an everlasting, perfect, legal righteousness for his people (Rom.

5:19; Jer. 23:6; John 17:4). Our Saviour also agreed to satisfy the penalty of the law as our substitute (Gal. 3:13; John 19:30). By his perfect obedience, in life and in death, the Lord Jesus Christ magnified the law and made it honourable in the redemption of God's elect (Heb. 10:5-14).

Second, Christ, our surety, agreed to bring all his elect safely to glory (John 10:16-18). This is the Father's will which he came to perform (John 6:39-40). Yes, the Lord Jesus Christ became responsible to bring God's Benjamins safely home. 'If I bring them not to thee, and set them before thee,' he said, 'then let me bear the blame for ever.' It is because of his suretyship engagements for his elect that the Son of God says, 'Them also I must bring.' What our surety has sworn to do he will do (Heb. 2:13).

He reconciled us to God by his sin-atoning death. He entered into heaven as our covenant-head, and claimed our eternal inheritance in our name as our surety. In the last day, he will present all of his elect faultless before the throne of his Father's glory with exceeding great joy (Eph. 5; Jude 1; Heb. 2:13). In that day, he will appear without sin; and we (all for whom he is surety) shall appear with him without sin. God the Father will say to Christ our surety and to all his people, 'Well done!'

Child of God, the suretyship engagements of Christ ought to cause your heart to leap with joy. The whole of our acceptance with God is in Christ our surety. Our relationship with the eternal God does, in great measure, determine what we do; but what we do does not, in any measure whatsoever, determine our relationship or acceptance with the eternal God, our heavenly Father. The whole of our assurance is Christ.

In my surety I am free!
His dear hands were pierced for me!

With his spotless garments on,
I am as holy as God's Son!

The whole of our security is Christ: his covenant engagements, his redemptive work finished at Calvary, his gospel
promise ('They shall never perish!'), and his glory as our
surety and Mediator upon the throne of universal monarchy.
These are the things, the only things, which give believing
hearts peace before God.

37.

Jacob's fear removed

Genesis 46:1-4

'And Israel took his journey with all that he had, and came to Beersheba, and offered sacrifices unto the God of his father Isaac. And God spake unto Israel in the visions of the night, and said, Jacob, Jacob. And he said, Here am I. And he said, I am God, the God of thy father: fear not to go down into Egypt; for I will there make of thee a great nation: I will go down with thee into Egypt; and I will also surely bring thee up again: and Joseph shall put his hand upon thine eyes' (Gen. 46:1-4).

When Jacob heard the report from his sons that Joseph was still alive and that he was governor over all the land of Egypt, the old man fainted. Then, when he was revived, being assured that it was so, he said, 'It is enough; Joseph my son is still alive: I shall go and see him before I die.' Bold, confident and full of joy, Jacob packed up all his family and everything he owned, and started out for Egypt.

Along the way to Egypt, Jacob came to Beersheba. There he worshipped the Lord his God. But God saw what Jacob never expressed. As the Lord looked upon the heart of his worshipping servant, he saw an old man whose heart was tossed about with many fears. So the Lord God graciously removed the fears of his beloved servant. This is another picture of grace. As God removed Jacob's fear, so he

graciously removes the fears of his people today by the revelation of himself to us, not in visions and dreams, but by
his Spirit and through his Word.

Flesh and spirit

Like all believers in this world, Jacob was a man with two
natures. He is called by two names: 'Israel took his journey... And God spoke unto Israel ... and said, Jacob, Jacob.'
Israel was the name God gave him, the name of his strength.
Jacob was the name his father gave him, the name of his
nature, the name of his weakness.

It appears that Jacob started out for Egypt, inspired by
the news concerning Joseph, without the least fear. The
old man had the sparkle of joy in his eyes. But when he
came to Beersheba, he seems to have halted by reason of
fear. Beersheba was on the border of Canaan. When he left
Beersheba, he knew he was leaving the land of promise
and was to be on his way to Egypt. Realizing what a momentous jourey he was about to make, the old man began to
tremble. We should ever be aware of these two facts, the
one very sad and lamentable, the other most blessed.

First, so long as we are in this world, God's chosen people
are men and women with two natures. Our name is both
Israel, prince with God who prevails, and Jacob, supplanter,
weakness and failure (Rom. 7:14-23; Gal. 5:17-23).

Second, our great God and Saviour sympathizes and ten-
derly cares for us in the state of weakness. The Lord God
saw Jacob's need and met it. He does not excuse, condone,
or approve of Jacob's fear. But he does not cast him off because of his fear. 'He knoweth our frame; he remembereth
that we are dust' (Ps. 103:14; 78:37-39; 1 John 2:1-2).

Worshipping

Before proceeding to Egypt, Jacob paused at Beersheba to worship God. This was to him a holy place. It was a place of significance for him. It was at Beersheba that God had met with Abraham and called upon him to sacrifice Isaac (Gen. 21:31). As that was a critical turning point in Abraham's life, Jacob paused there to worship God, because he had come to a critical turning point in his own life. He was about to go where he had never been before. He was about to break new ground. So he came to Beersheba and offered sacrifices to God, the God of his father Isaac. What wisdom he displayed.

As he began a new era in his life, he consecrated himself anew to his God. When Lot pitched his tent towards Sodom, we do not read of any devotion to God. But when Jacob was going to Egypt, before doing so, he consecrated himself to God again. He is wise who begins everything with God. Young people just beginning to set up their own homes, businessmen launching a new enterprise, churches and pastors setting out upon a new sphere of ministry, believers beginning a new day, first and foremost, all should begin with God.

Jacob 'offered sacrifices' to the Lord. He did so for at least three reasons.

First, he offered sacrifices to God to purge himself and his household ceremonially. This was also a type of sin. By an act of faith, by blood atonement, Jacob both confessed his sin and sought cleansing for it and for those of his family. He knew that he could not walk with God, enjoy God's fellowship or God's blessings, unless his sins were purged from him by the blood of Christ, God's Sacrifice.

Second, his sacrifices were also thank offerings to his
God for all that he had done. Benjamin had come back to
him safe and sound. Joseph was still alive and he was going
to see him. Once he had said, 'All these things are against
me.' Now, he is beginning to see that God had been working for him; and he humbly repents of his unbelief.

Third, I am sure that Jacob offered these sacrifices upon
the altar at Beersheba so that he might inquire of the Lord
as to what he should do. He was in a great dilemma. Shall
I go down to Egypt or not? He wanted to know God's will.
So he sought God's direction. What trouble and heartache
we would save ourselves if, before doing anything or making
any decision, we sought direction from our God (Prov. 3:5-6).

Troubled

The reason Jacob needed God's special direction was because his heart was troubled with fear at what lay before
him. I would not put words into his mouth, but it seems
that the cause of Jacob's fear is obvious. He was going down
to Egypt!

His grandfather, Abraham, once went down into Egypt
and found much trouble there. That is where he got Hagar.
Abraham's journey into Egypt was probably the greatest
mistake of his life. Isaac, Jacob's father, once started to go
down into Egypt, but God stopped him. Jacob was now an
old man, an experienced saint, experienced in his own
frailty. He must have paused with fear, asking himself, 'Is it
right for me to go to Egypt? What effect will this move have
upon me and my family? How will this move affect the
truth of God, the glory of God and the people of God?' These
were matters of great importance to Jacob.

He knew that Egypt was a notoriously idolatrous country. There learned, philosophical men worshipped everything from cats, calves and crocodiles to the vegetables they grew in their gardens. His associations in Egypt would be very trying for Jacob and his family. He knew, too, that God had told Abraham that his people would be afflicted in Egypt for four hundred years (Gen. 15:13-14).

Jacob knew that if he went down to Egypt, he was heading for trouble, unless God went with him. He knew that Joseph was there; but would God be there? He knew that corn was there; but would God be there? Everything seemed to draw him there; but would God be there? This was the matter of concern to Jacob. This ought to be the matter of concern to us in every decision we make.

I am a man with only one child, a daughter. As she began to mature and I tried to direct her concerning the kind of man she should consider for her husband, I told her several things which I am convinced are of paramount importance. I said to her, 'Find a man who worships God. Settle in a place where you can worship God. Do nothing that will interfere with, or keep, you and your family from the worship of God.' The worship and glory of God must ever be the dominant concern of the believer's life. All other things are indescribably less than secondary to this.

Fear removed

The Lord appeared to Jacob 'in the visions of the night' to say to him, 'Fear not.' Jacob's fear had to be removed. It is both displeasing and dishonouring to God for his people to walk in earthly fear (Matt. 6:19-33). Fear, fretting and worrying are things most unbecoming to men and women who claim to believe God. Fear robs us of joy (Phil. 4:4-5) and weakens us in the path of known duty and responsibility.

C. H. Spurgeon wrote, 'Before we begin a new enterprise, fear may be seasonable; we ought to be cautious as to whether our way is right in the sight of God. But when we once know God's will and begin we must say farewell to fear, for fear will be fatal to success. Go straight ahead. Believe in God, and carry the work through.'

Fear is an indication of a quarrel with God's will. Jacob had to go down to Egypt by God's command; but he was afraid. He was afraid to obey God's command. We must not judge him too harshly. Who has not been guilty of the same offence? God will never send us where he will not go with us. God will not require you to do anything he will not enable you to do. No believer will ever meet a trial or temptation in the path of obedience through which God will not sustain him (1 Cor. 10:13; 1 Thess. 5:24). His word to his servant is 'Fear not.'

The Lord removed Jacob's fear in the most tender and gracious manner imaginable. Our God always deals with his children in grace. What a picture we have here of God's grace dealing with poor, fearful Jacob, and with us. He removed it by letting him know that he knew him. 'God spake unto Israel in the visions of the night, and said, Jacob, Jacob.' In essence, he said, 'I know you. I know what you are going through, and I know what lies before you.' Then he allowed Jacob to know by experience that he was in communion with God. When the Lord spoke to Jacob, Jacob spoke to God and said, 'Here am I.' That is the language of a submissive heart in communion with God (Gen. 22:1; 1 Sam. 3:10; Isa. 6:8).

Next, the Lord assured Jacob of his covenant faithfulness. He said, 'I am God, the God of thy father.' That means

'I am the God of the covenant. The blessing I have promised I shall perform. I am the God who is for you' (Rom. 8:28-32).

Then the Lord promised Jacob that he would bless him in Egypt. 'I will there make of thee a great nation.' These things should ease us of fear, as we face the trials through which our heavenly Father is pleased to send us. Where God takes us, he will bless us. Peter, James and John 'feared as they entered into the cloud' (Luke 9:34). But they were blessed by God in that place; and we shall be blessed by God in whatever place or circumstance we find ourselves by following his direction.

The Lord also assured Jacob of his presence, saying, 'I will go down with thee.' He further promised his servant that, no matter what happened in Egypt, his inheritance in Canaan was sure. He said, 'I will also surely bring thee up again.' This is precisely what he says to us to assure, comfort and strengthen our hearts in the face of trial. Our inheritance in Christ is sure (Rom. 8:33-39).

The Lord gave Jacob one more word of promise by which he removed his fear. God told Jacob that he would die in peace with Joseph by his side: 'Joseph shall put his hand upon thine eyes.' He has done the same for every believer. For the child of God, death is a covenant blessing. 'So he giveth his beloved sleep!' At God's appointed time, the Lord Jesus will put his hand upon your eyes. It is written: 'Blessed are the dead which die in the Lord!' Therefore, the sons of Jacob are told to cease from fear (Isa. 43:1-5). For the believer, there is no cause for fear.

38.

Jacob's prophecy concerning Judah

Genesis 49:8-12

'Judah, thou art he whom thy brethren shall praise: thy hand shall be in the neck of thine enemies; thy father's children shall bow down before thee. Judah is a lion's whelp: from the prey, my son, thou art gone up: he stooped down, he couched as a lion, and as an old lion; who shall rouse him up? The sceptre shall not depart from Judah, nor a lawgiver from between his feet, until Shiloh come; and unto him shall the gathering of the people be. Binding his foal unto the vine, and his ass's colt unto the choice vine; he washed his garments in wine, and his clothes in the blood of grapes: His eyes shall be red with wine, and his teeth white with milk'

(Gen. 49:8-12).

Before the Word of God was given in written form, God revealed himself to chosen sinners, and spoke to them by giving them testimony by word of mouth and in various, supernatural ways concerning his Son, the Lord Jesus Christ, and the great work of redemption and salvation he would accomplish (Heb. 1:1-3). We have no way of knowing how much those early believers knew about the person and work of Christ; but they clearly knew and understood much more than most people seem to think!

Abel understood the necessity of blood atonement and brought a blood sacrifice to God by faith, showing that he knew salvation was by grace alone through the blood of Christ, the sinners' substitute (Gen. 4). Enoch walked with God by faith in Christ and even prophesied of Christ's glorious second coming (Jude 14). Abraham knew and believed much by God's special revelation (Gen. 22). The Lord Jesus Christ said of Abraham, '[He] rejoiced to see my day' (John 8:56). And Job, who probably lived about the same time as Abraham, spoke confidently of both redemption and resurrection by Christ (Job 19:25-27).

In this prophecy of Jacob concerning Judah, we see another example of the fact that these early saints were rich in knowledge and in faith. Jacob had called his twelve sons before him to tell them, by the Spirit of prophecy, how God would deal with the twelve tribes of Israel in the future. The dying patriarch had a word from God for each of his sons and the tribes that would descend from them. Judah was singled out and given special honour. Jacob praised him and prophesied many good things concerning him.

Particularly, we are told that Jacob prophesied that Messiah, 'Shiloh', would come from Judah. Both David and Solomon, Israel's greatest kings, sprang from the tribe of Judah. The Lord Jesus, the great King of God's Israel, our Redeemer-King, is 'the Lion of the tribe of Judah' (Rev. 5:5). When Jacob spoke to Judah and made this prophecy concerning him, he was speaking, by the Spirit of God, about the Lord Jesus Christ. Judah was a type of Christ. We see this in seven distinct ways.

1. Judah must be praised by his brothers (v. 8)

'Judah, thou art he whom thy brethren shall praise.' The name Judah means 'praise'. Matthew Henry wrote, 'God was

praised for him (29:35), praised by him, and praised in him; and therefore his brethren shall praise him.' Certainly, this speaks of Christ, our Messiah, Redeemer and King. He is worthy of praise and will have the sincere praise of his people.

Christ alone is to have our praise. 'He that glorieth, let him glory in the Lord' (1 Cor. 1:31; Ps. 115:1).

Praise him! Praise him! Jesus, our blessed Redeemer,
Heavenly portals, loud with hosannas ring!
Jesus, Saviour, reigneth for ever and ever;
Crown him! crown him! Prophet and Priest and King!

Believers delight to give all praise to Christ, because of the excellence of his person as the God-man, our Mediator. We praise him for the wonders of redemption, the abundant grace of God in him, and the goodness of his sovereign, providential rule.

As Judah's brethren praised him, so all Christ's brethren, all his people, give all praise to him. Some praise the pope, some praise the church, some praise preachers, and some praise themselves; but God's saints praise Christ. They praise him for ever in heaven (Rev. 5:9-10); but they learn to praise him on the earth! (Ps. 115:1). God's people are a praising people. We do not merely offer him the pretence of praise, or the hypocrisy of praise only from the lips. Believers give praise to God their Saviour. Nothing is more inconsistent with our profession of faith in Christ than murmuring, complaining and unhappiness. Murmuring is the fruit of unbelief. Praise is the fruit of faith.

2. Judah must be victorious over all his enemies (v. 8)

'Thy hand shall be in the neck of thine enemies.' When a man has his hand securely in the neck of his enemy, he has subdued him. At his pleasure, he can force him to the ground, snuff out his breath and destroy him. This, too, speaks of Christ (1 Cor. 15:25; Heb. 1:13; 10:13). He is in complete control of his enemies, and he will bring them down. Our Saviour met Satan and defeated him. In the wilderness of temptation (Luke 4:1-13), in the garden of Gethsemane, and upon the cross of Calvary, our Lord Jesus conquered and bound the devil, crushing his head, just as the Scriptures declared he would (Gen. 3:15; John 12:31-33; 19:30; Rev. 12:10; 20:1-3). Christ took our sins to the cross and vanquished them (Col. 2:15). The Son of God met death, bowed to it, and then conquered it (1 Cor. 15:51-58). There is no enemy of Christ, or of his people, that will not be finally destroyed.

3. All his father's children must bow down before Judah (v. 8)

'Thy father's children shall bow down before thee.' Without question, this prophecy refers immediately to the whole nation of Israel bowing before David and Solomon as their kings. But, behold, a greater than David and a greater than Solomon is here. This is a prophecy of that glory and honour which belongs to, and is reserved for, Christ alone. Christ is Lord of all. By virtue of his own deity (Rom. 9:5), by virtue of his Father's decree (Heb. 2:5,8), and by virtue of his sin-atoning death (Rom. 14:9; Phil. 2:8-11), the Lord Jesus Christ is that great Lord King who rules the universe, before whom all men must and will bow (Isa. 45:22-25). All of God's creation will one day bow before the Lord Jesus Christ and confess that he is indeed Lord of all. All God's elect bow to him in faith as their Lord (Rom. 10:9-10). But all the universe will bow before him and confess that he is Lord in the last day (Phil. 2:9-11).

4. 'Judah is a lion's whelp' (v. 9)

Our Lord Jesus is compared to a young lion, because he is
strong and courageous. The lion is 'the king of the jungle'.
He goes where he wants to go, does what he wants to do,
fears nothing, and is never in danger. Here is 'the Lion of
the tribe of Judah'. Our Saviour is not spoken of here as a
lion raging and ranging, but as a lion couching and resting.

'From the prey, my son, thou art gone up.' Christ Jesus,
the Son of God, left heaven and came to this earth to engage
the enemy and redeem his people by his own mighty arm.
Now, having accomplished his great work, he has 'gone
up,' ascended back into heaven again. 'The Lion of the tribe
of Judah ... hath prevailed!' (Rev. 5:5). There is no possibility of failure with Christ (Isa. 42:4). He is the Lion of
Judah. He has prevailed, and will yet prevail.

'He stooped down.' What a great stoop he made! (Phil.
2:5-8; 2 Cor. 8:9). God became man. The Son of God became
a servant to men. As a man, Christ was obedient to his Father
in all things, to establish righteousness for men. He was
obedient unto death, even the death of the cross, that he
might redeem us from the curse of the law.

*'He couched as a lion, and as an old lion; who shall rouse
him up?'* He stooped; he conquered; he took his prey; he
ascended; he sat down, having accomplished his pleasure,
having obtained what he sought, having fulfilled his mission (Matt. 1:21; Heb. 9:12; 10:10-14). Who will dare rouse
him? Who will be able to disturb him? Behold, the sovereign serenity with which the Son of God sits in heaven!

5. 'The sceptre shall not depart from Judah ... until Shiloh come' (v. 10)

This tenth verse is a great and notable prophecy. All of the
ancient Jewish writers have said that this verse is a prophecy

of the coming of Christ, by which God assured his people that the kingdom and civil government of Judah would continue until the Christ, the Messiah, came. That being the case, by their own instructors, the Jews should be convinced that Jesus Christ is the Messiah, because the kingdom and civil government of Judah ceased when Christ came.

The name which Jacob used for Christ is 'Shiloh'. Where did he get that name? God gave it to him. It was a special name, given by special revelation, for a special person, who would come at a special time. It is a name full of significance.

1. Shiloh means 'sent' (John 9:7). Christ is truly the 'sent one' (John 19:21).
2. Shiloh means 'son' (Isa. 9:6-7). Christ Jesus is the Son of God. He is the Son of David. He is the Son of Man.
3. Shiloh means 'the one to whom it belongs' (Ezek. 21:25-27). The sceptre, the crown, the throne, the kingdom, the worship, the praise belong to Christ alone. All others are impostors! (Col. 1:14-19).
4. Shiloh also means 'peace'. It comes from the same word as 'Salem, King of peace.' Christ is our peace. He made peace for us by the blood of his cross; and we have peace with God by faith in him (Rom. 5:1).
5. Finally, Shiloh means 'prosperous'. It is written concerning Christ that 'the pleasure of the LORD shall prosper in his hand' (Isa. 53:10).

6. 'Unto him shall the gathering of the people be' (v. 10)

The object of Christ's coming into the world, of his covenant engagements with the Father as our surety, of his death upon the cross for his people, was that he might redeem a people by his blood and gather them by the arm of his omnipotent grace to himself for ever. The people God has chosen will be gathered to him (John 6:37-39; 10:14-16; 17:1-10). At the appointed time of love, they will, each one, be gathered to Christ by the irresistible power and grace of his Spirit, gathered to him in repentance and faith, and in love and willing devotion (Ps. 65:4; 110:3). And all God's elect will be gathered to him in glory.

7. Judah will be strong and fruitful (vv. 11-12)

Without question, these two verses refer to the glorious work of redemption by Shiloh, the Lord Jesus Christ. When he came to redeem his people, he came into Jerusalem riding upon a colt, the foal of an ass (Zech. 9:9; Matt. 21:2-5). When he suffered and died upon the cross as our substitute, his garments (Isa. 63:1), his human nature and his clothing were washed in blood. Yet his eyes sparkled with joy, the joy of blood-bought redemption for his people, as he endured the cross, despising the shame (Heb. 12:2).

These two verses also refer to the manifold blessings of grace that are ours in Christ. Christ is the choice, true vine, a vine strong enough to have all burdens bound to him (v. 11). The blood of Christ is a fountain of cleansing and joyful refreshment for our souls (v. 11). Let us ever bind our burden to Christ. Cling to him. We find strength, when Christ is our strength. There is an abundance of grace in Christ to meet all the needs of his people (v. 12). There is wine for joy and milk for purity, wine for men and milk for babes. Every need of our souls, in all circumstances, is found in him, who is our all.

39.

Boundless blessedness

Genesis 49:22-26

*'Joseph is a fruitful bough, even a fruitful bough by a well;
whose branches run over the wall: The archers have sorely
grieved him, and shot at him, and hated him: But his bow
abode in strength, and the arms of his hands were made
strong by the hands of the mighty God of Jacob; (from thence
is the shepherd, the stone of Israel:) Even by the God of thy
father, who shall help thee; and by the Almighty, who shall
bless thee with blessings of heaven above, blessings of the
deep that lieth under, blessings of the breasts, and of the
womb: The blessings of thy father have prevailed above the
blessings of my progenitors unto the utmost bound of the
everlasting hills: they shall be on the head of Joseph, and on
the crown of the head of him that was separate from his
brethren'*

(Gen. 49:22-26).

In Genesis 49, we see Jacob on his deathbed; and here we
see him at his best. He showed himself a noble man in
many things; but his final scene is by far his best. Like the
sun at sunset, Israel appeared most glorious when he was
leaving this world. Spurgeon said:

Like good wine which runs clear to the very bottom, unalloyed by dregs, so did Jacob, till his dying hour, continue to sing of love, mercy, and goodness, past and future. Like the swan, which (as old writers say) singeth not all its life until it comes to die, so the old patriarch remained silent as a songster for many years, but when he stretched himself on his last couch of rest, he stayed himself up in his bed and, although with faltering voice, he sang a sonnet upon his offspring.

In verses 22-26, Jacob gives his richest, fullest benediction to his beloved son Joseph. Without question, the benediction given to Joseph speaks of the blessedness of him of whom Joseph was a type and picture, the Lord Jesus Christ. Because the one spoken of here is Christ our Lord, the blessedness bestowed upon him is also a declaration of that boundless blessedness which is the portion of God's elect. So, as we read these lines, I shall endeavour to show you how everything written in these verses applies first to Joseph, then to our Lord Jesus Christ, and then to all who are Christ's.

A fruitful bough

'Joseph is a fruitful bough, even a fruitful bough by a well; whose branches run over the wall' (v. 22). Joseph was made to be a fruitful bough. This prophecy refers to Joseph's seed, his children, which are compared to a tree so heavily loaded with fruit that its branches hang over the wall of the garden in which it stands. I do not doubt that the promise here given refers to Joseph's physical seed; but it goes beyond

that. This is a prophecy concerning the boundless fruitfulness of our great Joseph, the Lord Jesus Christ.

The fruit of our great Saviour's substitutionary sacrifice at Calvary is a great, innumerable host of redeemed sinners who will serve him for ever. The Lord Jesus Christ was cut off in the prime of his manhood, a single man, with no children. The question is asked, 'Who shall declare his generation?' It appeared that he would never have a seed to serve and honour his name; but that is not the case.

In fact, his death as our sin-atoning substitute is the very means by which his bountiful, innumerable seed is born. As an offering for sin, his death guaranteed the birth and everlasting life of his people.

He was taken from prison and from judgement: and who shall declare his generation? For he was cut off out of the land of the living: for the transgression of my people was he stricken. And he made his grave with the wicked, and with the rich in his death; because he had done no violence, neither was any deceit in his mouth. Yet it pleased the LORD to bruise him; he hath put him to grief: when thou shalt make his soul an offering for sin, he shall see his seed, he shall prolong his days, and the pleasure of the LORD shall prosper in his hand. He shall see of the travail of his soul, and shall be satisfied: by his knowledge shall my righteous servant justify many; for he shall bear their iniquities

(Isa. 53:8-11).

Therefore, we read in Psalm 22:30-31, 'A seed shall serve him; it shall be accounted to the Lord for a generation. They shall come, and shall declare his righteousness unto a people that shall be born, that he hath done this.'

This promise is also a promise concerning each of God's elect in Christ. Every child of God, every true believer will be a fruitful bough, bringing forth fruit to God, by the power of his grace. The Lord God declares, 'From me is thy fruit found' (Hosea 14:8); and he makes all his children fruit bearing trees. 'The fruit of the Spirit is love, joy, peace, longsuffering, gentleness, goodness, faith, meekness, temperance: against such there is no law' (Gal. 5:22-23).

A hated man

'The archers have sorely grieved him, and shot at him, and hated him' (v. 23). Joseph had to endure the envy of his brothers by which he was grieved, the temptations of Potiphar's wife, the slander she heaped upon him, and the unprovoked hatred of them all. All God's Josephs in this world are marked, hated men.

Our Master, like Joseph, was hated without a cause. He was tempted in the wilderness, envied by the Pharisees, hated by the Jews, slandered by his enemies, grieved in his very soul and, at last, slaughtered on trumped up charges as a common criminal.

Let none who follow the Son of God expect better treatment while living in this world. The disciple is not above his Master, nor the servant above his Lord. Though blessed by God, boundlessly, everlastingly blessed by God, in this world, every child of God has the lot of Joseph. 'We must through much tribulation enter into the kingdom of God.' Every believer must endure the temptations of Satan, the envy of men, the betrayal of friends, the slander of evil tongues and the hatred of men, even the hatred of men whose interests they serve. This is our lot in this world; but it is, surely, as much a part of our blessedness as the most pleasant things we experience (Luke 6:20-26).

A man made strong

'But his bow abode in strength, and the arms of his hands were made strong by the hands of the mighty God of Jacob; (from thence is the shepherd, the stone of Israel)' (v. 24). Joseph was a man made strong by the mighty God of Jacob. The text says nothing about Joseph's natural strength or superiority over his brothers. The text says he was 'made strong by ... the mighty God of Jacob'.

Though many archers took aim and shot their arrows at him, Joseph's bow abode in strength. That is to say, he was so strong that he never sought to retaliate. A warrior who draws a bow must release his arrow quickly, else his hand will quiver, and he will miss his mark. Joseph was made strong, so strong that though his bow was drawn, he held it steady, and never fired a return arrow at his adversaries.

When his brothers falsely accused him, Joseph said nothing, either in defence of himself, or against his accusers. When Potiphar's wife slandered him, he spoke not a word. When he was wrongfully imprisoned on trumped up charges, he said nothing. When the chief butler forgot his kindness to him, Joseph's bow still abode in his strength. His arm was still made strong by the hands of the mighty God of Jacob.

That is how our Master suffered evil at the hands of men. He never once opened his mouth in defence of himself. Rather, he recognized that those, who set themselves against him, were but instruments by which his Father was performing his will for him, instruments by which his Father was accomplishing his covenant promise to exalt him above all.

By his great example, our Lord teaches us to endure patiently the assaults of wicked men, without vengeance or retaliation, when we are the objects of their envy, slander, betrayal and hatred.

If, when ye do well, and suffer for it, ye take it patiently, this is acceptable with God. For even hereunto were ye called: because Christ also suffered for us, leaving us an example, that ye should follow his steps: Who did no sin, neither was guile found in his mouth: Who, when he was reviled, reviled not again; when he suffered, he threatened not: but committed himself to him that judgeth righteously: Who his own self bare our sins in his own body on the tree, that we, being dead to sins, should live unto righteousness: by whose stripes ye were healed.

(1 Peter 2:20-24).

The mighty God of Jacob still makes his Josephs strong by his grace. While a prisoner for the gospel's sake, one of them displayed this same, remarkable strength of grace. He wrote from his prison, 'I know both how to be abased, and I know how to abound: every where and in all things I am instructed both to be full and to be hungry, both to abound and to suffer need. I can do all things through Christ which strengtheneth me' (Phil. 4:12-13).

'From thence is the shepherd, the stone of Israel.' The Lord Jesus Christ, the shepherd and stone of Israel, is that one who was sent from 'the Mighty God of Jacob' to redeem and save his people. I cannot imagine two more encouraging, assuring, comforting titles by which Judah could have described our Saviour. The Son of God, our Lord Jesus Christ is the Shepherd of Israel. He is our almighty protector and provider, who carries his lambs in his bosom. He is also the stone, the rock of Israel, the one upon whom we build and upon whom we are built, our foundation and support.

Boundless blessedness

In verses 25-26, Jacob pronounced a sevenfold blessedness upon Joseph, a sevenfold blessedness upon all who are God's. This is boundless blessedness indeed!

1. *'Even by the God of thy father, who shall help thee...'* Here is a promise of help in every time of need. He who is the God of our fathers, the God of Abraham, Isaac, and Jacob; he who is the God of Judah, who helped them and fulfilled his word to them, will help us and fulfil his word to us.

2. *'And by the Almighty, who shall bless thee with blessings of heaven above.'* Here is the promise of all the blessings of heaven, grace, salvation, eternal life and heavenly glory in Christ (Eph. 1:3-6).

3. *'... with blessings of the deep that lieth under.'* Here is the promise that all the deep mysteries of providence, all the affairs of time, all the events of the world, the demons of hell, the beasts of the field and the adversities of life will prove to be a blessing from God to his people (Hosea 2:18; Rom. 8:28-30).

4. *'... with blessings of the breasts, and of the womb.'* This is a promise that 'goodness and mercy shall follow me all the days of my life'. Speaking by the Spirit of God, the old patriarch declares that God's elect are blessed in all things, all the days of their lives, even from their mother's breasts. Every believer may, with David and with the Lord himself, confidently speak these words of praise to God: 'Thou art

he that took me out of the womb: thou didst make me hope when I was upon my mother's breasts' (Ps. 22:9).

5. *'The blessings of thy father have prevailed above the blessings of my progenitors.'* Here Judah declares that this blessedness is indescribably greater than the blessings any earthly father could bestow upon his sons. This is the blessedness of grace upon grace, the blessedness of all things, the blessedness of all fulness in Christ (John 1:16; 1 Cor. 3:21; Col. 2:9-10).

6. *'The Almighty ... shall bless thee ... unto the utmost bound of the everlasting hills.'* Yes, the very fulness of heavenly glory obtained by the man Christ Jesus, as our Mediator, all of it, nothing excluded, will be ours for ever (John 17:5, 22). This is boundless blessedness indeed!

7. *'They shall be on the head of Joseph, and on the crown of the head of him that was separate from his brethren.'* This boundless blessedness is that which God freely bestows upon all who have been separated from the sons of Adam by election, redemption, effectual calling, and made to be the sons of God by grace in the Lord Jesus Christ (2 Cor. 6:14 - 7:1).

40.

Three lessons from Joseph

Genesis 50:15-21

'And when Joseph's brethren saw that their father was dead,
they said, Joseph will peradventure hate us, and will certainly requite us all the evil which we did unto him. And
they sent a messenger unto Joseph, saying, Thy father did
command before he died, saying, So shall ye say unto Joseph,
Forgive, I pray thee now, the trespass of thy brethren, and
their sin; for they did unto thee evil: and now, we pray thee,
forgive the trespass of the servants of the God of thy father.
And Joseph wept when they spake unto him. And his brethren also went and fell down before his face; and they said,
Behold, we be thy servants. And Joseph said unto them, Fear
not: for am I in the place of God? But as for you, ye thought
evil against me; but God meant it unto good, to bring to
pass, as it is this day, to save much people alive. Now therefore fear ye not: I will nourish you, and your little ones.
And he comforted them, and spake kindly unto them'

(Gen. 50:15-21).

We have already seen that Joseph is held before us in the
book of Genesis as a beautiful, instructive type of our Lord
Jesus Christ. In his betrayal, in his humiliation, in his exaltation, in opening the storehouses, in the saving of his family
and in many other ways the instruction of the type is crystal clear. A. W. Pink, in his *Gleanings in Genesis*, gives 101
comparisons between Joseph and Christ.

In Genesis 50, Joseph had finished the work God sent him to do. All Israel had been saved from death and dwelt in the peaceable habitations of Goshen. Jacob was now dead. Nothing remained but for Joseph's brothers to dwell in the land in peace, pursuing their ordinary work as shepherds, with gratitude to Joseph for his goodness to them. They now had nothing to fear. All was well.

Yet Joseph's brothers were uneasy. Their former transgressions made them fearful. Their guilt caused them to be suspicious of Joseph's goodness. In spite of all the kindness they had experienced at his hand, they were not assured of their acceptance with him. They feared that they might yet be made to suffer for what they had done. Therefore, they sued for mercy in the name of their father Jacob, whom they knew Joseph loved dearly.

They sent a messenger to Joseph with a message from Jacob (vv. 15-17). When Joseph heard their request, his tender heart broke and he wept (v. 17), because of his love for Jacob and for his brothers. But probably their suspicions of him, more than anything else, broke his heart. What an evil thing it is for sinners saved by the grace of God in Christ to be suspicious of his great goodness. Yet it is an evil of which we are all guilty, far too often.

Then Joseph's brothers themselves came before him (vv. 17-18). They confessed their sin. They sought forgiveness in Jacob's name, upon his word, and they bowed before Joseph as his servants. This was the thing they had refused to do before. It was this very thing which before had been the cause of their hatred. When they heard that they were to bow as servants to Joseph, they said, 'Shalt thou indeed reign over us?' (Gen. 37:8). Then they sold him into bondage. But now they are humbled. Now, they bow and say, 'We be thy servants.'

This is the issue that must be settled in the hearts of men. We must bow to Christ (Luke 14:25-33). He must be owned and acknowledged as our rightful Lord (Rom. 10:9-10). There is no salvation without the voluntary surrender of our hearts and lives to Christ's dominion as our Lord. When they bowed before Joseph as their rightful lord and master, he assured them of his good intentions towards them and comforted them (vv. 19-21). What a tender picture we have before us. It is a scene which needs no explanation. It is full of spiritual instruction for our souls. It clearly sets forth three lessons which we should take to heart.

1. A lesson about forgiveness

The first lesson is a lesson about God's abundant grace and forgiveness of sin in Christ. It is written: 'Where sin abounded, grace did much more abound' (Rom. 5:20). There is abundant grace for guilty sinners in Christ. Our God is a God who 'delighteth in mercy' (Mic. 7:18).

Let us learn from Joseph's brothers something about the nature of true repentance. The Spirit of God, who preserved this event for us and caused it to be recorded by Moses, gives us no reason to question the sincerity of these men. Joseph's penitent brothers show us what true repentance involves. Though fear is not itself repentance, repentance does involve a terrifying sense of guilt. These men were afraid because they were guilty of great sin, and they knew it. It also involves an acknowledgement and confession of sin (1 John 1:9). Like the publican our Lord mentioned (Luke 18:13), all who truly repent acknowledge and confess themselves to be sinners at heart, by nature, and in practice, without one shred of righteousness with which to commend themselves to God.

Pardon will never be granted until sin is confessed, confessed with a broken heart, and confessed completely. I do not mean that we must list all our sins. That would be impossible. But I do mean that we must not cover our sins (Prov. 28:13). We must confess our sin completely, offering no excuses for the evil of our sinful nature, our deeds of sin (our wicked thoughts and acts), or the corruption of our attempts at righteousness, acknowledging that even our 'good works' and personal righteousnesses are but filthy rags before the holy Lord God (Isa. 64:6).

In its essence, repentance is a voluntary surrender to Christ as our Lord and Master. It is taking his yoke upon us. Someone once said, 'He who abandons himself to God will never be abandoned by God.' We must lay ourselves at Christ's feet, if we would have him take us into his arms.

This grace of repentance, the gift of Christ to redeemed sinners (Acts 5:31) arises from faith in the Word of God. Joseph's brothers came to him and made their plea upon the basis of his father's word: 'Thy father did command...' So, too, penitent sinners come to Christ in hope of mercy upon the basis of what God himself has spoken in his Word (John 3:14-16). Believing God's record, we cast ourselves into the arms of the crucified Christ in hope of life eternal.

Let us ever remember the tenderness of our Saviour towards us. As 'Joseph wept when they spake unto him,' so our Lord Jesus Christ is 'touched with the feeling of our infirmities'. Our Saviour is as full of sympathy and tenderness for his saints now, though he is exalted, as he was when he dwelt upon the earth.

Let us, also, try to realize how thorough and complete God's forgiveness of our sin is. We nailed our Saviour to the cursed tree. We caused his blood to flow. His blood might justly be upon us for ever. But so great, so thorough, so complete is his forgiveness that our Saviour, rather than charging us with the sin and guilt of his death, blesses us through it! Joseph said to his brothers, 'Now therefore be not grieved, nor angry with yourselves ... for God did send me before you to preserve life' (Gen. 45:5). As John Newton put it:

> With pleasing grief and mournful joy,
> My spirit now is filled,
> That I should such a life destroy,
> Yet live by him I killed!

Let every believer understand clearly that Christ has forgiven us all our sin. We need never fear that he will deal with us upon the basis of our sin, neither by way of punishment, nor by loss of reward. Like Joseph, our great Saviour speaks comfortably to his people and assures them that he will nourish them. His word to us, with regard to all retaliation for sin is 'Fear not!' No wonder David sang, 'Blessed is the man to whom the Lord will not impute sin' (Rom. 4:8).

2. A lesson about providence

The second lesson in this passage is a lesson about the universal providence of our God (vv. 19-20). I am sure that when he was in that pit, when he was cast into prison, when he lay at night on the cold earth, shackled like a common felon, Joseph must have often wept in his loneliness, wondered why he was made to experience so much pain and sorrow, and wondered how his circumstances could be so bad when God had promised to bless him. But the end of his life vindicated God's promise and explained the necessity for every event in his life. Joseph's complicated life unravelled and was exhausted exactly as God had ordained it. With profound simplicity, Joseph said, 'I [am]

in the place of God!' The lesson from this man's life is 'the
LORD reigneth!'

Every child of God in this world should be constantly
aware of this fact: 'The LORD reigneth!' Let us ever rejoice
in this glorious fact and take to ourselves the comfort it
affords. May God give us grace to believe him. We ought to
trust him whose providence is so manifestly displayed to
us. Here are five areas in which the sovereignty of God in
providence[1] is clearly displayed.

1. God's sovereignty, his absolute control of the universe,
is seen in the accomplishment of redemption by the death
of Christ (Acts 2:23; 4:27-28).

2. God's sovereign rule of providence is manifest in the
exaltation and glory of Christ (John 17:2; Rom. 14:9). Like
Joseph, our Saviour is 'in the place of God ... to save much
people alive'. He came to be in that place by God's sovereign use of the wicked men who crucified him (Acts 2:22-36).

3. Certainly, we see the greatness of God's sovereignty
in providence, in the fact that he overrules evil for good
(Ps. 76:10). What Joseph's brothers meant to be evil, God
used for good. Adam's fall made way for our redemption
by Christ. Pharaoh's slaughter of the Hebrew children
brought Moses into his house. Thus the tyrant's wickedness was both the instrument of his own destruction and of
Israel's deliverance from Egyptian bondage for the fulfilment of God's covenant. Truly, 'all things work together'
for the eternal good of God's elect. As it is written: 'All things
are of God' (2 Cor. 5:18; Rom. 11:33-36).

4. Certainly, the history of every chosen sinner is a revelation of God's wise, good, adorable providence (Rom. 8:28).

Providence prepares the sinner for grace and preserves him for the appointed day of grace (Ps. 107; Hosea 2:8). The old writers called this 'prevenient grace,' that grace that goes before and prepares the way for grace. Our heavenly Father's secret providence orders all the affairs of our lives, yes, all the affairs of the world, for the good of his people.

5. God's great and glorious, good and wise providence will be so manifest at the conclusion of history that everything will render praise to him (Rev. 5:11-14). A. J. Gordon, who succeeded C. H. Spurgeon as pastor at the Metropolitan Tabernacle in London, England, said, 'God's providence is like the Hebrew Bible; we must begin at the end and read backward in order to understand it.'

3. A lesson about brotherly love

The third lesson to be learned from this story is a lesson about brotherly love. Do you see how this man, Joseph, loved his brothers? He loved them so much that he not only forgave their crimes against him, but spoke kindly to them and sought to remove all their fears. His heart was so tender towards them that he wept when they were suspect of his kindness. Let us ever seek grace from our God to love our brethren truly in Christ in this way, and to show that love by our attitude and actions.

When we have wronged a brother or a sister in Christ, we must with humility seek forgiveness and reconciliation with them. 'Confess your faults one to another' (James 5:16). To wrong a friend is great evil; but to compound the wrong by refusing to acknowledge it is even more wicked. That will soon destroy a friendship (Matt. 5:23-24).

When we have been wronged, we must freely forgive the wrong and the wrongdoer (Matt. 6:14; Eph. 4:32 - 5:1).

Nothing in this low, ruined world so beautifully reflects the character of the Son of God as forgiveness. As Joseph forgave his brothers, let us forgive one another. As God, for Christ's sake, has forgiven us, let us, for Christ's sake, forgive one another.

Let us take these three lessons to heart. First, God's grace is abundant and free in Christ. We have great reason to give thanks to him. Second, God's providence is always good for his people. We should always be content with what our heavenly Father brings to pass. Third, the love of God in Christ, when experienced, teaches saved sinners to love and forgive one another.

Notes

Chapter 1. Creation

1. The creation of the world was a work that involved all three persons in the Holy Trinity: Father, Son and Holy Ghost, even as the works of redemption and providence involve all three of the divine persons.

2. I am aware of the opposition of many faithful, highly esteemed expositors to this interpretation. Perhaps there are those who embrace it as an attempt to reconcile scientific speculation with biblical revelation. That is not my purpose. I am not at all concerned about the conflicts which exist between the changing speculations of science and the facts of divine revelation. I simply believe this to be the most accurate interpretation of the text.

Chapter 2. The first week

1. Pink, Arthur W. *Gleanings In Genesis,* Moody Bible Institute of Chicago, Chicago, IL, USA, 1922, p.20.

Chapter 5. The fall of man

1. The fall of Adam was not an accident (Ps. 76:10). Either God could have prevented it, or he couldn't . If he couldn't then he is not God and the whole Bible is a myth. If he could, but wouldn't, then it came to pass according to his will, though he did nothing to cause it.

Chapter 12. **God's covenant with Noah**

1. Do not allow the infidels of our day to influence your thinking. Scientists, environmentalists and politicians may fret and worry themselves about 'global warming' and the disappearance of the seasons. But God has declared that 'while the earth remaineth, seedtime and harvest, and cold and heat, and summer and winter, and day and night shall not cease!'

2. God could not and would not bless and save even the people whom he loved with an everlasting love, apart from the satisfaction of his justice by the blood of Christ.

Chapter 14. **Noah and his sons**

1. As it is expanded in the giving of the law and by our Lord Jesus in his sermon on the Mount, this prohibition of murder is much more than just a prohibition of murder. It requires that we love and care for one another, that we protect both the lives of others and the name and well-being of others. As we shall see, it is precisely at this point that Ham's rebellion and sin were manifest. He hated his father and sought to destroy his character.

2. This covenant and its token (the rainbow) are used by the Spirit of God as a type and of the covenant of grace, according to which our heavenly Father rules the universe for the salvation of his elect (Rev. 4:1-3; Rom. 8:28-30).

3. In so far as it relates to spiritual things, the curse, is not upon the physical descendants of Cain and Ham, but upon those who walk in the way of Cain and Ham, in the way of self-righteous, free-will, works religion. In other words, all idolaters are the descendants of Cain and Ham.

Chapter 22. **El-Shaddai — the covenant of God**

1. We must never endeavour to accomplish the purpose of God by the arm of the flesh. This is a lesson for God's servants in every age. We long for seed, spiritual seed, God's promised seed. We long to see chosen sinners born into the kingdom of God. Far too often, men who themselves believe God (as did Sarai and Abram), employ carnal means to accomplish what God alone can accomplish. The result is always trouble. Let us rather wait on him who is 'the Almighty God' to perform his work. The best our efforts can produce is Ishmael. The fruit of grace is Isaac.

2. The Old Testament rite of circumcision has absolutely nothing to do with the New Testament ordinance of believer's baptism. There is not a single passage of Scripture in which the two are connected. As it is explained in the New Testament, circumcision pointed to the work of God the Holy Spirit in the hearts of chosen, redeemed sinners. It was a picture of the new birth. As circumcision was the seal of God's covenant with Abraham to his children, so the coming of the Holy Spirit in his saving operations of grace is the seal of the new covenant to God's elect, Abraham's true children (Eph. 1:13-14; 4:30). Circumcision is a picture of regeneration. Believer's baptism is a picture of redemption (Rom. 6:3-6).

Chapter 23. Lot

1. Homosexuality is still an abomination to God. It is the perverse practice of wicked men with perverted hearts and minds, acting in a manner that is against nature. Wherever homosexuality becomes commonly accepted, reprobation is evident. Any society that permits, accepts and condones the practice of homosexuality is under the judgement of God (Rom. 1:24-32).
2. Strife between brethren is often, if not usually, about money, wealth and earthly possessions. Abraham was a godly man. He chose the way of peace. Lot was a greedy man. He chose the way of prosperity. His choice was indescribably costly!

Chapter 24. Sarah and Hagar

1. We do not have the liberty to take any historical event revealed in Scripture and make it teach what we want it to teach, or think it might teach. But we do have a responsibility to interpret honestly every historical event revealed in Scripture in the light of revealed gospel truth, making every event a type, or an allegory, of redemption by Christ.

Chapter 27. Isaac

1. Our sons and daughters are far more likely to imitate our vices than our virtues. Be careful how you live before them.

Chapter 29. **Jacob's ladder**

1. Henry, P., *Christ All in All*, Reiner Publications, Swengel, PA, USA, p.308.

Chapter 31. **Jacob at Peniel**

1. Christ frequently appeared to the saints of the Old Testament in human form. These pre-incarnate appearances were tokens and pledges of his incarnation.

Chapter 40. **Three lessons from Joseph**

1. Providence is the unfolding of God's purpose. It is God bringing to pass in time what he purposed to do in eternity.